WHO CHOSE THE GOSPELS?

WHO CHOSE THE GOSPELS?

Probing the Great Gospel Conspiracy

C. E. Hill

OXFORD
UNIVERSITY PRESS

OXFORD
UNIVERSITY PRESS

Great Clarendon Street, Oxford OX2 6DP

Oxford University Press is a department of the University of Oxford.
It furthers the University's objective of excellence in research, scholarship,
and education by publishing worldwide in

Oxford New York

Auckland Cape Town Dar es Salaam Hong Kong Karachi
Kuala Lumpur Madrid Melbourne Mexico City Nairobi
New Delhi Shanghai Taipei Toronto

With offices in

Argentina Austria Brazil Chile Czech Republic France Greece
Guatemala Hungary Italy Japan Poland Portugal Singapore
South Korea Switzerland Thailand Turkey Ukraine Vietnam

Oxford is a registered trade mark of Oxford University Press
in the UK and in certain other countries

Published in the United States
by Oxford University Press Inc., New York

British Library Cataloguing in Publication Data
Data available

Library of Congress Cataloging in Publication Data
Library of Congress Control Number: 2010930294

Typeset by SPI Publisher Services, Pondicherry, India
Printed in Great Britain
on acid-free paper by
Clays Ltd., St Ives plc

ISBN 978–0–19–955123–1

1 3 5 7 9 10 8 6 4 2

ACKNOWLEDGEMENTS

THE English translation of the Bible used throughout is the New Revised Standard Version, unless otherwise noted. I wish to thank Tom Perridge and Elizabeth Robottom at OUP for all their helpful guidance and suggestions, and the Oxford readers who in many ways made this a better book. Thanks also to Michael Farrell and Karen Middlesworth for their tireless and cheerful efforts in securing library materials and to Rick Bennett for his help in obtaining permissions. I owe special thanks to Sean Hill for reading the manuscript and offering his valuable comments, to Charity, Jamie, and Megan Hill for their artistic consultation, and to Marcy Hill for her great patience and for her inspiration to attempt an 'accessible' book.

This book is lovingly dedicated to Marcy—*cara et amica*.

CONTENTS

LIST OF ILLUSTRATIONS

Jacket Illustration: The Four Gospels. Brass rubbings from the tomb of Gijsbert Willemszoen de Raet, Art: Marcy A. Hill. Photo: Charity R. Hill.

LIST OF TABLES

ABBREVIATIONS

AH	Irenaeus, *Against Heresies*
ANF	Ante-Nicene Fathers
ApocJas	*Apocryphon of James*
EH	Eusebius, *Ecclesiastical History*
EpApost	*Epistle of the Apostles*
GJ	*Gospel of Judas*
GT	*Gospel of Thomas*
IGT	*Infancy Gospel of Thomas*
JCEC	Charles E. Hill, *The Johannine Corpus in the Early Church* (Oxford: Oxford University Press, 2004, corrected, paperback edition, 2006)
OECT	Oxford Early Christian Texts
WUNT	Wissenschaftliche Untersuchungen zum Neuen Testament

INTRODUCTION:
DROWNING IN A SEA
OF GOSPELS

> 'Who chose which gospels to include?' Sophie asked. 'Aha!'
> Teabing burst in with enthusiasm. 'The fundamental irony
> of Christianity! The Bible, as we know it today, was collated
> by the pagan Roman emperor Constantine the Great.'
>
> (Dan Brown, *The Da Vinci Code*, 231)

The recent excitement over the well-publicized unveiling of the
Gospel of Judas in the spring of 2006 provided a glitzy showcase for
the views of certain scholars of early Christianity. Such collabor-
ations between the media and the academy seem to be much
more common today than they used to be. One result of this
partnership has been the wider promotion of the idea that Christianity's early centuries were something of a free-for-all with
regard to Gospel literature—books which purported to describe
the life and teachings of Jesus of Nazareth. Since there were once
many other Gospels besides the four now in the Bible, why
should we simply assume that the church chose the best ones?
Shouldn't we in fact presume that the church simply selected the
Gospels that best promoted its own causes to the detriment of its
competitors? Who was it that conspired to give us the books we
have? Who chose the Gospels anyway?

If many informed laypeople, believers or unbelievers, now have the impression that the ancient church was a veritable breeding-ground for Gospels, it is for good reason. For this is precisely what several well-placed scholars have been telling the public, even before the *Gospel of Judas* hit the airwaves and made a big splash on the internet. In the words of William Petersen: 'Whoever wanted to write a gospel could—and often did.'[1] Petersen speaks of a 'sea of multiple gospels,' and quips that 'gospels were breeding like rabbits'.[2] Another deservedly famous scholar, Elaine Pagels, has written of her astonishment on learning as a graduate student at Harvard that two of her professors each 'had file cabinets filled with "gospels" and "apocrypha" written during the first centuries', books which, Pagels says, revealed a 'diversity within the Christian movement that later, "official" versions of Christian history had suppressed so effectively'.[3]

So, we may now ask, how did the Christian church, apparently drowning in a sea of Gospels, finally end up with only four? The educated reader of today may already have come to the conclusion that the story was attended with a good bit of bullying, intrigue, and skullduggery. Many perhaps picture councils of bad-tempered bishops voting on which books to include in the Bible one minute, and voting to execute heretics the next. It is now widely believed, in any case, that the four canonical Gospels emerged into prominence only fairly late from a long and drawn-out battle within early Christianity, a battle finally won in the fourth century after the establishment of the church by Constantine the Great. While academics might not, as Teabing does in Dan Brown's novel, attribute the collation of the Bible to 'the pagan emperor Constantine', many even in the academic community insist that the question of which Gospels the church ought to endorse was still up for grabs in the fourth century. As Boston University professor and author of *American Jesus* Stephen Prothero says:

There are many places to begin this search for the American Jesus, but the fourth-century Council of Laodicea may be the most appropriate. At that gathering, early Christians met to close the canon of the still evolving Christian Bible. Some, following the second-century theologian Marcion, insisted that the one true Church should have only one true Gospel. Others, citing Marcion's contemporary Irenaeus, fought for four (one for each corner of the earth). Inexplicably, Irenaeus got his way.[4]

It is true that the Council, meeting in 363 or 364 CE, issued a statement that no 'uncanonical books be read in church, but only the canonical ones of the New and Old Testament'. And some later manuscripts of the Council's proceedings give the list of the books which the Council in all probability understood as 'canonical'.[5] But there is no reason to believe that any of the thirty or so church leaders in attendance would have suggested the acceptance of only one Gospel as opposed to four, let alone that any would have called upon the example of Marcion, a well-known but widely denounced Christian heretic, as a rallying-point. Prothero calls the Council's alleged selection of the four 'inexplicable'. And why wouldn't he think so, for, again, the common idea is that the church's canon is the result of a great power-struggle between rivals among early Christianity. The four Gospels, like the other books in the canon of the Christian New Testament, achieved their place only by finally out-muscling their many competitors.

When one of my son's professors at the University of Florida recently asked his class who decided which books would be included in the Bible, one student confidently responded, 'the people with the biggest army'. The professor could add nothing to the student's brilliant riposte, and simply returned to his lecture. While no respectable scholar of early Christianity would put the matter quite so crassly, the writings of some scholars today make it easy to understand why such conceptions are rampant. Bart Ehrman, Professor of Religious Studies at the University of North Carolina, does not speak of armies, but still uses political, even military, terms to describe the process:

In brief, one of the competing groups in Christianity succeeded in overwhelming all the others. This group gained more converts than its opponents and managed to relegate all its competitors to the margins . . . This group became 'orthodox,' and once it had sealed its victory over all of its opponents, it rewrote the history of the engagement—claiming that it had always been the majority opinion of Christianity, that its views had always been the views of the apostolic churches and of the apostles, that its creeds were rooted directly in the teachings of Jesus. The books that it accepted as Scripture proved the point, for Matthew, Mark, Luke, and John all tell the story as the proto-orthodox had grown accustomed to hearing it.[6]

The present book intends to examine critically some of the foundational scholarship used to support and promote this now popular narrative of how the church ended up with four, and only four, Gospels (and, indeed, the rest of the New Testament as well). On what bases do scholars such as Ehrman, Petersen, and Pagels make their cases? In the chapters which follow we'll look at the major arguments of these and other scholars and test them against the evidence. We'll review the fascinating papyrus discoveries of the last century-and-a-quarter and see what can be learnt from the study of the codices (early 'book' manuscripts, as opposed to scrolls) which contain the Gospels. Then the writings of Irenaeus of Lyons and a few of his contemporaries in the late second century will be examined to see where the Gospels stood in their day. We'll also discuss the promotion in the late second century of the *Diatessaron*, a 'Gospel Harmony', constructed by a reportedly disaffected orthodox Christian named Tatian who sought to combine the words of all four Gospels into a single, consistent narrative. Moving to an earlier period, we'll ask how writers in the middle of the second century, both orthodox and unorthodox, were treating written Gospels. And finally, we'll seek to ascertain just how early a four-Gospel collection was being received as authoritative in the church and seek to answer the question: 'Who chose the Gospels?'

Before moving on, a word needs to be said about the use of the terms 'canon' and 'canonical'. In common usage today 'canon' refers to the contents of any received 'list' of books or ideas, but particularly to the contents of the Bible: 'the canon of Scripture' or simply 'the canon'. The reader should know that there is ongoing debate among scholars about the proper use of 'canon' and 'canonical' when speaking of Gospels, or other books, in the early church. The disagreement is about when we can or should speak of a 'canon' of New Testament writings existing in the church. Two prominent scholars of an earlier generation, the erudite Theodor Zahn and the no less erudite Adolf von Harnack, argued over whether a New Testament canon can be said to have existed by the end of the first century (Zahn) or the end of the second (Harnack).[7] There should be no mistaking who was perceived as winning that debate! Today, the disagreement is between those who still speak of the end of the second century (a 'core canon') and those who insist instead on the middle or end of the fourth (a 'closed canon').[8] As John Barton has observed, in both the earlier and the present debates much depends on what

5

exactly one means by 'canon'. Does it require the existence of a securely closed list of books endorsed (or 'chosen') by an authoritative ecclesiastical body, or may it be used more loosely for a more or less well-defined set of books which the church is, or at least individual churches are, treating as divine, written authorities, that is, as Scripture?[9]

In the following pages, instead of employing some unwieldy expression like, 'the Gospels which were at some time canonized as part of the New Testament', or 'the Gospels which most Christians today treat as canonical Scripture', I shall simply on occasion refer to 'the canonical Gospels' as a term of convenience, without staking out a position on just when they attained either 'Scriptural' or 'canonical' status. Finding out when they did attain such status is, after all, what the rest of this book is about.

THE PROOF IS IN THE PAPYRI? GOSPEL BESTSELLERS FROM EGYPTIAN GARBAGE DUMPS

Rabbit Trails

I HAVE already cited the words of William Petersen comparing the production of Gospels to the breeding habits of rabbits. So, just how many Gospels were there? Using the dates given in J. K. Elliott's collection, *The Apocryphal New Testament*,[1] 'or other standard works', Petersen gives a list of Gospels written by 175 CE (this would include the *Gospel of Judas*). Of course, new Gospels continued to be produced by certain groups after 175 but it would be a little hard to imagine that Gospels originating so late would ever seriously have rivalled the four in the mainstream church (in fact, none did). The list of Gospels is not in the thousands, or in the hundreds. Petersen, somewhat anticlimactically, finds a grand total of *nine* other Gospels which might have sought to compete with the four.[2] Not an insignificant number, to be sure, but hardly what we might expect from all the hype. (As I learned from the internet, one female rabbit can produce nine bunnies in a single litter.) Moreover, including the *Infancy Gospel of James* in the category of 'Gospels' is a bit of a stretch, as

Table 1.1. *Petersen's 'partial list' of non-canonical Gospels composed before 175 CE*

Gospel of the Ebionites	*c.*125?
Gospel of the Egyptians	*c.*125?
Gospel of the Hebrews	*c.*125?
Gospel of the Nazoraeans	*c.*125?
Gospel of Thomas	*c.*140?
Gospel of Peter	*c.*150?
'Unknown Gospel' [P. Egerton 2]	*c.*150?
Gospel of Judas	*c.*170?
Infancy Gospel of James	*c.*170?

its genre is quite different. More realistically, then, we are talking about eight or so alternative Gospels (see Table 1.1). Perhaps rabbit habits were different in antiquity.

Granted, Petersen calls this a 'partial list.' It is not unlikely that more Gospels might have circulated before 175. But if they once existed they have left no record, even in later lists of books to be avoided, and this in itself may be an indication of their perceived value at the time. But whether eight or eighty, this does not yet answer for us which Gospels, if any, were being used and valued by most Christians in the second century. If almost anybody *could* write a Gospel (that is, any 'literate' body with ample time, resources, and inclination), this did not mean just anybody did. And if anybody did, this did not guarantee that the new Gospel would find readers, let alone that it would become acceptable to significant numbers of Christians as in any sense an authentic or trustworthy account of the life, words, and deeds of Jesus.

It should be observed that Petersen, when listing the Gospels and probable dates given above, also lists what many consider the most probable dates for the canonical Gospels (see Table 1.2). These dates are fairly standard among historians today, although

Table 1.2. *Petersen's dates for the canonical Gospels*

Gospel of Mark	*c.*70?
Gospel of Matthew	*c.*85?
Gospel of Luke	*c.*90?
Gospel of John	*c.*100?

some very competent scholars would argue that not only Mark, but also Matthew and Luke (and a small minority would say John too) were in circulation before 70 CE. In any event, to state the obvious, the four canonical Gospels are acknowledged by Petersen and the vast majority of scholars of all persuasions to be the earliest *known* Gospels.

Now, the average reader might be tempted to conclude that the four Gospels now in the Bible might always have been considered by *most* Christians to have the best claim to authenticity, simply because these Gospels were around longest in the life of the church. But many scholars are quick to dismiss such an easy conclusion. Do they have reason for this scepticism? They believe they have material proof for it. Enter the evidence of the papyri.

Papyrus Trails

In his *National Geographic* article introducing the *Gospel of Judas* to the public, Andrew Cockburn intimates that the prominence of the four canonical Gospels over others in the church was a relatively late phenomenon. 'In ancient times,' he writes, 'some of these alternative versions [i.e. other Gospels] may have circulated more widely than the familiar four Gospels.'[3] For support, Cockburn quotes Bart Ehrman, who declares: 'Most of the manuscripts, or at least fragments, from the second century that we have found are copies of other Christian books.'[4] Those of us who try to keep abreast of the discoveries of New Testament manuscripts may wonder if the bestselling author of *Misquoting Jesus* was not misquoted himself here! Does he really mean to claim that most of the earliest Gospel fragments discovered to date do not represent any of the familiar four? Cockburn certainly seems to understand the statement in this way. And, in any case, the contention that non-canonical Gospels equalled or outnumbered canonical ones in the early period has the support of other prominent scholars of early Christianity.

James M. Robinson is a veteran researcher whose extensive scholarly output has contributed a great deal especially to our understanding of the (mostly gnostic) texts discovered at Nag Hammadi in Egypt. A recent article by Robinson supports the claim just mentioned. 'When Matthew, Mark, Luke, John, and Thomas were written,' says Robinson, 'there was no New Testament canon, and hence no distinction between canonical and non-canonical. They stood on equal footing, and it was only gradually that some were elevated into canonical status, others not.'[5] Later he concludes, 'in the second century, Gospels that were later to lose out, as non-canonical, were about as common as Gospels that were later to win out, as canonical'.

If there once were other Gospels which stood on equal footing with the four among Christians, or Gospels even more widely used than the four, this would certainly be important. It would surely seem to support the popular notion that some mischief must have occurred for these now almost forgotten Gospels to have been supplanted. But is the claim true? The general public seldom has direct access to the records and to the serious scholarship on manuscript discoveries, so it will now be necessary to take some time to show that claims such as this one outrun the evidence.

There are several problems in Robinson's statements cited above. First is the assumption about the date of the *Gospel of Thomas*, that it is contemporary with the other four—let's say, from sometime before the year 100. This would be a view held by a very small minority of scholars. Many do believe that perhaps a portion of the 114 sayings recorded in the *Gospel of Thomas* circulated from this time or before, but almost nobody asserts that a written document closely resembling what we know as the *Gospel of Thomas* existed in the first century. Many scholars in fact do not believe the *Gospel of Thomas*, as a literary work, came into existence until much later; Petersen thinks not until the 140s, others not until the 170s or 180s.

Second, Robinson's use of plurals, 'some were elevated into canonical status, others not', gives the clear impression that not just the *Gospel of Thomas* but other Gospels too were 'on equal footing' before the gradual elevation of the four we know. Robinson has not told us which Gospels these were, and probably for good reason. For it would be very difficult to show that any others approached anything like equal footing in the church as a whole.

A third difficulty concerns Robinson's conclusion from the assertion that 'there was no New Testament canon' when the four Gospels, and *Thomas*, were written, and hence no distinction between canonical and non-canonical. From this he concludes that all these books stood on 'equal footing'. If it is true that there was no New Testament canon by about the year 100 (certainly the church had given no *official pronouncement* about the canonicity of books by then), there was obviously no distinction between 'canonical' and 'non-canonical'. But Robinson infers that this means there were no distinctions at all. Despite claims to the contrary, there is simply no positive evidence to support an assertion that *Thomas*, in the event that it was around at that time, would have stood on 'equal footing' with the others. One might as well say that Caesar's *Gallic Wars* stood on equal footing with the four Gospels, for it too was in existence at this time when there was 'no New Testament canon'. Of course, this comparison is not entirely fair. The *Gallic Wars*, unlike the *Gospel of Thomas*, is not a religious text and the *Gospel of Thomas*, whenever it first began to circulate, presumably circulated among some who considered themselves Christians. Most likely it was among these Christians that it held its highest influence. Perhaps among these Christians it stood on 'higher footing' than any of the four Gospels. We simply do not know. What we do know is that among those communities of Christians who eventually showed their clear adherence to the four canonical Gospels there is no evidence of a positive adherence of any kind to the *Gospel of Thomas*. Our first recorded mention of a book with this title by any Christian writer comes in about 235 CE in the work of Hippolytus of Rome, who says it was used by the Naassene gnostics (*Refutation* 5.7.20). Only slightly later, Origen of Alexandria lists it as spurious (*Homilies on Luke* 1), and the third writer, the church historian Eusebius (early fourth century), charges that it is not only spurious, but to be 'shunned as altogether wicked and impious' (*EH* 3.25.6).[6]

But it is time to get more specific. What is the actual state of play with regard to the discovery of early Christian manuscripts? In order to proceed towards an answer, we'll need a little background information. In what follows I shall be referring to 'papyri', that is, to copies of early Christian writings written not on parchment but on papyrus, a common writing material made from the stalk of the papyrus plant which grows along the Nile. I shall refer to these papyrus manuscripts by their customary reference 'P' followed by a number. The 'P' stands for papyrus, and the number reflects the order in which each document was discovered and catalogued by scholars known as textual critics. Every papyrus fragment of a New Testament writing so far discovered and published has been assigned a number. For example, P^{52} and P^{90} refer to the fifty-second and the ninetieth papyrus manuscripts catalogued which contain a portion of a New Testament writing (both of these happen to be fragments of John). These manuscripts may also be identified by other abbreviations which designate the collections to which they now belong. Early Christian writings which are not in the New Testament do not have a 'P number' but are identified only by their collection numbers. For example, 'P.Egerton 2' stands for the second manuscript in the Egerton collection of papyri; 'P.Oxy. 4009' refers to the 4009th manuscript catalogued in the collection of papyri discovered in Oxyrhynchus, Egypt. When speaking of papyrus discoveries, this exotic-sounding place called Oxyrhynchus (it's meaning in Greek is as odd as its sound in English: city of the sharp-nosed fish) must take pride of place. Excavations of the ancient Oxyrhynchus rubbish heaps conducted in the late nineteenth and early twentieth centuries, mainly by two Oxford scholars, Bernard P. Grenfell and Arthur S. Hunt, have provided the world with about 500,000 pieces of papyrus to study—only about a tenth of which have so far been published.[7] It is from Oxyrhynchus, more than from any other single place, that the flow of once-lost New Testament papyri has come. Scholars are now able to work with a total of 126 papyrus fragments of New Testament texts from the first several centuries of Christian history (along with over 5,000 later, parchment manuscripts), at least fifty-four of which were discovered at Oxyrhynchus.

When scholars speak of 'the early Christian papyri', then, they mean the discoveries of Christian writings written on papyrus, many of which have been dated by experts to the third century CE and a handful even to the second. It is these earliest surviving Christian manuscripts which will now be our concern. Robinson states that from the second century we have

Two fragments of the Gospel of John (P^{52} and P^{90}), one of the Gospel of Matthew (P^{104}), one of *The Gospel of Peter* (P. Oxy. 4009), and two of the so-called *Unknown Gospel* (P. Egerton 2 and P. Köln 255). That is to say, in the second century, Gospels that were later to lose out, as non-canonical, were about as common as Gospels that were later to win out, as canonical. Around 200 CE this began to shift, as the concept of canonicity began to take over, with the three copies of Matthew ($P^{(4+)64+67}$, P^{77}, and P^{103}), one of Luke $P^{4(+64+67)}$), one of John (P^{66}), and one of *The Gospel of Peter* (P. Oxy. 2949).[8]

As for the *Gospel of Thomas*, Robinson says that the three fragments known from the second or third century (all discovered at Oxyrhynchus: P.Oxy. 1, P.Oxy. 654, P.Oxy. 655) compare well with the third-century statistics for canonical Gospels: five of Matthew, one of Mark, four of Luke, and twelve of John. He cites the views of one scholar (Soren Giverson), who has argued that 'the three Greek copies of *the Gospel of Thomas* should actually be dated back to the second century', which would put it then 'in first place in terms of fragments of copies surviving from that century!' He speaks again of the earliest centuries as a time 'when 'canonical' and 'apocryphal' are largely anachronisms, and popularity was rather evenly distributed'.[9]

Here, unfortunately, we find several more problems with Robinson's presentation. First, his reference to two copies of 'the Unknown Gospel' is wrong. P.Egerton 2 and P.Köln 255 are actually two fragments from the same manuscript.[10] (A few tugs on the corners of P.Egerton 2 could, by this means of counting, greatly increase this Gospel's attestation.)

Then there is the matter of the dating of papyri, which, it is no secret, is not an exact science. When papyrologists—those who study works written on ancient papyrus—date a manuscript at 'around 200', they mean it could be from the late second century or the early third century. Generally speaking, they allow at least twenty-five years on either side of the date they give. And how do they have any idea at all when a manuscript was written? The writing materials (papyrus as opposed to parchment, certain kinds of ink) tell them some things, but it is mainly a matter of evaluating the forms of the letters. Fortunately, some ancient documents are actually dated by their scribes, or they refer to some datable historical event, and the forms of writing on these documents can help papyrologists determine when different forms of writing passed into and out of use. This knowledge then can be applied to other manuscripts which are not dated by their scribes. If the independent judgements of several, trained papyrological experts agree on a rough date for a given document, we can place a lot of confidence in their evaluations. But, as one can imagine, unless the scribe has somehow indicated a hard date, these methods can only produce approximate results. In fact, it is often the case that experts disagree to a greater or lesser extent in their datings of manuscripts. This is why one cannot speak as if the year 200 was some kind of exact cut-off date after which everything began to change, whether because of a notion of canonicity or for some other reason.

On specific manuscripts, the dates given by Robinson do not always seem to be representing a scholarly consensus. For instance, most scholars ascribe the *Gospel of Thomas* fragments to the third century, not to the second.[11] Many experts conclude that the three fragments known as $P^{4/64/67}$ came from a single volume which contained at least the Gospels of Matthew and Luke. These experts date the volume to the late second century.[12] Both these examples show that the second-century count can easily shift, and in fact, many would not agree with Robinson's totals. Robinson reports only three attestations of one of the four Gospels in manuscripts from the second century, but J. K. Elliott claims that experts have identified six to eight.[13] Martin Hengel says there are 'about seven or eight' attributed to 'the very early third or to the second century'.[14] Others would add one more manuscript of Matthew (P^{77}), one, two, or three of John (P^5, P^{75}, and/or P^{108})[15] and one more of Luke (P^{75}, which contains Luke and John).

Thus, without insisting on a definite number, this means that there are in our possession anywhere from seven to thirteen manuscript attestations of one of the four canonical Gospels which some qualified experts today believe could plausibly date from around the year 200 or before.[16] In Table 1.3 and 1.4 I have put in bold letters the manuscripts on which there seems to be a consensus among papyrologists.[17] I have placed asterisks beside the two fragments of the *Gospel of Peter* because there is significant doubt as to whether either of them (particularly P.Oxy. 4009) actually represents the *Gospel of Peter*.[18] In any case, they apparently represent some kind of 'Gospel literature' and thus

Table 1.3. *Possible second-century manuscripts of canonical Gospels* (consensus in bold)

Matthew	$P^{64, \ 67}$ (Mag.Coll.Gr. 18 + P.Barc.inv. 1)
	P^{77} (P.Oxy. 2683 + 4405)
	P^{103} (P.Oxy. 4403)
	P^{104} (P.Oxy. 4404)
Mark	
Luke	P^4 (Paris Supp.Gr.1120)[a]
	P^{75} (P. Bod. XIV–XV)
John	P^5 (P. Oxy. 208 + 1781)
	P^{52} (P.Ryl. 457)
	P^{66} (P.Bod. II)
	P^{75} (P. Bod. XIV–XV)
	P^{90} (P.Oxy. 3523)
	P^{108} (P.Oxy. 4447)
	P^{109} (P.Oxy. 4448)

Table 1.4. *Possible second-century manuscripts of non-canonical Gospels* (consensus in bold)

Egerton Gospel	**P.Egerton 2 + P.Köln 255**
Gospel of Peter	**P.Oxy. 4009**[*]
	P.Oxy 2949[*]
Gospel of Thomas	P.Oxy. 1
	P.Oxy. 655

Note: Because $P^{4,64,67}$ were catalogued separately and many years apart, they were not dated to exactly the same time. Many (including C. H. Roberts and T. C. Skeat) now believe they all came from the same manuscript and date from the late second century.

may be included here. This makes a total of at least seven and up to thirteen manuscript attestations of one of the four canonical Gospels (actually one of the three, as Mark is not represented), as opposed to two or at the most five attestations of all non-canonical Gospels from the second century. Needless to say, it is simply not true that 'most of the manuscripts, or at least fragments, from the second century that we have found are copies of other Christian books', if by 'other Christian books' we mean other Gospel books.

Robinson says 'the concept of canonicity began to take over' at around the year 200.[19] His words imply that at about this time the use of other, popular Gospels began to be curtailed in the church. And yet, if we look at the papyrus finds from the third century, we cannot affirm that the ratio of non-canonical to canonical Gospels changes very much in that century. Ehrman has recently said that of all Gospel or Gospel-like texts from the second or third century combined, there are thirteen fragments representing seven non-canonical Gospels and thirty fragments representing the four canonical ones.[20] Martin Hengel says the ratio of apocryphals to canonicals is fourteen to thirty-six,[21] and Larry Hurtado would put the numbers at ten to thirty-six.[22] In addition, since these scholars wrote, fragments of two more third-century copies of John have been published.[23]

Again, we are obviously unable to give precise numbers because of the imprecise nature of the science of dating manuscripts. Perhaps it is thirteen to thirty-two, perhaps ten to thirty-eight. In any case, we cannot say with any confidence that the ratio changed very dramatically in the third century as compared with the second. It may be that the same sorts of people who used Matthew (Mark), Luke, and John at the beginning of the third century continued to do so throughout the century and that it was the same for people who used other Gospels. In both centuries, remnants of canonical Gospels outnumber remnants of non-canonical ones at least somewhere between two (plus) to one and three (plus) to one, and perhaps closer to four to one.

Reading Random Samplings

We have seen how the numbers used by Robinson are a bit fishy. But there are also problems with the method he employs. First, when he concludes that 'popularity was rather evenly distributed'[24] among canonical and non-canonical Gospels, this assumes that the random discovery of ancient manuscripts in a limited number of archaeological sites is an accurate and sufficient barometer of a document's popularity, and the *only* such barometer. But this is hardly the case. Counting the fragments which have been discovered is only one aspect of the attempt to determine the popularity of a book, and by itself it is not necessarily very trustworthy. This is because the count is always changing as new discoveries are made, and because the sampling is necessarily spotty. We obviously can only know what has been dug up, and only a tiny fraction of possible ancient sites have been dug up, and these only in Egypt, where the dry conditions are more conducive to the survival of papyrus materials. We have no first-, second-, or third-century Gospel papyri from the northern Mediterranean. It may be that the finds from Egypt are representative of the whole Christian world, but we do not know that—more on this question in a moment. Even with regard to Oxyrhynchus, whose rubbish heaps have yielded the lion's share of our relevant papyri, we cannot be sure that what has emerged there is representative even for that city, let alone for the entire Christian population across the empire. For one thing, all the documents rescued from Oxyrhynchus are fragmentary; in most cases the greater part of each manuscript has not survived due to decay (and possibly mutilation). Of some works we have only a tiny fragment, and surely that means that of other works we have nothing left at all.

That is, by far most of the tonnage of papyri which once existed there has completely perished. Therefore, there is no way of knowing how many copies of a given text might once have been deposited there by the residents.

To take one very pertinent example, we have only one manuscript attestation for the Gospel of Mark (P^{45}) before the end of the third century. That no more fragments of Mark have survived may well reflect the fact that it was not as popular as several others. Christian writings up to this time show many more quotations of Matthew, for instance, than of Mark. Perhaps also there were more people who read the *Gospel of Thomas* or the *Gospel of Peter* at Oxyrhynchus in this period than read Mark. Yet while this is entirely possible, it is still a precarious conclusion to draw from the evidence. This is because, first, contemporary literary sources (Irenaeus of Lyons, Clement of Alexandria, Tertullian of Carthage, and so on) show us that the churches which were using the Gospels of Matthew, Luke, and John were also using the Gospel of Mark.

Second, we know that at least by the early third century (if not before) books were being produced which contained more than one of the four Gospels bound together (we'll have more to say about such books in Chapter 5). The earliest known codex containing all four Gospels is the third-century P^{45}, which also contains the book of Acts. From an earlier period is P^{75}, a codex containing Luke and John, and $P^{4,64,67}$, evidently originally containing at least Matthew and Luke. This practice of binding two or more of the four Gospels together means it is quite possible that some fragments of Matthew, Luke, or John now in our possession, some of which are no more than scraps of single pages, might have belonged to codices which contained Mark too. Thus, there is reason to believe that at this time Mark was more widely used in

Christian churches than the statistics of papyrus discoveries would, by themselves, lead us to believe.

While these papyrus finds may not give us an entirely accurate measure of a document's popularity, even in a given locale, they remain hugely important. They have provided us with our earliest forms of the texts which millions of Christians have honoured as Holy Scripture down through the centuries and which have played a very large role in western culture. They have also provided valuable attestation of some fascinating religious texts which are *not* in our Bibles but which tell us something about the beliefs of some ancient Christians.

The Papyri: Conspiracy Killers

Something else we can say about the discoveries is that they are *impartial*. This is important because when orthodox writers of the period such as Irenaeus of Lyons report on the use of Gospels in their day, they could be, and have been, accused of skewing their reports in favour of the four Gospels, as if involved in a conspiracy. But nothing like this can be said about the papyrus discoveries—that is, unless we want to suppose that the 'proto-orthodox' had their agents stationed at the rubbish heaps to make sure that only proto-orthodox and not proto-heretical documents were dumped off! The papyri are, in this sense, 'conspiracy killers' (as will be made clearer in the following paragraphs). And, so far, when we look just at these random and impartial discoveries, the canonical Gospels still outnumber non-canonical ones by about three to one.

Something too needs to be said about the views of a man named Walter Bauer, a twentieth-century German historian and lexicographer of early Christianity, and the influence these views have had on scholars such as Robinson, Ehrman, and others. Ehrman regards Bauer's 1935 book *Rechtgläubigkeit und Ketzerei im ältesten Christentum* ('Orthodoxy and Heresy in Earliest Christianity') as 'possibly the most significant book on early Christianity written in modern times'.[25] Bauer is famous for his attempt to show that the forms of Christianity which we now call orthodoxy and heresy were not clearly delineated in the early centuries, that in many places what was later considered heresy was in fact the first and dominant form of Christianity, and that 'orthodoxy' did not have a better claim on the original religion founded by Jesus than did some brands of 'heresy'. Various points of Bauer's construction of early Christianity have been challenged, some even discredited, over the years. But some of the most influential and prolific of the present generation of scholars of early Christianity, including Helmut Koester, Elaine Pagels, James Robinson, and Bart Ehrman, assume at least the broad strokes of Bauer's thesis as the very basis of their work. A full evaluation of the Bauer thesis is not possible here. I only draw attention to two aspects of his overall theory which are particularly relevant for our purposes.

First, it is remarkable how Bauer's thesis seems to predispose many of its advocates to what we might call a 'conspiracy theory' mentality. That is, to explain what now may appear to be the prominence of one 'mainstream' church before the fourth century, many lay great weight on the notion of the ultimate 'winners' *rewriting* history. We have already noted Ehrman's words: 'This group became "orthodox," and once it had sealed its victory over all of its opponents, it rewrote the history of the engagement—claiming that it had always been the majority opinion of Christianity'.[26] This is why Ehrman and others restrict their use of the terms 'orthodox' and 'heretical' to fourth-century and later phenomena (after the victory was sealed) and use 'proto-orthodox' and 'proto-heretical' to describe people or groups before that. For, until the victory was sealed, there was no 'orthodoxy', no main or intrinsically more genuine stream of Christianity. The reason, then, why we don't see more evidence of these other streams arising from the second and third centuries is that their writings were later suppressed and destroyed by 'the winners'.

Whatever amount of truth might be present here, one can see that this approach opens itself to the tendency to assume the operation of injurious plots among the orthodox to stifle and obliterate evidence in their efforts to rewrite history. But where does one take confiscated heretical treatises when one sets out to destroy them? Probably to the rubbish heaps! And yet what has been salvaged out of Egyptian rubbish heaps so far shows a strange and embarrassing preponderance of 'proto-orthodox' as opposed to 'proto-heretical' materials.

The second aspect of Bauer's thesis which interests us here is something to be kept in mind when we consider that the place where these discoveries have been made is Egypt. Egypt is one of the regions where, Bauer claimed, what would later be called heretical forms of Christianity were actually the first and dominant forms. As Ehrman says, 'the earliest Christians in Egypt were various kinds of gnostic'.[27] Kurt and Barbara Aland, in their widely used textbook on New Testament textual criticism, say, 'Egypt was distinguished from other provinces of the Church, so far as we can judge, by the early dominance of gnosticism'.[28] Eldon J. Epp concurs: 'Certainly heterodoxy... was the mark of the earliest Egyptian period.'[29] Until things began to change in the early third century, then, Egypt is considered to have been a centre of Christian free-thought, home to a colourful variety of what Ehrman would call 'Lost Christianities'. Amid this boisterous diversity, the form later identified as orthodox was but one, and (according to these scholars) a minority one at that.

That gnostics and other heterodox groups were the *first*[30] forms of Christianity to establish themselves in Egypt, and that they formed the numerical *majority* of Christians there, are both debatable assertions. Yet no one should contest the fact that such groups formed a very significant presence throughout the early period, from the 'Basilidians' in the early part of the second century to a not-inconsiderable number of 'Valentinians' near its end. The orthodox Clement of Alexandria and his successor Origen devoted a great deal of energy to answering these other forms of Christianity. Heterodox groups do seem to have flourished in Egypt more than in some other places in the empire such as Rome or Asia Minor. But this means that an obvious conclusion (even more obvious for the followers of Bauer) must follow. If there is any place in the empire where we should expect to see a high concentration of heterodox or non-canonical texts, it is Egypt.

Let's try to imagine a modern analogy. Just for the sake of illustration let's imagine that the entire topographical United States was obliterated—God forbid—by some natural or man-made disaster, and the only place where anything survived for future archaeologists to study was at Salt Lake City, Utah. Knowing that Salt Lake City was the world centre of Mormonism, reasonable people might naturally expect that the proportion of copies of the *Book of Mormon* to copies of the Bibles discovered there would be higher than in most other places in the United States. But if future historians were to claim, based *only* on what they found in Salt Lake City, that in twentieth- and twenty-first-century America the *Book of Mormon* was more popular than the Bible, we might have questions either about the competency of those historians or their objectivity. And yet scholars who believe that Egypt was dominated by heterodox forms of Christianity in the early period do not blink at drawing conclusions for all of Christianity based on findings from Egypt.

But the most remarkable thing is that the Egyptian rubbish heaps, which are no respecters of persons but which *are* a constant threat to conspiracy theories, so far attest that even in diversity-rich Egypt non-canonical Gospels were perhaps a third as popular as the canonical ones. And what we know about Egypt naturally suggests that elsewhere in the empire, in places where Christianity was apparently not so diverse, alternative Gospels might have made an even worse showing than they have so far in Egypt.

More Secrets of the Papyri

Two other interesting aspects of the papyrus discoveries await our attention. They have to do with the forms of the manuscripts themselves. For many centuries we in the West have been accustomed to thinking of a 'book' as a stack of sheets of paper, bound together at one end, able to be opened to any page with ease. But in the ancient world this was not the case. A 'book' was a scroll, or roll, a long sheet of papyrus or parchment rolled up with rods attached at each end to serve as handles. For reasons which are still not entirely clear to scholars, Christians from a very early time adopted the very much less common *codex* form, that is, a stack of folded sheets bound together at the folded end, for the production of their Scriptural books, and in time, for all of their books. The popularity and eventual supremacy of the codex form from late antiquity to today is arguably a cultural transition which owes a great deal to the spread of Christianity.[31]

It is a curious fact that all of our early copies of the Gospels of Matthew, Mark, Luke, and John were written on codices. In fact, Larry Hurtado observes: 'So far as biblical texts are concerned...there is no New Testament text copied on an unused roll among second- or third-century Christian manuscripts.'[32] Hurtado mentions 'unused' rolls because occasionally a scribe wrote on the back side of a roll which already contained writing. These scrolls written on both sides are called opisthographs (from Greek, meaning 'written on the back'). In the case of opisthographs, the scribe seems simply to have used whatever writing materials were at hand, and no conclusion can be drawn in such cases about whether the scribe considered the text he was copying to be sacred or not. Nor may we conclude that every piece of early Christian literature written in codex form was necessarily considered sacred or Scriptural— this form of publication eventually became the preferred format for virtually all Christian writings. Yet Hurtado makes an interesting point:

given this general Christian preference for the codex, particularly for scriptures, plus a noteworthy readiness to use the roll for a variety of other Christian texts, it is reasonable to judge that the use of a roll to copy a text signals that the copyist and/or user for whom the copy was made did not regard that text (or at least that copy of that text) as having scriptural status.[33]

Illustration 1.1 P.Oxy. 3525, the earliest-known fragment of the Gospel of Mary. A roll. Third century. Courtesy of the Egypt Exploration Society.

It is appropriate, then, to note the 'book' form of each of our other Gospel fragments. Our only copy of the Egerton Gospel, the earliest of our non-canonical Gospel fragments, is a codex. Based on what we know of the use of codices, it is possible (though not certain) that the scribe who copied this text in a codex wanted it to be considered a Scriptural document alongside (or perhaps replacing) these other Gospels. However, of the three early copies of *Gospel of Thomas* known, only one is a codex. One was copied on an unused roll and one is an opisthograph, written on the back of a land survey. Of the two third-century copies of *Gospel of Mary*, one is a codex and one is a roll. Of the two copies of what is possibly the *Gospel of Peter*, one is a codex and one is a roll.[34] The only existing fragment of the so-called Fayum Gospel is also a roll.

It is at least a sound working hypothesis that the non-codex form of these texts indicates that their owners would not have viewed them as Scriptural or as in the same category as the Gospels of Matthew, Mark, Luke, and John. If this is valid, then five of the nine earliest non-canonical Gospel fragments discovered in Egypt disqualify themselves as actual rivals to the four canonical Gospels in terms of their perceived Scriptural status. This means that in terms of our second- or third-century manuscripts, the ratio of the four canonical Gospels represented *in codex form* to the five non-canonical Gospels represented *in codex form* (if anyone is still keeping score) currently stands at about thirty-eight to four (or 9.5 to 1).

A second aspect of the papyrus fragments which has not received enough attention is their original size. Exacting work has been done by some scholars to determine the original page-sizes of the ancient codices, including early Christian codices, and to compare and categorize them.[35] Why does this matter? Hurtado writes, 'the physical dimensions of a manuscript constitute important data that may . . . suggest the intended usage of the manuscript'.[36] Some of the early codices produced for Christian readers were executed in what is now called 'miniature' format, smaller-than-normal writing on smaller-than-normal pages. These miniatures would have been cheaper, more portable editions, making it easier for individuals (as

Illustration 1.2 P[104] (P.Oxy. 4404), the earliest-known fragment of the Gospel according to Matthew. A papyrus codex. Late second century. Courtesy of the Egypt Exploration Society.

opposed to churches) to own them, and easier to carry them about or store them in personal libraries. It is clear that these copies were intended for private reading by those who commissioned them, and not for public reading.[37]

There are examples of New Testament, Old Testament, and apocryphal documents written in miniature format. The small size of the copy did not mean the document could not have been considered Scripture, it just meant the scribe or the commissioner of the volume most probably intended it for private reading. By contrast, however, other copies of texts, including texts of the canonical Gospels, have been found which would have been more suitable for public reading in church. They are somewhat larger or much larger, executed with great care, usually with comfortable margins around the writing space, written with a more formal or regular script, and often with certain 'reader's aids', like punctuation, paragraph markings, breathing marks, and so on, evidently designed to help the person reading the text aloud to a congregation. Some scholars have referred to a few of these as 'pulpit editions'.

Now let us take the two early copies of (what is thought by some to be) the *Gospel of Peter* cited by Robinson as evidence of the 'equal' popularity of canonical and non-canonical Gospels in the early period. As we just saw above, one of these two copies (P.Oxy. 2949) was made on a roll, not a codex, which is most likely an indication that the person who wrote or commissioned this copy did not regard the text as sacred Scripture. The other early copy of the *Gospel of Peter* (P.Oxy. 4009) is on a codex, but there is a strong possibility that this codex was a miniature.[38] Of the two extant copies of the *Gospel of Mary*, both third century, one is a roll (P.Oxy. 3525) and the other (P.Ryl. 463), measuring 8.9 cm wide by about 13.4 cm high, may also be classified as a miniature,[39] and thus was apparently also intended for private use. That is, while the scribe or commissioner of these small codices may or may not have considered these Gospels to be Scripture (we do not know), these particular copies were evidently not intended for reading in public but in private.[40] While the discovery of these fragments of other Gospels indicates a certain popularity of these texts for private reading (whether for scholarly purposes or for personal enjoyment), it offers no good evidence that these texts were ever read in the services of a worshiping community, and thus enjoyed a place on a par with the four Gospels.

On the other hand, most Christian codices of Old Testament and New Testament texts are not miniatures or even 'compact' in size. From the dimensions Hurtado reports we may observe that there are no less than twenty-one surviving second- or third-century papyrus codices containing one or more of the canonical Gospels which are at least 16 cm high, of which fifteen are at least 20 cm high and eight at least 25 cm high. The larger format as well as the presence of various 'readers aids' in many of them would have made them more suitable for public reading in services of worship.[41]

Here, then, is one more reason why simply counting the numbers of papyrus fragments is inadequate. Whereas most of our early papyrus copies of the canonical Gospels are from codices which were at least suitable for the purpose of public reading in the churches, none of our surviving copies of the *Gospel of Peter* or the *Gospel of Mary* was. Of all the early apocryphal Gospels from the second or third centuries, only the single copy of the Egerton Gospel and one of the three copies of the *Gospel of Thomas* were written in formats which could have made public reading a likely possibility. This, of course, does not mean they ever were so used, nor does it tell us what sort of Christians would have used them in this way if they ever were used in this way.

Conclusion

The papyrus discoveries do not support the claims which have often been made from them by some scholars, and now by *National Geographic* magazine. They certainly do not show that non-canonical Gospels were ever 'about as popular' as the canonical ones. And the kind of popularity that Gospels like the *Gospel of Peter*, the *Gospel of Thomas*, and the *Gospel of Mary* did enjoy was most likely not the same *kind* of popularity that the canonical Gospels had. Many scholars have in fact argued[42] that a high proportion, at least, of the apocryphal Gospels and apocryphal 'Acts of the Apostles' were 'popular literature' produced for private reading for various groups of Christians, much like the Christian novels and other popular Christian literature one sees on bookstore shelves today. Even Walter Bauer said that many of these writings depict 'a pious yearning to know more, a naïve curiosity, delight in colourful pictures and folktales'.[43] This assessment of the popular or folk character of these books now receives some support from the physical aspect of the papyri discoveries, as we have seen. We know from literary sources that the four canonical Gospels, on the other hand, were being copied not only for private reading but also for reading in services of worship already at some point in the second century (as we shall see in later chapters). This too can now be supported from the papyri. No one should make hard-and-fast claims based only or primarily on the manuscript discoveries. But both the *numbers* of

Christian texts discovered so far and the *formats* in which they were written, if they tell us anything, attest to the prominence of at least the Gospels of Matthew, Luke, and John in Egyptian Christianity from the earliest time from which we have evidence (the second half of the second century CE). This, obviously, is long before the emperor Constantine and long before any of the church councils of the fourth and fifth centuries.

As important as the manuscript discoveries are, they still leave us with a very incomplete picture of the state of Gospel literature in early Christianity. The manuscripts are crucial evidence but they must be supplemented by other kinds of evidence, most importantly by the writings of Christian authors of the period, of every theological stripe. And when one speaks of the 'choosing' of Gospels in the second century, one has to speak of one central figure in particular. Ironically, the name of Irenaeus—a name which means 'peace'—has become a lightning-rod for controversy in discussions of the status of Gospels in the early church. In the next two chapters we shall see what the storm is all about.

2

SILENCING THE BISHOP, PART I: THE LONELY IRENAEUS

Irenaeus and the Gospels: Argument and Artistry

ON one wall of my family room hang four handsome brass rubbings of the symbols of the four Gospels, taken from a mould from the tomb of Gijsbert Willemszoen de Raet (d. 1511, original in the Rijksmuseum). They were expertly made by my wife in the autumn of 1988 at the Cambridge Brass Rubbing Centre, located then at the Round Church, a famous Cambridge landmark. The Gospel of Matthew is depicted in the form of a man, Mark in the form of a lion, Luke in the form of an ox, and John in the form of an eagle, these forms being based on the description of the four living creatures who surround the throne of God in heaven, in the book of Revelation, chapter 4. And what do these distinguished brass rubbings have to do with Irenaeus of Lyons and the subject of the present chapter? I think of Irenaeus often when I see them because he is the first known source for the well-known symbolism of the four Gospels which they represent (even though in his original version the symbols for Mark and John are switched).

Illustration 2.1 The Four Gospels. Brass rubbings from the tomb of Gijsbert Willemszoen de Raet. Photographs by Charity Hill.

If anyone has viewed, to take just one more example, folio 27V of the Book of Kells, housed in the Old Library of Trinity College, Dublin, or any number of representations of the four Gospels in stained-glass windows or in other church art, one has participated in the visual legacy bequeathed to the world through Irenaeus. As Irenaeus explains:

It is not possible that the Gospels can be either more or fewer in number than they are, for, since there are four zones of the world in which we live, and four principal winds [cf. Ezek. 37.9], while the Church is scattered throughout all the world, and the 'pillar and ground' of the Church is the Gospel and the spirit of life; it is fitting that she should have four pillars, breathing out immortality on every side, and vivifying men afresh. From which fact, it is evident that the Word, the Artificer of all, He that sitteth upon the cherubim, and contains all things, He who was manifested to men, has given us the Gospel under four aspects, but bound together by one Spirit. As also David says, when entreating His manifestation, 'Thou that sittest between the cherubim, shine forth' (Ps. 80.1). For, [as the Scripture] says, 'The first living creature was like a lion' (Rev. 4.7), symbolizing His effectual working, his leadership, and royal power; the second [living creature] was like a calf, signifying [His] sacrificial and sacerdotal order; but 'the third had, as it were, the face as of a man,'—an evident description of His advent as a human being; 'the fourth was like a flying eagle,' pointing out the gift of the Spirit hovering with his wings over the Church. And therefore the Gospels are in accord with these things, among which Christ Jesus is seated. (*AH* 3.11.8)

Irenaeus then, with a touch of artistry, goes on to remark on how the character of each of the four cherubim, fittingly, 'is in accord with' the way one of the four Gospel writers commences his Gospel: John's, for instance, is like a lion, relating Jesus' 'original [or 'ruling'], effectual, and glorious generation from the Father, thus declaring, "In the beginning was the Word, and the Word was with God, and the Word was God" '. So established are these four Gospels in the mind of Irenaeus that they may be compared to the angelic quartet which surround the very throne in heaven, according to the prophetic books of Ezekiel (chs. 1 and 10) and John (Revelation 4). Moreover, just as there are four winds, four corners of the earth, and four major biblical covenants, so there must be four Gospels. It is with such confidence that Irenaeus writes about the Gospels of Matthew, Mark, Luke, and John.

And it is this type of confidence that causes problems, as I'll now explain. Many popular authorities today claim that the four Gospels were not 'chosen' for the church until sometime in the fourth century. It may be that many *scholarly* authorities would like to do the same, but they know they cannot quite do so. And why not? Mostly because of Irenaeus. Based on a study of Irenaeus' writings, Graham Stanton is able to conclude that: 'By the time Irenaeus wrote in about 180 AD, the fourfold Gospel was very well established. Irenaeus is not defending an innovation, but explaining why, unlike the heretics, the church had four gospels, no more, no less: she has received four written accounts of the one Gospel from the apostles and their immediate followers.'[1] Well established by 180 AD? As the reader might guess, other scholars take strong exception to Stanton's evaluation.[2] Indeed, it seems far too easy to refute Irenaeus' argument in *Against Heresies* 3.11.8. 'Irenaeus's speculation that there are four gospels because there are four winds and four cardinal directions is simply implausible, even as humor', writes Robert W. Funk.[3] McDonald reports that 'Irenaeus employs arguments that by today's standards are considered strange, and even in the ancient world his reasoning for limiting the Gospels to four was not the most convincing line of argument'.[4] One might, then, surmise that Irenaeus must be trying desperately to convince his contemporaries of his position, otherwise he would not resort to arguments so 'fanciful' and 'tortured'.[5]

One thing this shows, however, is how easy it is to mistake the nature of Irenaeus' argument in *Against Heresies* 3.11.8. Despite his statement that 'It is not possible that the Gospels can be either more or fewer in number than they are', Irenaeus' argument is not one of logical necessity but of aesthetic necessity, of harmony, beauty, or proportion.[6] 'It is fitting', he says, that there are four

37

and only four; the characters of the four cherubim are 'in accord with' the characters of the four Gospels. Later in the passage he reiterates, 'there cannot be more or fewer than those we have mentioned. For since God made everything with harmony and proportion, it was necessary for the form of the Gospel to be harmonious and in proportion' (*AH* 3.11.9).[7]

Eric Osborn traces the background for Irenaeus' oft-recurring notions of 'fittingness' or 'appropriateness' in earlier Greek and Latin philosophical and artistic sources, from Plato and Aristotle to Irenaeus' day.[8] He aptly summarizes that, for Irenaeus, 'the aesthetic unity of the Gospels . . . reflects the unity of the creation'.[9] Thus, objections to Irenaeus' argument in *AH* 3.11.8 as logically uncompelling are a bit beside the point. To meet his 'argument' here one would probably have to begin by arguing that there is no harmony, proportion, or beauty to creation. This is an argument some might make today, but not one that many would have made in Irenaeus' day.

In any case, to focus on this aesthetic argument in *AH* 3.11.8 as the sole reason for accepting or rejecting Irenaeus' contentions about the 'givenness' of the fourfold Gospel is to miss a lot. For, whatever one ultimately thinks about such an argument, it is not the real 'argument'; it does not constitute the strength of the case for the kind of conclusion Stanton draws. Irenaeus 'argument' both here and elsewhere relies on these Gospels already having an underlying plausibility to his readers.

Before making the comparisons in 3.11.8 Irenaeus had declared: 'We have learned from none others the plan of our salvation, than from those through whom the Gospel has come down to us, which they did at one time proclaim in public, and, at a later period, by the will of God, handed down to us in the Scriptures, to be the ground and pillar of our faith' (*AH* 3.1.1). He then proceeded to describe the origins of these four Gospels:

Matthew also issued a written Gospel among the Hebrews in their own dialect... Mark, the disciple and interpreter of Peter, also handed down to us in writing what was being preached by Peter. Luke also, the companion of Paul, recorded in a book the Gospel preached by him. Afterwards, John, the disciple of the Lord, who also had leaned upon his breast [see John 13.23], himself published a Gospel during his residence at Ephesus in Asia.[10]

Even if one rejects his claim that these Gospels go all the way back to the apostles and their companions, the claim was apparently quite believable to Irenaeus' contemporaries. We happen to know (as we'll see in more detail in Chapter 10) that at least the first two traditions, those concerning Matthew and Mark, were already in circulation some sixty-to-eighty years before Irenaeus wrote, and there is reason to think that the traditions about the other two Gospels were circulating then too. Irenaeus' assertions about the normativity of these four Gospels were plausible to his readers because they knew these same four Gospels and knew that they had already had a long history of use in the church. Thus it was easy to believe that they had always been in use, since the time they were handed to the church by the apostles or their co-workers.

Readers of *Against Heresies* were familiar with these Gospels, and familiar with the portrait of Jesus that they offered. The same could not be said of most of their competitors. Churches with whom Irenaeus was aligned knew and worshipped Jesus as the one promised through the prophets of the Jewish Scriptures, as each of these four Gospels presented him. They knew him as one born miraculously of a virgin, but truly born a human infant, as one who lived subject to the normal travails of human existence, as these Gospels presented him. They knew Jesus as one who performed miracles and works of compassion, a preacher of the kingdom of God, and as one claiming the authority to forgive sin, as these Gospels presented him. They knew him as one who was betrayed, tortured, and crucified as a criminal, who died as a ransom for many, who was then raised bodily from the dead by the power of God, as these Gospels presented him.

The plausibility for Irenaeus' assumption of four Gospels, laying the foundation for his much-maligned comparisons in Book 3 is perhaps best seen simply in his comfortable, self-confident, and unapologetic use of these Gospels throughout the treatise. From beginning to end, he uses these Gospels in theological argument and as sources for Christian teaching and worship as if nothing were more natural. It is only in Book 3 that he pauses to say anything specific about the authoritative Scriptural sources that he had been using without apology up to that point.

The only people who do not acknowledge all four, and only these four, are, according to Irenaeus, those who teach doctrine which is unacceptable in the church. Irenaeus criticizes these people for either expanding the number of Gospels or shrinking them to a single Gospel. When he does so he speaks as if these people are deviating from what was standard among Christians in his day. 'Wherefore also Marcion and his followers have betaken themselves to mutilating the Scriptures, not acknowledging some books at all; and curtailing the Gospel according to Luke and the Epistles of Paul, they assert that these are alone authentic, which they have themselves thus shortened' (*AH* 3.12.12).

All this presents a rather sticky problem. Recall that in Professor Ehrman's political interpretation of church history it isn't until the fourth century that the 'orthodox' party finally 'sealed its victory over all of its opponents'. At that time 'it rewrote the history of the engagement', claiming that its views were passed down from Jesus' apostles. And yet here is Irenaeus, nearly two centuries earlier, already 'rewriting history' long before the victory was sealed. At a time when, many prominent scholars insist, the issue was still very much in doubt, Irenaeus writes as if the church had been nurtured by these four Gospels from the time of the apostles.

The problem with Irenaeus is that he simply wrecks the popular paradigm. His views about the emerging New Testament canon, and about the four Gospels in particular, are simply too well-developed, too mature, to fit the scheme that many have invested themselves in today. As a *second-century* Christian author who argued that there are, and can only be, four legitimate Gospels—because they alone teach the truth about Jesus and because they alone had been handed down in the church from the time of the apostles—Irenaeus lies like a fallen Redwood in the path of those who would see the choice of the four Gospels as a late and politically motivated manoeuvre of the fourth century.

How do you solve a problem like Irenaeus? The first thing people often do when confronted with a crisis is to attempt to isolate it. If we can first contain a fire, a flood, or the outbreak of a virus, confine it to a restricted area, we can at least limit the damage and then try to muster the forces to defeat it. This common-sense procedure has been employed to good effect in the effort to cope with the difficulty which is Irenaeus. The result is that in terms of his views of the four Gospels or the developing New Testament canon, Irenaeus is often presented as a bold innovator, a meteoric Da Vinci figure, brilliant perhaps, but nonetheless a solitary individual with no predecessors, no peers, and even very few followers for quite some time. Irenaeus of Lyons becomes the originator not merely of the popular symbolic representations of the Gospels in Christian art, but of the fourfold Gospel itself, and perhaps of the New Testament canon too.

The Lonely Lyonian

One supposed aspect of Irenaeus' persona which emphasizes his remoteness from others is his creativity, his pioneering spirit. Lee McDonald observes that Irenaeus was 'the first to promote a four-Gospel canon'.[11] Elaine Pagels states it more colourfully:

Irenaeus resolved to hack down the forest of 'apocryphal and illegitimate' writings—writings like the Secret Book of James and the Gospel of Mary—and leave only four 'pillars' standing. He boldly declared that 'the gospel,' which contains all truth, can be supported by only these four 'pillars'—namely, the gospels attributed to Matthew, Mark, Luke, and John. To defend his choice, he declared that 'it is not possible that there can be either more or fewer than four . . .'[12]

Like an axe-happy frontiersman of bygone days, blind to ecological realities, Irenaeus destroyed a perfectly good stand of Gospel trees in order to create his four-Gospel canon. As a consequence it was Irenaeus, writes Arthur Bellinzoni, who 'essentially created the core of the New Testament canon of Holy Scripture. It was he who placed side by side with the Old Testament a New Testament canon consisting of the Pauline letters, some of the Catholic epistles, and the four separate gospels of Matthew, Mark, Luke, and John.'[13]

Just as an aside, Irenaeus' New Testament also included the book of Acts (*AH* 3.15.1), the Revelation of John, and possibly Hebrews, resulting in a collection that would have looked essentially like our own.[14] In any case, what stands out in all of these presentations is Irenaeus' creative initiative. Virtually single-handedly he is said to have created the New Testament, and in particular, the canon of four Gospels.

If it was Irenaeus who 'chose the Gospels', was the wisdom of his choice immediately perceived by other Christians? Not exactly, say many scholars. The fourfold Gospel 'sponsored by Irenaeus was not broadly, let alone universally, recognized'.[15] According to McDonald, 'Irenaeus's acceptance of the four canonical Gospels alone was not generally shared by his contemporaries or even by many Christians at a later time'.[16]

Pagels grants that 'Ireanaeus and his successors among church leaders did strive to compel all believers to subject themselves to the "fourfold gospel" and to what he called apostolic tradition'.[17] But one gets the impression that these ecclesiastical arm-twisters were late (nearly two centuries late) in arriving on the scene. The next ones she mentions are a group of fourth-century Egyptian bishops, in particular Athanasius of Alexandria, who 'took up and extended Irenaeus's agenda'.[18] It was Athanasius, 'the zealous bishop of Alexandria—an admirer of Irenaeus'[19] who, in his Easter Letter of 367 CE, specified the contents of the New Testament as consisting of the twenty-seven books that are in our Bibles today.[20] 'Athanasius included in his annual Easter Letter detailed instructions that would extend and implement the guidelines his predecessor [i.e. Irenaeus] had sketched out nearly two hundred years before.'[21]

But despite disagreements which persisted among church leaders in the intervening years, and even in later years, about some of the books of the New Testament, one cannot truthfully say that anyone had to 'compel . . . believers to subject themselves to the "fourfold gospel" '. These four Gospels remained very much in use and were looked to as the church's Scripture by Christians throughout the empire. Just to nail down this point, I mention here the following examples.

Hippolytus of Rome (or Asia Minor)

Early in the third century (probably about 202), a writer named Hippolytus, either in Rome or in Asia Minor, wrote a commentary on the Old Testament book of Daniel. At one point Hippolytus draws a comparison between Christ and the river in the garden of Eden, which divided into four as it flowed from the garden: 'Christ, himself being the river, is preached in the whole world through the fourfold Gospel' (*Commentary on Daniel* 1.17).[22] In another treatise, *On Christ and Antichrist* 58, he refers to the Law, the Prophets, the Gospels, and the Apostles, and in the next chapter says that the church, like a ship, is steered by 'the two Testaments'. This author, writing at the beginning of the third century, knows the Scriptures as consisting of Old Testament and New, each of these consisting of two broad categories, 'Law and Prophets' in one, 'Gospels and Apostles' in the other. The number of those Gospels is four.

Tertullian of Carthage

Writing sometime between 207 and 212 in his treatise *Against Marcion* 4.2.2, Tertullian of Carthage says: 'Of the apostles, therefore, John and Matthew first instil faith into us; whilst of apostolic men,

Luke and Mark renew it afterwards.' In chapter 5 of the same book, speaking about Luke's Gospel, he says:

The same authority of the apostolic churches will afford evidence to the other Gospels also, which we possess equally through their means and according to their usage—I mean the Gospels of John and Matthew—whilst that which Mark published may be affirmed to be Peter's, whose interpreter Mark was. For even Luke's form of the Gospel men usually ascribe to Paul.

Tertullian affirms later in the same chapter that Luke's Gospel is 'on a par with them in permanency of reception in the churches'.

Origen of Alexandria and Caesarea

Writing around 226 in Alexandria in his *Commentary on John* 1.6, Origen says straightforwardly that 'the Gospels are four. These four are, as it were, the elements of the faith of the Church.' That is, so utterly basic are these four that they are like earth, air, fire, and water, the very building-blocks of the church.

It is not as though Origen had only ever heard of the four. He knew many more. In his *Homilies on Luke*, preached in Caesarea, Palestine, in about 240, he reiterates:

The Church has four Gospels. Heretics have very many... 'Many have tried' to write [referring to Luke's wording in Luke 1.1] but only four Gospels have been approved. Our doctrines about the Person of our Lord and Savior should be drawn from these approved Gospels. I know one gospel called *According to Thomas*, and another *According to Matthias*. We have read many others, too, lest we appear ignorant of anything, because of those people who think they know something if they have examined these gospels. But in all these questions we approve of nothing but what the Church approves of, namely only four canonical Gospels.[23]

A few years later, in his *Commentary on Matthew*:

As I have understood from tradition, respecting the four gospels, which are the only undisputed ones in the whole church of God under heaven. The first is written according to Matthew...who having published it for the Jewish converts, wrote it in the Hebrew. The second is according to Mark, who composed it, as Peter explained it to him, whom he also acknowledges as his son in his general Epistles... And the third according to Luke, the gospel commended by Paul which was for the converts from the Gentiles, and last of all the gospel according to John.[24]

These four Gospels were not recent inventions, or recent acquisitions by the church. Origen attests that he has learned about them 'from tradition', and adds that they are the only ones which are unquestioned in the entire church. His testimony is quite in harmony with that of Irenaeus.

Dionysius of Alexandria

One of Origen's successors as leader of the catechetical school at Alexandria was a man named Dionysius. In his *Letter to Basilides*,[25] written sometime before the year 251, Dionysius attempts to deal with the question of when one ought to end the fast before celebrating Easter, at sundown on Easter eve, or to wait until cockcrow on Easter morning. In order to do this Dionysius runs through the Scriptural presentations of Jesus' resurrection and decides that since nothing tells us exactly at what hour Jesus rose, while it is good to keep the longer fast, church leaders ought to grant liberty to those with weak constitutions. He takes as his objects of consultation 'the divine Gospels' and examines what each one says. The divine Gospels he consults are Matthew, Mark, Luke, and John. He omits the witness of none of these; he adds the witness of no other. No arm-twisting here; clearly, these are the very Gospels Basilides is expecting Dionysius to use. Dionysius shows how natural a thing it was to advert to the authority of just these four Gospels in the mid-third century.

Cyprian of Carthage

We see the same thing in Cyprian of Carthage, writing at about the same time. In a treatise composed of Scriptural testimonies designed to meet the Jewish arguments against Christianity, he cites texts taken from the Gospels of Matthew, Mark, Luke, and John, and no others. The witness of these Gospels, he knows, will be readily accepted by those Christians who will read his work. In a letter written to Iubaianus in 256 he writes: 'The Church is like Paradise: within her walls she encloses on the inside fruit-bearing trees ... And those trees she waters by means of four rivers—that is, by the four Gospels ... ' (*Epistle* 73.10.3).[26]

Victorinus of Pettau

A younger contemporary of Origen and Dionysius was a man named Victorinus, bishop in Pettau, which is Ptuj in modern Slovenia. He died a martyr, either in the persecution of the emperor Diocletian in about 304, or, as some now think, about twenty years earlier in a local persecution.[27] Victorinus wrote commentaries on several books of the Bible, including one on the book of Revelation. In this commentary, speaking of the four

47

living creatures in Revelation 4, he writes quite in the tradition of Irenaeus that: 'the four living creatures are the four Gospels.' In his book *On the Creation of the World*, commenting upon God's work on the fourth day of creation in Genesis 1, he echoes Irenaeus, Hippolytus, and Origen: 'Therefore this world of ours is composed of four elements—fire, water, heaven, earth . . . The sun, also, and the moon constitute throughout the space of the year four seasons . . . And to proceed further still from that principle, lo, there are four living creatures before God's throne, four Gospels, four rivers flowing in paradise . . . ' As with his predecessors, so with Victorinus, that there are four Gospels is as much a part of the natural order of things as that there are four elements, four seasons, and a number of foursomes revealed in Scripture.

Marinus of Caesarea

Most writers of the third century simply assume the four Gospels and use them, without calling attention to any controversies about them and without reference to any rivals. By this time some churches were using copies of the four bound together into a single codex, sometimes called a *megalios*, or 'big book'.[28]

Eusebius tells the story of a certain Marinus in Caesarea, Palestine, a prominent military man, who in the 260s was exposed to the authorities as a Christian and was given three hours to deny his faith. In that space of time he was met by Theotecnus, the local bishop, who accompanied him to the place where the church held its meetings.

Once inside, he placed him [i.e. Marinus] close to the altar itself, and raising his cloak a little, pointed to the sword with which he was girded; at the same time he brought and placed before him the book of the divine Gospels, and bade him choose which of the two he wished. Without hesitation he stretched forth his right hand and took the divine book. 'Hold fast then,' said Theotecnus to him, 'hold fast to God.' (*EH* 7.15.4)[29]

Marinus soon stood before the judge again. Refusing to sacrifice to the emperors, he instead confessed his faith in Christ and so was led away to his death. One of his last acts was to grasp the 'divine Gospels' in a single book. Eusebius, a successor of Theotecnus in the bishopric of Caesarea, tells us he came to know some of Marinus' friends (*EH* 7.16.1); perhaps he knew the very codex which had been held in the martyr's hands.

Euplus of Catania[30]

One of the means used by the emperor Diocletian in the year 303 in his attempt to wipe out Christianity was to outlaw its sacred books (see Eusebius, *EH* 8.2.4). In the next year one Christian in the city of Catania, Sicily, for reasons unknown, actually turned himself in! One of the accounts of this incident (there are two, one in Greek, one in Latin) says: 'When the blessed Euplus came into the council-chamber carrying the holy Gospels with him, the illustrious Maximus said to him: "This is a wicked thing you have there, especially when it is against the edicts of our emperors"' (1.1–2 Greek). Euplus was asked where he got the writings, but would only answer that 'I received them from the Lord Jesus Christ, the Son of God.' (1.5 Greek). Euplus was then asked what the books were and was ordered to read from them. 'He read from the holy Gospels according to Matthew, Mark, Luke, and John' (1.4 Greek). The Latin version reports that what he read from Matthew was, 'Blessed are they who suffer persecution for justice' sake, for theirs is the kingdom of heaven' (Matt. 5.10), and what he read from Mark was 'Whoever wishes to come after me, let him take up his cross and follow me' (Mark 8.34). At his later trial he again refused to recant and refused to offer sacrifices to the gods. The Latin reports that the Gospel book he had brought in was then tied around Euplus' neck and, so adorned, his neck was presented to the waiting swordsman (3.2 Latin).

By the time Eusebius published the first edition of his *Ecclesiastical History* in the early fourth century, still about half-a-century before Athanasius' 39th Easter Letter, he could say in all honesty that the four Gospels were the only ones received by every church under heaven, calling them 'the holy tetrad of the Gospels' (*EH* 3.25.1).

It is quite true that several of those mentioned above (we don't know about Theotecnus, Marinus, or Euplus) had read Irenaeus, but it is highly unlikely that they had all been 'persuaded' by reading Book 3 of *Against Heresies* to adopt four Gospels that they were not already used to using in their churches. The salient fact is that these Christian believers, some clerics, some laymen, give some indication of how prevalent was the acceptance of a fourfold Gospel in the time between Irenaeus and Athanasius. These Christians represent the mainstream of the 'Great Church' of the third century, in widely separated regions of the empire. All attest to the church's acceptance of the same four Gospels. None includes any Gospel under the name of *Thomas*, *Mary*, *Peter*, or *Judas* as one of the church's Gospels.

Conclusion

Some say it was Irenaeus who chose the Gospels for the church and that he was more or less alone in his day. But if he was ever alone, he soon found friends. The church after him seemed quite ready to endorse his 'choice'. If indeed it was his choice. For that readiness all around the empire in fact arouses suspicions that perhaps Irenaeus may not have been the first to choose the four Gospels at all, that their prominence perhaps dates from an even earlier time. This reminds us that the attempt to isolate any problem carries with it some risk. If one guesses wrong about where the heart of a problem lies, the problem can simply break out elsewhere. In this chapter we have only begun to see signs of a containment problem.

But before moving on to examine the church in Irenaeus' own day, as well as what had led up to it, there is another way in which the witness of Irenaeus about the four Gospels can be muted. It is sometimes called the *ad hominem* argument, and it takes its power from the psychological fact that we are less disposed to credit someone's words or ideas if that person is, or is made out to be, unappealing to us.

3

SILENCING THE BISHOP, PART II: THE UGLY IRENAEUS

S OME today evidently find Irenaeus and what he stood for to be truly and genuinely unappealing. Perhaps this is not too surprising. The title of his great literary work was *Exposure and Overthrow of Knowledge Falsely So-Called*, or, in its better-known, short title, *Against Heresies*. Its object was first to inform Christians of the systems of belief which Irenaeus regarded as counterfeits of the true Christian faith, and then to refute those systems. Clearly, this kind of writing is not an easy sell today. Moreover, in dealing with the views of his opponents, Irenaeus often indulges in sarcasm and parody. He openly calls certain people heretics, demeans their intellects, questions their motives and sometimes their morals, even charges that some are either wittingly or unwittingly in league with the devil—all of which verges on the side of what most people today would consider less than polite! And so, whatever good things Irenaeus may have said or done, some will find his aims and his rhetoric off-putting from the start.

Inflamed Rhetoric

The expectation that participants in theological disputes should maintain a consistent posture of detached objectivity and only use language which cannot be construed as offensive to anyone is, however, probably a modern one. Our sincere craving is for a civil mode of discourse, more especially in matters which tend to excite the emotions. But we'll also have to admit that such an ideal is strictly adhered to very infrequently, even in our own day. One need think back no further than the latest national political campaign for reminders of this. Not only are distortions and personal attacks still too common even in our 'enlightened' age in political and religious disputes; I would go so far as to suggest that even normally dispassionate scholars sometimes find it hard to avoid doing to Irenaeus what they accuse him of doing to his opponents.

And to understand Irenaeus' rhetoric a little better, something more should probably be said about the social and religious context in which he wrote. No matter what one might think of his polemical language, Irenaeus' detractors will find it difficult to take refuge in the thought that his theological targets modelled the kind of balanced and fair-minded treatment we all would be proud of. We happen to know that before publishing the first book of *Against Heresies* Irenaeus had come across something called the *Gospel of Judas* (*AH* 1.31.1). Most scholars think this is the same book, or at least an early version of it, that was released to the world amid shouts of acclaim just prior to Easter 2006. After devoting much study to the book, April DeConick describes the 'Sethian'[1] Christians responsible for the *Gospel of Judas* as people who were 'completely opposed to apostolic Christianity and did not consider the apostolic Christians to be real Christians'.[2]

According to this gnostic book, catholic Christians like Irenaeus are ignorant of Jesus (34.15–17); they are ruled by the stars and cannot be saved (37.2–8); they are fornicators (54.25) and murderers of their children (54.26). They are 'those who sleep with men...people of pollution and lawlessness and error' (40, lines 10–14). Whatever else one might say about the people behind this book, they can hardly be held up as models of religious toleration and the acceptance of 'alternative lifestyles'.

Scholars are well aware of this aspect of the *Gospel of Judas* and generally have no trouble maintaining a proper scholarly detachment when discussing it. 'In sum,' writes Frank Williams matter-of-factly, 'Gos. Judas exhibits the traits we would expect in a work of religious controversy, in its period or in any...'[3] We are evidently permitted a yawn. While Williams believes these same traits are characteristic of the catholic heresiologists like Irenaeus and Tertullian and of several of the gnostic works from Nag Hammadi, there is one aspect of its polemic that apparently sets the *Gospel of Judas* apart. '[T]o accuse the entire leadership of one's own community, *en bloc*, of immorality seems strange, whatever accusation one might bring against one leader or another.'[4]

The blistering accusations of the *Gospel of Judas* provide some interesting background for Irenaeus' literary work. For they eerily resemble slanders which had recently placed some of Irenaeus' fellow Christians on trial and had led to their brutal execution as forms of public entertainment. An account written soon after the atrocities which took place in the year 177, only a few years before Irenaeus would begin writing *Against Heresies*, reports that the Christians of Lyons and nearby Vienne were falsely accused . . . of Thyestean feasts and Oedipodean intercourse, and things which it is not right for us either to speak of or to think of or even to believe that such things could ever happen among men. When this rumour spread all men turned like beasts against us, so that even if any had formerly been lenient for friendship's sake they then became furious and raged against us, and there was fulfilled that which was spoken by our Lord that 'the time will come when whosoever killeth you will think that he doeth God service' (Jn. 16.2). (*EH* 5.1.14–15)

A 'Thyestean feast', from Greek mythology, refers to a meal in which Thyestes was tricked by his brother Atreus into eating the flesh of his own sons. Oedipodean intercourse refers to incest. And these were the slanderous charges that the writer thought he could mention! In such a context, in which he and his fellow Christians had been accused by the local populace and by the *Gospel of Judas* of such monstrous acts as the killing and eating of their children[5] and the practising of incest, most of Irenaeus' polemical rhetoric may seem rather pale and unimaginative.

It might also be worth mentioning one tactic employed by Irenaeus that seems to distinguish him from his opponents, at least from those whose writings survive. He prays for them. He says he prays for them, 'loving them to a better purpose than they imagine they love themselves. For our love, since it is true, is for their salvation, if they will accept it . . . Wherefore it does not weary us to extend our hand to them with all our strength . . . May we be able to persuade them to cease from their error and to stop their blasphemies against their Maker . . .' (*AH* 4.25.7). Now, some may read this and say: 'See, even when praying for them he insults them, accusing them of blasphemy. How can anyone be sincere who is so unwilling to acknowledge the legitimacy of diverse views?' And, indeed, this points to another real and legitimate question. Should there be limits to acceptable theological diversity among Christians?

Quashing Diversity

Quite obviously, Irenaeus believes that theological diversity should have limits, though it is a distortion to say that Irenaeus 'insists that only what he teaches is true'.[6] Instead he insists on the necessity of reading Scripture in community with the recognized elders of those churches which were founded by the apostles. Moreover, from some recent treatments one can easily get the impression that Irenaeus sought to enforce conformity to a rather complex theological system, to step outside of even the minor points of which would be to invite his rhetorical wrath. It will then surprise those who actually read his works to discover how much of Irenaeus' five-volume manifesto is taken up in defence of what has to be called a very basic, 'vanilla' brand of Christianity, a Christianity which Greek Orthodox, Roman Catholic, and all manner of Protestants would hold in common.

To take one important example, readers of this book will surely be familiar with certain basic ways in which world religions are commonly classified. Christianity, Judaism, and Islam are known as the great *monotheistic* religions. 'Monotheism' denotes belief in one, almighty God who made the world, and thus this broad term describes all three major religions. There is a lot it doesn't tell us about the three, for they all differ from each other in important ways, but all may be described as monotheistic. Monotheism, then, is a very basic characteristic. The Valentinians whom Irenaeus opposed, who saw themselves as Christians, were not monotheists. Neither were the Marcionites, the Basilideans, the Cerinthians, the Saturnilians, or those commonly designated 'gnostics'.[7] If any of these groups had won the day, 'Christianity' would not share with Judaism and Islam even a belief in monotheism.[8] Thus, already, Irenaeus might be seen to have some grounds for making a distinction between the 'Great Church' and these others. While it is certainly true that the figure of Jesus played some role in each of these systems (as indeed he does even in Islam), to Irenaeus, as to the modern student of world religions, what he called Christianity and what his opponents called Christianity could reasonably be categorized as different religions altogether.

But there was another problem, in Irenaeus' mind, with what these groups taught about God (to say nothing yet about what they taught about Jesus). It was a problem even graver than their belief in multiple gods. Nearly all the groups whose views he criticized (all except the Ebionites, who were Jewish) believed that the God revealed in the Jewish Scriptures, whom Irenaeus and other Christians worshipped as the only true God, was in fact one of the lesser deities, hardly fit to be called a deity. In the Valentinian system, for instance, a being given the name Sophia (Greek for 'wisdom'), the last and least of their pleroma or fullness of thirty gods, suffered a tragic moral lapse when she fell into passion. In the anxiety and grief produced by this passion, she somehow brought forth and then abandoned a horrible deformity, who grew up ignorant of his own origins. Not realizing he was the misbegotten offspring of a fallen deity, but puffed up with pride, he reasoned that he was the only, eternal God. He proclaimed, 'I am the LORD, and there is no other, besides me there is no God', a statement some readers may recognize as coming from the God of Isaiah the prophet (Isa. 45.5).[9] This self-deceived demigod, full of hubris, jealousy, and spite, is presented as the god who created matter and the world. He is the God of Abraham, Moses, David, the God of Second Temple Judaism, and the God Irenaeus and other Christians worshipped as the true God.[10] For such Christians this advanced Valentinian doctrine could be nothing but blasphemy, pure and simple. It could not be considered Christian.

Thus, whether one has any sympathy with Irenaeus and his religious views or not, his refusal to consider Marcionites, Valentinians, and gnostics as real Christians cannot be said to be grounded in hair-splitting theological distinctions.

Destroying Books

As we have seen, Irenaeus had very definite ideas about the four Gospels, and about other Christian books which he alleges were accepted as authoritative by churches throughout the empire. Irenaeus also valued other, non-Scriptural, Christian literature such as the letters of his former teacher Polycarp, or those of the martyr Ignatius, the popular allegory *The Shepherd* written by a Christian named Hermas, the traditions collected by Papias of Hierapolis, or the apologetic writings of Justin of Rome. But Irenaeus definitely did not welcome books which embodied the heretical views he thought were so harmful to people and dishonouring of the God of the Jewish and Christian Scriptures. This being the case, it is sometimes hard for scholars to resist overstating his methods of dealing with opponents. We have already cited Pagels's statement that Irenaeus resolved to 'to hack down the forest of "apocryphal and illegitimate" writings'. Just how does she think Irenaeus undertook to accomplish his literary deforestation project? According to Pagels, 'Irenaeus confronted the challenge . . . by demanding that believers destroy all those "innumerable secret and illegitimate writings" that his opponents were always invoking . . .'[11] Again, she calls attention to Irenaeus' 'instructions to congregations about which revelations to destroy and which to keep . . .'.[12]

Censoring books would be bad enough. But ordering their destruction sounds positively barbaric! Based on this practice alone, it is easy to form a conception of Irenaeus as a cruel inquisitor willing to employ extreme measures to achieve and enforce theological uniformity. The only problem is, the charge isn't true. Nowhere in the five books of *Against Heresies* does Irenaeus demand that anybody destroy any rival, holy books. Nor in his other surviving theological work, *Proof of the Apostolic Preaching*, does he make any such demand. Without question, he would have preferred that heretical books should not exist, and that no Christian should ever have to read them—he clearly advocates that rank-and-file Christians avoid them (*AH* 5.20.2). But ordering their destruction—as if he had the authority to give such instructions to churches and expect them to be obeyed—is another matter.

Much as Origen would later do, Irenaeus had apparently made his own collection of heretical books which he used for study and response (*AH* 1.31.2). In fact, he notes in one place that previous apologists for his brand of Christianity had been ineffective precisely because they were not sufficiently studied in the doctrines of their gnostic opponents (*AH* 4.preface.2). And so, Irenaeus took the trouble to read their books and to hold personal conversations with those of different persuasions. This part of Irenaeus' library may have consisted of at least the *Gospel of Judas* (1.31.1);

the *Gospel of Truth* (3.11.9); a version of the *Apocryphon of John* (1.29.1) (these last two have been preserved in the Nag Hammadi finds); some writings of the Carpocratian sect (1.25.4, 5); certain Valentinian 'commentaries' or 'notes' on Scriptural passages (1.preface.2), including comments by a man named Ptolemy on the Prologue to the Gospel of John; and he had at least read, if he did not also own, some written work of Marcion's.

Irenaeus had also come across some books by a man named Florinus, and it is in connection with these that we find the closest thing there is in the writings of Irenaeus to a demand to destroy heretical books. This comes not in *Against Heresies* but in a letter/ treatise Irenaeus wrote to Victor of Rome shortly after the latter's election as bishop in 189 CE. In this letter Irenaeus informs his younger colleague about the writings of Florinus, who was at that time advocating Valentinianism. Irenaeus and Florinus had been acquaintances decades earlier when Irenaeus was a youth in Smyrna in Asia Minor and Florinus was a young government official assigned to Smyrna and an admirer of the well-known Smyrnaean bishop, Polycarp. Florinus later drifted away from the teaching of Polycarp and (after flirting for a while with Marcionism) had embraced the doctrines of the Valentinians. At the time of Irenaeus' letter to Victor, Florinus was living in Rome, teaching in what was probably a house church and writing books which espoused Valentinianism while still claiming to be a presbyter of the orthodox church in Rome.[13] Irenaeus calls Victor's attention to Florinus' books, 'that for the sake of your reputation you may expel these writings from among you, as bringing disgrace upon you, since their author boasts himself as being one of your company. For they constitute a stumbling-block to many, who simply and unreservedly receive, as coming from a presbyter, the blasphemy which they utter against God' (Fragment 51, ANF; Syriac Fragment 28).[14]

It was not, then, simply that Irenaeus disapproved of the contents of Florinus's writings—he disapproved of the contents of any number of heretical books, as we know from *Against Heresies*. Florinus' books were not rival Gospels; they were not books which were in any sense contenders for inclusion in the canon. What was it, then, that moved Irenaeus to advise that Victor 'expel' these particular books from his midst? Evidently it was that Florinus was still passing himself off as a presbyter of the Roman church in fellowship with Victor, thus gaining for himself an illegitimate endorsement, as well as bringing notoriety to the church in Rome. This fits a pattern noticed by Irenaeus and confirmed by other evidence, that Valentinians considered themselves free to confess in public the doctrines of the mainstream church but to teach in private things which were diametrically at odds with them (*AH* 3.15.2).

Irenaeus requests that Victor 'expel' this man's writings from his midst. Irenaeus' words may mean that if some of Florinus' books should have somehow slipped into the Roman church's library, they ought to be removed. Perhaps Victor would go as far as to issue a public disavowal of the writings and a warning to house churches in fellowship with Victor not to read or be taken in by them. Yet not even here is there any instruction, much less any 'demand', to destroy these books. At this point in history, as Raymond Starr points out, even the emperor had trouble pulling off such a demand. Because books were all copied by hand and privately circulated, 'suppression or official discouragement could never be entirely successful nor were they expected to be. When a book was removed or barred by order of the emperor from the imperial public libraries, the author would be disgraced, but his writings were not destroyed, since they could still circulate in private hands.'[15]

Needless to say, no church—not Irenaeus's church in Lyons nor the church in Rome—had anything resembling the kind of imperial power (the kind which would later be exercised against Christians by the Roman government) to search out private copies of a detested book, seize them, and destroy them. In sum, Irenaeus did not demand that congregations destroy any Gospels, alleged apostolic letters, or revelations he had not 'chosen' for them.

Sex, Lies, and Anti-heretical Tracts

It is clear that many today believe Irenaeus was ruthless in dealing with his opponents and unfairly tried to prevent their voices from being heard. On the question of his accuracy in representing the theological views of his opponents Irenaeus has, perhaps surprisingly, been largely acquitted by recent studies, even after the discovery of the Nag Hammadi library.[16] But what about his personal attacks on his opponents? Did Irenaeus' palpable frustration with these people and their teaching ever lead him to misrepresent their characters? It would be very remarkable if it never did.[17] As we have seen, it is difficult enough for today's scholars, schooled in the ideals of objective impartiality, trained with the exacting methods of modern scholarship, and backed up by eagle-eyed copy-editors, to avoid distorting the views and the characters of those in the ancient world whom they find unattractive.

Yet there is one portion of his report in particular which has prompted some scholars to call Irenaeus' honesty into question, and this one is particularly interesting in the light of our present knowledge about sexual abuse. Irenaeus claims that a certain Valentinian teacher named Marcus, whom Irenaeus calls 'a perfect adept in magical impostures' (*AH* 1.13.1), duped and then sexually violated certain women of the church. Some of the women who had been induced to join Marcus later confessed—or alleged—that they had been seduced by him and succumbed after participating in his sexually charged rituals (1.6.3; 1.13.5). These are very serious charges. Obviously, if they are true, it was exceedingly disturbing to the church in Irenaeus' day. If they are not true, it is disturbing that Irenaeus would repeat such libel. Disturbing too, however, is the number of scholars today who ignore, downplay, or dismiss the report altogether, assuming or explicitly charging that it is nothing more than typical Christian slander on Irenaeus' part, made for polemical purposes. Writes one: 'Lying behind such slurs is the notion that those who side with God will lead moral, upright lives . . . the charges of immorality continued for as long as there were orthodox polemicists to make them. They continue today, among Christian groups inclined to accuse others of heresy.'[18] Another says: 'For the most part, Irenaeus' information about Marcus seems to be nothing more than malevolent rumors.'[19] Viewed as standard, Christian polemical fare, such charges as Irenaeus makes against Marcus are taken seriously only as reflecting poorly on the person who made them.

Malevolent rumours can at times have deadly consequences. We have seen that Irenaeus' Christian community in Gaul had been on the receiving end of such not many years earlier. Some of his friends suffered the ignominy of having to deny with their dying breaths charges that they ate their children or slept with their daughters.

And theirs was not the first, nor would it be the last, community of Christians so to suffer. Earlier in the century Melito of Sardis in Asia Minor had written to the emperor Marcus Aurelius (161–80 CE) complaining of people pillaging Christians' property and of Christians being put to death because of lies and false accusations (*EH* 4.26.5–11). Intermittent exposure to public scorn for 'immorality' or 'atheism' dogged catholic Christians for centuries. Any natural disaster or danger to the public good might even be seen as retribution by the gods for public toleration of the Christians. Tertullian would write in about 200 CE: 'They think the Christians the cause of every public disaster, of every affliction with which the people are visited. If the Tiber rises as high as the city walls, if the Nile does not send its waters up over the fields, if the heavens give no rain, if there is an earthquake, if there is famine or pestilence, straightway the cry is, "Away with the Christians to the lion"' (*Apology* 40). Irenaeus had witnessed some members of his congregation thrown to the lions, others burned alive, others tortured and left with permanent physical handicaps. And this persecution was fed by anti-Christian smears. Coming back to Marcus, then, was an embittered Irenaeus, still stinging from the recent distresses of his own Christian community, simply doing to Marcus what others had done to them? The seriousness of the charges on all sides makes the matter deserving of a little more attention.

The acts attributed to Marcus, as outrageous as they are, are not beyond belief (like, for instance, charges of child murder and cannibalism). The financial and sexual seduction of women by charismatic, itinerant male teachers was not at all unknown in that day. The contemporary philosopher and satirist Lucian of Samosata, in his satire *The Runaways*, inveighs against the Cynic philosophers:

When beauty comes within the reach of these grave and reverend gentlemen, they are guilty of excesses that I will not pollute my lips with mentioning. They have been known, like Trojan Paris, to seduce the wives of their own hosts, and to quote the authority of Plato for leaving these fair converts at the disposal of all their acquaintance . . . I will not tire you with a description of their drunken orgies; observe, however, that these are the men who preach against drunkenness and adultery and avarice and lewdness. Could any contrast be greater than that presented by their words and their deeds? . . . To hear them, you would say they were at war with pleasure, and Epicurus their bitterest foe: yet nothing do they do but for pleasure's sake. (*The Runaways* 18–19, see also 30–1)[20]

If this is 'standard polemical fare', it is at least not standard *Christian* polemical fare. Lucian, far from being a Christian, was in fact a well-known opponent of Christianity.

Nor does Irenaeus rest in blanket charges that indict the entire Valentinian community or its leadership, like those made against the apostolic Christians in the *Gospel of Judas*. That is, he alleges no similar crimes on the parts of other Valentinian teachers,[21] such as Ptolemy and Heracleon, or Valentinus himself. In fact he allows that 'There are those among them who assert that that man who comes from above [that is, the Valentinian] ought to follow a good course of conduct' (*AH* 3.15.2). But both Irenaeus and others in his community had personal knowledge of many of Marcus' current and erstwhile followers, first in Asia Minor and later in Gaul (*AH* 1.preface; 1.13.7).

Most notable in this matter is Irenaeus' mention of one particular woman, the wife of a deacon in his church when he lived in Asia Minor, where Marcus taught.[22] The woman, after consorting for a while with Marcus and eventually being coaxed by church members to leave him and return to her husband, 'spent her whole time in the exercise of public confession, weeping over and lamenting the defilement which she had received from this magician' (*AH* 1.13.5). Irenaeus presents this as a very public case which occurred in a specific locale with a specific woman, the wife of a deacon in his church. If he is making this up it surely will have aroused many suspicions and finger-pointings within his old church back in Asia Minor where his writings were read. Moreover, many in the congregations in Gaul had come with Irenaeus from Asia Minor, and would have known if the story about the church officer's wife was his invention or not. These considerations, then, make it hard for me to agree with those who assume that Irenaeus simply invented the story as part of a smear-campaign against Marcus and his followers.

But what about the woman herself? Perhaps it was she who fabricated the story about Marcus' unseemly exploits. But if so, what was her motive? Her constant confession of her unfaithfulness could not have brought her a notoriety she or her deacon husband would have sought. There were no civil damages to collect by taking her alleged victimizer to court, no tabloids offering money for her story. And according to Irenaeus, this was not an isolated occurrence. It had been repeated time after time during the 'ministry' of Marcus in Asia Minor and then in the Rhône valley, where some of Marcus' followers had emigrated. Shall we assume that the stories of these women too were fictitious, and that they all simply wanted to titillate their listeners or cover up their mistakes in order to gain readmittance into the church? Irenaeus says that the women who eventually left Marcus often confessed 'that they have been defiled by him, and that they were filled with a burning passion towards him'. That is, it appears they did not simply make Marcus the scapegoat, but owned responsibility for their illicit excitations.

Marcus is not here to defend himself, and the women cannot now be cross-examined. Should we, then, in cases of doubt, simply *assume* that the deacon's wife concocted her story, along with the other women Irenaeus mentions? Recent scholarship has given us empathetic and valuable studies of many women from the history of early Christianity, including Mary Magdalene, Junia, Thecla, Blandina, Perpetua, and Felicitas. But nobody (to my knowledge) has risen up in defence of this woman or her fellow injured. She gets no sympathy from scholars, even female scholars, even feminist female scholars, whom we might expect to be alive to the plight of women in patriarchal societies.[23]

The refusal of modern scholars to take the testimony of this woman and her co-plaintiffs seriously, and on the other hand, their tendency to speak glowingly of Marcus (perhaps the strongest argument for crediting Irenaeus' report is that Marcus still has a mysterious ability to make people swoon today!) may seem a little disconcerting, particularly given what we have learned in recent years about society's tendency to dismiss women's stories of abuse.[24] Could it be that the risk for some is simply too great? For admitting that the stories of exploitation might be true could seem to remove one demerit from the reputation of Irenaeus.

Conclusion

While it will be evident that I think the efforts of some in the academic community have overreached—to the point that they have done to Irenaeus just what they accuse him of doing to others—in the end, no matter how ugly Irenaeus looks, no matter how unpleasant his rhetoric might be or how outdated his intolerance of substantive theological pluralism seems, the effort to spotlight these features can only have limited success. This is because it still belongs to an *ad hominem* argument which can only temporarily distract from the real question. And that is, is Irenaeus simply a blip on the radar screen, an inexplicable eruption appearing out of nowhere and quickly sinking back into oblivion? Or, does he represent a wider phenomenon, one that had real precedents and left other collateral effects? In short, was this 'arch-conspirator' acting alone, or did he have any accomplices, any 'co-conspirators', in his 'plot' to set the four Gospels of Matthew, Mark, Luke, and John, as the standards for the church?

4

IRENAEUS'
'CO-CONSPIRATORS':
A TEACHER, A PREACHER,
AND A CANON-LIST MAKER

IF a four-Gospel canon was Irenaeus' idea, as some assert, it was an idea which caught on quickly. As we have seen, a four-Gospel canon soon became standard (if it was not already standard) among churches throughout the empire. Those who argue that Irenaeus was the inventor or first promoter of the four-Gospel canon of course believe that his views were not shared by other Christians in his day. Lee McDonald, for example, tries to establish the point that 'in Irenaeus's day few Christians limited the number of Gospels to be read in their churches to the same four that he did. In fact, Irenaeus is the only witness in his generation who acknowledges only the four canonical Gospels in his NT Scripture collection.'[1] He goes on to speak about the worship practice of the churches: 'At the end of the second century, a canonical Gospel might likely be read alongside one or more noncanonical gospels.' As the records of very few churches of that period are available to us, how does one prove or disprove such an assertion?

McDonald cites five examples of individuals or groups from the last half of the second century which he believes show Irenaeus to be a loner: Clement of Alexandria, Serapion of Antioch, a group of people called 'the Alogi', another known as the Ebionites, and Tatian the Syrian. In this chapter we'll take a closer look at all of these but the last, who is postponed till Chapter 5. In addition, we'll take a look at a famous, and controversial, early list of New Testament books, the *Muratorian Fragment*.

Clement of Alexandria and the 'Hand-me-down' Gospels

Alexandria, Egypt, where Clement lived, is a long way from Gaul. This is true not only in terms of distance but also culture. Irenaeus in Gaul lived on the frontiers of the Roman empire. Clement lived in a city long renowned for its high culture and its institutions of learning. Its great library of 700,000 volumes was a wonder of the ancient world. And Clement moved among some of the best-educated, upper-class, Greek-speaking Egyptians in Alexandria. As a Christian intellectual he wanted to advertise the benefits of the Christian faith to people who were by birth and/or education among society's elite. Both Clement and Irenaeus were well read, both were incisive thinkers, and both inveighed against Christian heresies which they believed were destructive to people. But the types of people they interacted with day to day probably tended to be on different ends of the economic and educational scale.[2]

As we noted in Chapter 1, various forms of gnostic thought (both Christian and non-Christian versions) flourished in the Egypt of Clement's day, and in his efforts to make Christianity more broadly known and accepted he had to deal with the confusion created by the existence of rival claimants to the Christian name. Thus, while Clement and Irenaeus shared many basic assumptions, the attitude towards pagan literature displayed by Clement the cosmopolitan differed from that of Irenaeus. In the freer intellectual environment of Alexandria, Clement was much more apt to look for points of agreement between Christianity and what he considered the best of Graeco-Egyptian literature and morals, the literature and morals accepted by the crowds in which he moved.

It would hardly, therefore, be surprising if Clement should also display an attitude towards the use of some apocryphal Gospels and other Christian literature different from that of Irenaeus. Indeed, Clement cites some of these lesser-known works and at times he seems confident of the truth of what he cites. This, of course, has been keenly noted by scholars. Some point to his 'liberal use' of, or his 'frequent reference' to, Gospels other than the canonical ones.[3] In his surviving works Clement, it is said, uses the *Gospel of the Egyptians* no less than eight times,[4] and the *Gospel of the Hebrews* and something called the *Traditions of Matthias* three times each.[5] Most scholars today seem happy to leave the impression that these Gospels, not to mention several other non-Gospel texts,[6] were esteemed by Clement every bit as highly as the four. Thus, Clement was surely at odds with Irenaeus.

Or was he? One thing missing from these listings commonly used by scholars is any comparative information about how many times the canonical Gospels are referenced by Clement. According to a recent monograph by Bernard Mutschler, Clement uses the Gospel according to Matthew 757 times in his extant works, Luke 402 times, John 331 times. Even the Gospel of Mark, so sparsely attested among the discovered papyrus fragments mentioned in Chapter 1, is cited by Clement 182 times.[7] That makes a total of 1,672 references to one of the four canonical Gospels, fourteen to the three non-canonical ones, a ratio of about 120 to 1. To the casual but now better-informed observer, it might appear that the *Gospel of the Egyptians*, the *Gospel of the Hebrews*, and the *Traditions of Matthias* (and whatever other Gospel-like materials he might have known) were not close rivals to the four canonical Gospels in Clement's mind.

Also worth noting is Clement's complete lack of interest in those Gospels which some today like to promote as the most popular rivals to the four in the early church. That is, Clement cites the *Gospel of Thomas* and the *Gospel of Peter* a combined total of zero times.[8] Throw in the *Egerton Gospel*, the *Gospel of Judas*, and the *Gospel of Mary*, and the number remains zero.

It is likely that Clement used the *Gospel of the Egyptians*, the *Gospel of the Hebrews*, and the *Traditions of Matthias* in particular because they happened to be in circulation in Alexandria at the time and were known to some of his contemporaries. One expert on Clement's writings, Annewies van den Hoek, points out that Clement may not even have known the *Gospel of the Egyptians* first-hand, but only through quotations of it he had read in the

Table 4.1. *Clement of Alexandria's citations from Gospel-like sources*

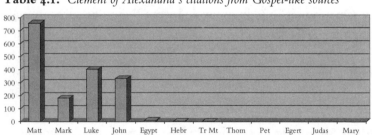

writings of a man named Julian Cassian, whom Clement was attempting to refute.[9] Van den Hoek also notes that: 'Even when the discussion is provoked by his opponents and the texts to which they refer may not have been his favourites, he still plunges into the discussion without reservation. He usually takes their texts seriously; he questions the interpretation of the words but not the words themselves . . .'[10]

The numbers mentioned above would certainly suggest that if Clement ever found anything valuable in these other books, it was not very often. But even more significant than the gaudy numbers is what Clement actually says about the books in question. Here is another place where information routinely passed over by certain scholars turns out to be quite essential.

In chapter 5 of his book *Who is the Rich Man That Shall Be Saved?* Clement refers to the Gospel of Mark and to the other 'acknowledged Gospels', showing that, in his mind, certain Gospels had already been 'acknowledged' or 'agreed upon' by the church, and others had not.[11] In his treatise entitled *Stromateis*, written in the early or mid-190s, he specifically calls Matthew, Mark, Luke, and John 'the four Gospels that have been handed down to us' (*Strom.* 3.13.93). This is important, because in speaking of only these four Gospels as 'handed down' Clement sounds very much like Irenaeus, who also spoke of the very same four as handed down to the church, ultimately from the apostles (*AH* 3.11.9). In the context, Clement is contrasting the 'hand-me-down' Gospels with something written in the *Gospel of the Egyptians*, something he is here rejecting precisely because it was written in that Gospel and not in Matthew, Mark, Luke, or John! 'On this account he [Cassian] says: "When Salome asked when she would know the answer to her questions, the Lord said, When you trample on the robe of shame, and when the two shall be one, and the male with the female, and there is neither male nor female".' Clement immediately objects: 'In the first place we have not got the saying in the four Gospels that have been handed down to us, but in the Gospel according to the Egyptians.'[12]

Eusebius had a copy of one of Clement's books which has not survived, his *Hypotyposeis* (*EH* 6.14.5–7). In this book Clement repeats an earlier tradition which he had received about the Gospels. This tradition probably came from his older colleague Pantaenus, who in turn attributed it to primitive elders. It said that the Gospels which contain the genealogies of Jesus, that is, Matthew and Luke (no other Gospel we know of contains a genealogy of Jesus), were the first of the four to be written,[13] that Mark was written for those in Rome who had heard the apostle Peter's preaching and wanted a record of it, and that John, 'last of all . . . composed a spiritual Gospel'. Calling John the 'last of all' clearly sets these four Gospels apart from any others which might have been produced by others at a later time. Clearly, these four are in a class by themselves. And, just as significant, Clement is here repeating what he had received ultimately from 'primitive elders'. This means that Clement, who wrote only just after Irenaeus, did not derive this view of the uniqueness of these four from Irenaeus or anyone of his generation. It was a tradition of long-standing.

And so we come away from Clement with the same impression we got from Irenaeus: there are only four Gospels, Matthew, Mark, Luke, and John, which are acknowledged by the church and 'handed down' from earlier generations. While Clement does not report specifically on the liturgical practices of his church in Alexandria, his evidence gives us no reason to think that his church would have read any Gospels alongside these four 'hand-me-down' Gospels as Scripture.

Do Christians Read Other Books?

If there is a difference between Clement and Irenaeus it is that while Clement was willing to use critically at least two or three other works when it suited his purposes, Irenaeus apparently was not. But were Clement and Irenaeus in fact so entirely different? Often forgotten is the fact that Irenaeus once cites the fourth volume of Papias' work in which Papias preserves three sayings of Jesus not written in any of the Gospels (*AH* 5.33.3–4). What is most surprising is that Irenaeus seems to vouch for the authenticity of these sayings. No scholar I know of seriously entertains the idea that these words were actually spoken by Jesus. This is not only because they seem so unlike anything Jesus says in the canonical Gospels, but also because they in fact mirror words that are contained in the pseudepigraphal Jewish work *2 Baruch* from around the beginning of the second century CE. Somehow, Papias or one of his sources had mistakenly attributed these words to Jesus through the alleged means of John the apostle. But Irenaeus was not aware of that history, and accepts the report that Jesus actually said them. Even so, it is clear that these sayings of Jesus do not carry the weight of the words of Jesus recorded in the authoritative Gospels. When Irenaeus cites the non-Gospel sayings, he does not introduce them straightforwardly as the words of Jesus, but as the words of the elders who heard from John what Jesus said. By comparison, he never cites the word of Jesus recorded in the Gospels as, for instance, 'as Luke has reported, who heard it from those who had heard Jesus, that Jesus said . . . '.

This sort of qualification we also have in Clement. Clement, like Irenaeus, seems to hold open the possibility that some words Jesus actually spoke might have been preserved more or less intact, passed down in other sources. So what did Clement think of these other sources?

It may be natural for modern readers to assume that when an ancient writer quotes another book, he or she accepted the entire book as authoritative. In the majority of cases the assumption may be correct. But not always, and often there was actually a principle involved. The principle is observed in a comment made by Origen, Clement's successor at the Alexandrian catechetical school, about a book called *The Preaching of Peter*. This *Preaching of Peter* is not a Gospel, but an 'apologetic' work written in defence of the Christian faith. Its fictional style has the apostle Peter declaiming like a second-century apologist, though it also contains some alleged sayings of Jesus. Noting that Heracleon the Valentinian had used citations from this book, Origen says, 'We would also have to examine that little book to see if it is genuine at all, or spurious, or a mixture' (*Commentary on John* 13.104).[14] We may be confident that Origen did not think any examination would find this work to be 'genuine', as he shows no interest in investigating the matter. Did he, then, regard it as spurious? Some scholars think this *Preaching of Peter* is the same book Origen mentions elsewhere under the title *The Doctrine of Peter*. Origen says that if anyone should refer to a certain statement of Jesus recorded in the latter, 'the answer must be given him, in the first place, that this book is not included among the books of the church, and further it must be pointed out that this writing comes neither from Peter nor from any other person inspired by the Spirit of God' (*On First Principles*, praef. 8). Clearly Origen regards *The Doctrine of Peter* as spurious and unacceptable. Whether this spurious book is the same as the *Preaching*, unfortunately, we do not know. In any case, it is interesting that Origen in his *Commentary on John* mentions another category for certain writings, those that are 'mixed', that is, writings which might contain some truth or perhaps even some genuine teaching of the apostle Peter, but this will be mixed in with spurious material.[15]

This same *Preaching of Peter*, which Origen thought was either spurious or mixed, which he reports that Heracleon the Valentinian had used, had also been cited several times by Clement. It appears that it was a popular book making the rounds in Alexandria near the end of the second century. Some have observed that Clement seems to cite from it as if it really contained the apostle Peter's authentic testimony. Origen's notion of 'mixed' writings, mentioned specifically with regard to *The Preaching of Peter*, enables us to see how Clement too might have thought himself able to take from this work what he gauged was authentic material but without endorsing the entire book.

In his *Commentary on the Song of Solomon* Origen makes another illuminating comment about 'mixed' books. Here he observes that the authors of the New Testament themselves sometimes used apocryphal books, books written after the Old Testament books and not considered to be Scripture by the Jews. If these books are not sacred Scripture, how is it that the inspired New Testament authors occasionally used them?

Not that the apocryphal writings are to be given a place in this way: we must *not overpass the everlasting limits which our fathers have set* [citing the words of Proverbs 22.28]. But it may be that the apostles and evangelists, being filled with the Holy Spirit, knew what was to be taken out of those writings and what must be rejected; whereas we, who have not such abundance of the Spirit, cannot without danger presume so to select.[16]

The apostles had such an abundance of the Spirit that they could discern what was true and good in writings which were otherwise questionable, or at least not Scripture. We, who are not so wise, can only do what they did with hesitation and some 'danger'. It is clear that Origen thought he had enough of the Spirit to brave the danger on occasion himself! He, Clement, and others read and occasionally cited for their useful testimonies books which 'are not to be given a place', that is, a place among the authoritative books of Scripture.

The point is that the four Gospels of Matthew, Mark, Luke, and John did have 'a place' among the Scriptures. And the scriptural status of the four Gospels was not, to Clement's mind, something they had acquired anytime recently, or something he had to argue for. On the contrary, these four had been passed down in the church from what were already in Clement's day 'ancient' times.

So much, then, for the conflict between Clement and Irenaeus. The two seem instead rather boringly, monotonously, the same. They seem like allies, or, shall we say, 'co-conspirators' in their acceptance and promotion of the church's four acknowledged Gospels. But around the corner and up the coast from Alexandria, in Antioch of Syria, lived an influential bishop who, experts say, had a radically different idea.

Serapion of Antioch and the *Gospel of Peter*: For Every Church a Different Gospel?

Antioch, in Syria, was a thriving metropolis in antiquity and is well known to readers of the New Testament. According to the Acts of the Apostles, Antioch is where the followers of Jesus were

first called Christians (Acts 11.26). Paul, Barnabas, and Peter had
ministered there. Early in the second century the Antiochene
bishop Ignatius was arrested and taken to Rome, where he suffered martyrdom. Several decades later another bishop of Antioch, Theophilus, wrote an apologetic work, *To Autolycus*,
intended to answer charges against the Christians and to win
over sceptics. The church in Antioch, then, already had a long
and storied history and enjoyed high esteem as an important
centre of apostolic Christianity. Surely, the views of the Antiochene bishop would command an automatic respect in the wider
church.

Such respect is put on display not long after Serapion was
elected bishop (*c*.189 CE) when he played some role in settling
a dispute in a nearby town called Rhossus. This dispute and
Serapion's response to it also shed much light on ecclesiastical
attitudes towards Christian Gospels at that time and in that
region. The dispute, as Eusebius relates in the sixth book of his
Ecclesiastical History, concerned a book known as the *Gospel of
Peter*. On a visit to Rhossus Serapion was asked about this book
and initially gave his consent to its being read. But later, after
returning home and examining the book himself, he wrote a
letter to the church in Rhossus in which he criticized the *Gospel
of Peter* as a Gospel which had been interpolated by 'docetists',
those who denied the incarnation of Jesus and taught that his
suffering was not real. McDonald summarizes the story in the
following way:

when asked by the Christians in Rhossus for permission to read the
Gospel of Peter in the church, [Serapion] agreed at first to let it be read.
He would not have done so presumably if he had already accepted
Irenaeus's notion of a closed four-Gospel canon. It was only after

reading for himself the *Gospel of Peter* at a later time that Serapion saw that it denied the humanity of Jesus, and so he reversed his earlier decision. He did so not on the basis of a widely accepted closed Gospel canon, but on the basis of a canon of truth that was circulating in the churches.[17]

McDonald's summary would be fairly typical of several recent scholarly treatments of this incident. These scholars tend to agree on three important points:[18]

1. That the church at Rhossus at the time of Serapion's visit either was requesting to use,[19] or already had an established custom of using, the *Gospel of Peter* for public reading in church 'as its sacred text'.[20] 'There is no way of knowing', says one scholar, 'whether... the Christians of Rhossus ever had heard of Matthew, Mark, Luke, and John. Their Gospel was the *Gospel of Peter*...'[21]

2. That Serapion's initial permission meant he approved of the *Gospel of Peter* being read thus in Christian services of worship as a Scriptural or authentically Petrine document. 'Not knowing the character of the book, but assuming that it must be acceptable if Peter himself had written it, Serapion allowed its use...'[22]

3. That the reason for his eventual banning of the book was 'not because he objected in principle to gospels other than Matthew, Mark, Luke or John—we know nothing about his acquaintance with or regard for them—but simply because he found theological fault with its contents'.[23]

It is easy, then, to draw a clear contrast between Serapion and Irenaeus in their respective attitudes towards Gospel literature.[24] Here we seem to have proof that there was no accepted canon of four Gospels at the end of the second century, and evidence for Irenaeus' isolation from his contemporaries. We cannot forget, however, that Clement in Alexandria at the same time was very much on the same page with Irenaeus. So, if Serapion had a different approach to Scripture and a looser attitude towards the reading of Gospels in the church, perhaps he, not Irenaeus, was the odd one out.

But as it happens, the three points mentioned above, on which several recent scholars have found a consensus, are not borne out by Serapion's letter. A re-examination will show, I think, that this consensus was arrived at prematurely.

What Does One Read in Church? Or, Ancient Liturgical Book Clubs

Was the church at Rhossus using, or requesting to use, the *Gospel of Peter* for public reading in church during its gatherings for worship? Here is what the relevant part of Serapion's letter to the church at Rhossus says: 'For I myself, when I came among you, imagined that all of you clung to the true faith; and, without going through the Gospel being put forward by them in the name of Peter, I said: If this is the only thing that seems to cause you dissension, let it be read' (*EH* 6.12.4).

The first thing to notice from this account is that at the time of Serapion's visit to Rhossus this new Gospel was 'being put forward'. That is, not only was it at that time unknown to Bishop Serapion, it must have been fairly new to the church in Rhossus too. Clearly it had not been functioning as the Rhossians' Gospel or their sacred text. This is confirmed by the distinction in

Serapion's letter between 'you' and 'them'. This Gospel was 'being put forward by them', that is, by one group in the church, not by the whole church. And this group must not have represented the leadership of the church because Serapion addresses his letter to 'you', obviously those who officially represent the church, and distinguishes 'you' from 'them', the ones who were putting forth the novel Gospel at the time of Serapion's visit. Later in the letter Serapion mentions the name of an apparent leader of this group, a person named Marcianus, and speaks of him in the third person, as if he didn't expect that Marcianus would ever read the letter. At the time of his visit Serapion assumed that everyone's motives were pure. But he has since learned about the promoters of the *Gospel of Peter* that, as he puts it, 'their mind was lurking in some heresy'.

And when Serapion said, 'If this is the only thing that seems to cause you dissension, let it be read', was he approving it for reading in worship services as Scripture? To many people today who perhaps are not accustomed to regarding anything as 'Holy Scripture' this may not seem hard to believe. It is a bit more surprising that scholars, who know more about how people in antiquity regarded their Scriptures, would think that a bishop, when presented by some laypeople with a book he'd never seen before, a book he'd just been informed had been 'causing dissension' in the church, 'without going through' the book himself and without consulting the church's leadership, would have consented in so offhand a manner to a request to use the book as Scripture. As far as we know, Christian worship was not a liturgical book club, with every individual or faction able to suggest his, her, or its choice.

What was The Gospel of Peter?

But why would Bishop Serapion agree even to the private reading of a book such as the *Gospel of Peter*? This is indeed puzzling, and if one assumes that Christians of that period read the Bible and only the Bible, it will be a tough question to answer. But when we look at actual Christian practice both in that period and beyond, perhaps the question is not so difficult after all. We have just seen that Serapion's contemporary, Clement of Alexandria, was not averse to reading non-Scriptural books, even Scripture-like, non-Scriptural books. Granted, he did not recommend them or approve them for other Christians to read. But his example may have implied to others that he didn't think they were so bad (his example has certainly given modern scholars the idea that he admired them very much!) Even Irenaeus endorsed Papias' books, which purported to give a few sayings of Jesus not recorded in the authentic Gospels. The author of the *Muratorian Fragment* (which we shall examine below) even encourages Christians to read two works, the *Apocalypse of Peter* and *The Shepherd* of Hermas, which he or others think 'cannot be read publicly to the people in church'.

What kind of book was this *Gospel of Peter*? Just about all we know about it for certain is what Serapion tells us in the few words of his letter recorded by Eusebius. It was apparently a Gospel in genre and, as Serapion said after studying it, 'most of it was of the orthodox teaching of the Saviour', though some heretical parts had been added. Eusebius knew a book of this title and listed it as among those put forth by heretics (*EH* 3.25.6, probably thinking of the incident at Rhossus).

In 1886–7 French archaeologists discovered in an Egyptian cemetery, at a place called Akhmim (ancient Panopolis), a strange parchment codex. It has often been reported that this codex was found in the grave of a monk, and that the monk therefore must have specially prized the codex and the writings it contained, even more than he treasured the canonical Gospels. This is part of a legend which has grown up around the discovery. We don't know if the person in whose grave it was found was a monk or not, or what that person thought of the book.[25] As far as we know, the gravedigger could have thrown it into the grave to get rid of it! In any case, the late sixth- or early seventh-century codex contained, among other writings, part of a Gospel which told the story of Jesus from the point of view of Peter. Could this be the *Gospel of Peter* known to Serapion?

In later years a few papyrus fragments discovered in Egypt have been suggested to be fragments of the *Gospel of Peter* by some scholars. Mentioned in Chapter 1, these are the fragments known as P.Oxy. 4009 (from a codex) and P.Oxy. 2949 (from a roll), plus a third fragment, containing the so-called Fayum Gospel, which has been claimed by a few scholars as belonging to this Gospel. Unfortunately, none of these contains any text that overlaps with the Gospel found at Akhmim, and the case for the Fayum Gospel seems particularly weak. Moreover, the identification of any of these, including the Akhmim Gospel, with the *Gospel of Peter* has recently been called into question,[26] leaving us with only a set of probabilities and no certainty that we have the document seen by Serapion.

If the Akhmim Gospel is the *Gospel of Peter* in question, as most scholars have assumed, there is also no guarantee that the text found at Akhmim has not undergone many changes from the text which was known to Serapion. The Akhmim Gospel, as we have it, is a retelling of the story only of Jesus' passion and resurrection,

Illustration 4.1 The Akhmîm Fragment, commonly identified as the *Gospel of Peter*. A parchment codex. Sixth or seventh century. Used by permission of the Center for the Study of Ancient Documents, Dr A. Bülow-Jacobsen, and the Cairo Museum.

though the original may have contained more than this. J. K. Elliott reports that: 'Nowadays it is generally concluded that this gospel is secondary to and dependent on the accounts of the passion in the canonical Gospels.'[27] This Gospel adds many details to those accounts and a few weird twists, to be sure, including a portrayal of the resurrected Jesus as so exalted in stature that his head extended beyond the heavens, and a talking cross! Noticeable also is its amplification of the responsibility of the Jews for Jesus' death, and its general anti-Jewish slant.[28] In only a couple of places, however, could its modifications be called potentially docetic or heretical in flavour, and even these are ambiguous.[29]

What, then, was the aim of the person who wrote this Gospel? In his recent treatment of this question Joseph Verheyden concludes that the Akhmim *Gospel of Peter* 'rather echoes the voice of somebody living in and addressing a more popular, though perhaps not completely uncultivated milieu. The really "novel" things, such as the detailed description of the resurrection, would only demonstrate that GP indeed is the kind of popularizing account that would have appealed to these circles.'[30]

The character of the Akhmim Gospel (if it is virtually what Serapion saw) reinforces the idea that Serapion would not have been approving the *Gospel of Peter* for use as Scripture in the church at Rhossus. Put on the spot, he gave the scroll (or codex) a cursory look and couldn't see what all the fuss was about. He probably assumed it was a pious, popular attempt to amalgamate the better-known Gospel accounts of the story of Jesus, with no obvious harmful agenda. No doubt he had seen this kind of popular Christian literature before.

The *Gospel of Peter*, like the Egerton Gospel,[31] offers a popular retelling of the familiar Gospel story with some fictional elements.

But there were other pseudepigraphal books which were fiction through and through. And though we often associate pseudepigraphal writing with the tactics of 'heretics', those wanting to argue for what they considered an under-appreciated agenda, we know that the genre was sometimes co-opted by orthodox writers as well. Sometimes the object was apparently to offer a fictional orthodox counterblast to a fictional heretical work. An example of such is the writing known as *The Epistle of the Apostles*, to be examined in a later chapter. Sometimes the overriding object of these fictions seems to be nothing more than simply pious (one presumes), popular entertainment, much as one finds even today in religious bookstores. The *Infancy Gospel of Thomas* (not to be confused with the better-known *Gospel of Thomas*) was probably written as Christian children's literature.[32] Particularly interesting, because we happen to have a report about its origin, is the case of the *Acts of Paul*. Tertullian tells us that this fictional work describing the exploits of the apostle was written by a presbyter in Asia Minor who, in his self-defence, said he wrote it out of love for Paul (*On Baptism* 17). But perhaps because they wanted to prevent any more incidents like the one that took place at Rhossus, his fellow clergy members tried to put an end to this by relieving the presbyter of his office. Nevertheless, the work gained a certain popularity.

Other fictional *Acts* of apostles could be mentioned and possibly other works as well. Perhaps Serapion was familiar with the apologetic work, *The Preaching of Peter*, cited positively by Clement of Alexandria and Heracleon. Besides fictional works like these, we know that at least two Gospel Harmonies, sober attempts to combine the separate elements of multiple Gospels into a single narrative, had lately been produced and were known in the region by that time. We'll hear more about them later as well. The *Gospel of Peter* is not a Gospel Harmony, but it shares in common with a Harmony and with certain other works like the Egerton Gospel an attempt in some way to produce a single retelling of the story of Jesus with some indebtedness to existing written sources. While a Harmony does this in a very exacting way as the result of a thorough comparison of the sources, these other Gospels do so less reflectively, with no concern for preserving the source material with any verbal precision. Serapion was surely acquainted with them as well. With this kind of literature in circulation, it is not difficult to imagine that even a bishop might look at some of these popular works as spurious but relatively harmless for private reading.

Ehrman thinks that Serapion assumed, at first glance, that he was looking at a genuine writing of the apostle Peter. It seems instead that the bishop simply viewed it as harmless and not worth fighting about. Ehrman, in an imaginary scenario, posits that the pastor of the church in Rhossus might have written back protesting Serapion's high-handeness in banning their sacred Scripture.[33] I imagine instead he would have written back thanking Serapion for putting out a flame he had inadvertently fanned.

Serapion's Hand-me-down Library

We can safely conclude that the church in Rhossus had not been using the *Gospel of Peter* as its sacred Scripture. We have also seen several reasons to think that Serapion did not accept its title at face value, did not assume that it was a genuine work of St Peter, and was not approving of the book for reading in church. But there is an often neglected part of Serapion's letter which would seem to lay this last theory to rest once and for all. The letter, Eusebius tells us, carried the title *Concerning the So-called Gospel according to Peter*, and the portion he preserves begins with Serapion saying: 'For we ourselves, brothers, receive both Peter and the other apostles as Christ, but the pseudepigraphal writings (written) in their name we reject, as having experience in such things, knowing that we did not receive such writings by tradition' (*EH* 6.12.3–6, my translation).

Four points about Serapion's words here stand out. First, he knows a category of books 'received by tradition'. That is, surprisingly, just like Clement and just like Irenaeus, Serapion too had a library of 'hand-me-down' books he had inherited from previous generations in the church. He claims he knows very well which ones they are, and the 'so-called *Gospel of Peter*', no matter how harmless or how edifying it might be for personal reading, was not one of them. Second, he also knows a number of books which went under the names of apostles, but falsely. As one who has experience in such things, he says he and others rejects these books. This would not necessarily mean he regarded all such books as evil or heretical, but certainly they had to be rejected as belonging to the 'received' books. Third, he confesses that he 'receives the apostles as Christ', that is, he recognizes that apostolic authority is tantamount to the authority of Christ himself. Fourth, Serapion obviously means to imply that this apostolic authority belongs not simply to the persons of the apostles—none of whom was around in the year 190—but to certain *books*, books which he must assume the apostles wrote or perhaps approved to be passed down.

In these last two points too, Serapion sounds just like Irenaeus. At the beginning of the third book of *Against Heresies* Irenaeus wrote: 'The Lord of all gave his apostles the power of the Gospel, and by them we have known the truth, that is, the teaching of the Son of God. To them the Lord said, "He who hears you hears me, and he who despises you despises me and Him who sent me"' (citing Luke 10.16). Then, after naming the four Gospels and the truths they declare, Irenaeus continues: 'If any one does not agree to these truths, he despises the companions of the Lord. Even more, he despises Christ himself the Lord, indeed, he despises the Father also . . . ' (3.praef.; 1.2). Serapion and Irenaeus agree: to receive the apostles of Jesus and their testimony is to receive Jesus and the God who sent him; to reject his apostles is to reject Jesus and his Father.

Serapion, like Irenaeus, received from former generations a set of sacred books. Were they the same books Irenaeus received, a slightly different set, or a significantly different set? We would love to know, but unfortunately, in the part of the letter cited by Eusebius there is no explicit mention of their titles (only that they didn't include the *Gospel of Peter*). Thus, one scholar concludes, 'we know nothing about his acquaintance with or regard for' the Gospels of Matthew, Mark, Luke, and John. But is this really the case?

What Serapion Had Received: The Legacy of Theophilus

Serapion became bishop of the church in Antioch in about 189 (*EH* 5.22.1). His immediate predecessor was a man named Maximinus, about whom we know next to nothing. But according to Eusebius, Maximinus immediately succeeded Theophilus (*EH* 4.24.1), whom we mentioned above, and about whom we know a bit more. Theophilus died sometime in the 180s, thus only a few years before Serapion became bishop. Almost certainly, then, Serapion knew Theophilus personally, and as his next-to-immediate successor was surely well acquainted with Theophilus' published writings.

The only one of those writings that has survived is a three-volume treatise called *To Autolycus*. In the first volume of *To Autolycus* Theophilus speaks of his own conversion to Christianity, which took place after 'I encountered the sacred writings of the holy prophets, who through the spirit of God foretold past events in the way that they happened, present events in the way they are happening, and future events in the order in which they will be accomplished' (*To Autolycus* 1.14).[34] In his attempt to lead Autolycus to a more favourable view of Christianity, Theophilus responds to the objection that the Christians' writings 'are recent and modern' (3.1) by citing the venerable antiquity of the Hebrew prophets, who spoke by the Spirit of God. 'All these things are taught us by the Holy Spirit which spoke through Moses and the other prophets; so that the books which belong to us, the worshippers of God, are proved to be writings not only more ancient but also more true than all historians and poets' (2.30). Theophilus, of course, could not claim that any of the writings that now make up the New Testament were so ancient. Thus his written testimonies are mostly taken from the Old Testament books. What he must do, then, is to link the newer writings with the prophets of the Old Testament. He does this by stating that they share the same teaching and the same ultimate authorship by the Holy Spirit. '[C]oncerning the justice of which the law spoke, the teaching of the prophets and the gospels is consistent with it because all the inspired men made utterances by means of the one Spirit of God' (3.12).

These words show us that Theophilus not only considered the authors of the Gospels to be 'inspired', but also that the books they produced were inspired books.[35] The Gospels as inspired books are linked here with 'the Law' and 'the Prophets', both major categories of the Old Testament Scriptures. But which Gospels did he have in mind? Later, when reporting what 'the holy word' has to say about marital faithfulness, he quotes from Solomon in the book of Proverbs and from 'the voice of the Gospel' (3.13), in this case, Jesus' words recorded in Matthew 5. Earlier, when speaking of God's power to create the universe out of nothing, he had cited Jesus' words, 'For the things which are impossible with men are possible with God', in the form in which Luke 18.27 alone records them (2.13). At one point he even reveals the name of one of the inspired Gospel writers: 'Hence the holy scriptures and all those inspired by the Spirit teach us, and one of them, John, says, "In the beginning was the Logos, and the Logos was with God" [John 1: 1]' (2.22).

Thus, we know that Theophilus, bishop of Antioch and Serapion's predecessor, had multiple Gospels, and that he considered these Gospels to be inspired and part of God's holy word. Simply from his one surviving work, *To Autolycus*, it appears that his Gospel collection must have included Matthew, Luke, and John.[36] Did it also contain Mark?

Though *To Autolycus* is the only one of Theophilus' works which survives today, Jerome in the early fifth century had several more, and reports that Theophilus composed a book in which he 'put together into one work the words of the four Evangelists'.[37] By 'the four Evangelists', of course, Jerome means the authors of the four canonical Gospels, Matthew, Mark, Luke, and John. That is, like Tatian the Syrian, whom we shall meet in the next chapter,

Theophilus produced a Gospel Harmony, a book which combined the accounts of the four Gospels into a single, continuous narrative.

Robert Grant notes: 'Scholars sometimes claim that Irenaeus' stand on the New Testament books was decisive for Christian theology. This seems unlikely in view of his devotion to older teaching, as well as the very similar collection in use by his older contemporary Theophilus of Antioch.'[38] The collections of both men included the four Gospels and a corpus of Paul's letters (*To Autolycus* 3.14). Eusebius tells us that, in his now lost work against Marcion, Theophilus also used testimonies from the Apocalypse of John (*EH* 4.24.1). Now, all of this naturally has implications for Serapion.

For Serapion, determining the books of Scripture was not like being in a book club. Members did not take turns suggesting which books they wanted read in church as Holy Scripture. For him, novelty was not good. So, when Serapion in around 190 claims he had received a number of authentic writings from his predecessors, now, through one of those predecessors, we have an excellent idea of which writings they were. Despite the statements of some present-day scholars, there is every reason to think that the Gospels handed down to Serapion from the previous generations of clergy in Antioch before him were the very same ones that had been handed down to Irenaeus in Gaul, the very same ones handed down to Clement in Alexandria, namely, Matthew, Mark, Luke, and John.

The Alogi and the Ebionites

The examples of Clement and Serapion, brought out to prove that Irenaeus' view of the four Gospels 'was not widely accepted in his day', not only fail to prove this but only serve to establish the contrary. But other evidence remains. McDonald points out: 'Another group roughly contemporary with Irenaeus, the so-called "Alogi," a group of heretics in Asia Minor (ca. 170), opposed the use of Hebrews and both the Gospel and the Revelation of John in their churches.'[39] Yet, right away, the admission that the Alogi were 'a group of heretics'[40] would seem to disqualify them as evidence against John and the church's Gospel canon. For it should not be entirely unexpected that 'heretics'—that is, those who reject one or more of the central teachings embraced by the church—might also reject at least one of the church's Gospels. In this case it was the church's teaching about the Holy Spirit which was in question, and according to Irenaeus it was John's teaching on the work of the Spirit which was tied to this group's rejection of John's Gospel (AH 3.11.9). Irenaeus implies that these people may have had trouble with Paul's letters too.

It is the much the same with the next example cited by McDonald, a group known as the Ebionites. The Ebionites were Jewish followers of Jesus who did not, however, accept the belief that Jesus was the divine Son of God. According to Irenaeus, they not only restricted their Gospels to one, Matthew (or a version of it), but also rejected the apostle Paul and all of his writings (AH 1.26.2; 3.11.7). It is hardly surprising that people who rejected the deity of Jesus would find it difficult to accept John's Gospel in particular, or the epistles of Paul. If, on the other hand, they accepted either of these, it would have been very difficult not to accept Jesus' deity.

Irenaeus singles out groups like the Ebionites, the Marcionites, the Valentinians, and those who rejected the Gospel of John in AH 3.11.9 precisely because they stood apart from what he and others understood to be the Christian faith. Irenaeus, however, did take special note of the fact that even the Ebionites used Matthew, even some docetists (those who claimed that Jesus Christ only 'seemed' to be human) used Mark, even the Marcionites used a version of Luke, and even the Valentinians made special use of John's prologue. To him, the fact that even those who departed from the church's teaching could not completely avoid using the church's Gospels was further proof of the firm ground on which these Gospels stood (*AH* 3.11.7).

A Canon-list Maker: The *Muratorian Fragment*

Since we are in the period roughly contemporary with Irenaeus I'll mention here the *Muratorian Fragment*. The reason it is not considered by McDonald and some others is because the dating of this work has been the subject of much controversy of late.

The *Muratorian Fragment* is a portion of a longer text which enumerates the books its author says are received by the church. The work was discovered in 1740 in the Ambrosian Library in Milan by Lodovico Muratori, hence its name. The beginning of the fragment is as follows:[41]

... at which nevertheless he was present, and so he placed [them in his narrative]. (2) The third book of the Gospel is that according to Luke. (3) Luke, the well-known physician, after the ascension of Christ, (4–5) when Paul had taken him with him as one zealous for the law, (6) composed it in his own name, according to [the general] belief. Yet he himself had not (7) seen the Lord in the flesh; and therefore, as he was able to ascertain events, (8) so indeed he begins to tell the story from the birth of John. (9) The fourth of the Gospels is that of John, [one] of the disciples. (10) To his fellow disciples and bishops, who had been urging him [to write], (11) he said, 'Fast with me from today for three days, and what (12) will be revealed to each one (13) let us tell it to one another.' In the same night it was revealed (14) to Andrew, [one] of the apostles, (15–16) that John should write down all things in his own name while all of them should review[42] it. And so, though various (17) elements may be taught in the individual books of the Gospels, (18) nevertheless this makes no difference to the faith of believers, since by the one sovereign Spirit all things (20) have been declared in all [the Gospels]: concerning the (21) nativity, concerning the passion, concerning the resurrection, (22) concerning life with his disciples, (23) and concerning his twofold coming; (24) the first in lowliness when he was despised, which has taken place, (25) the second glorious in royal power, (26) which is still in the future. What (27) marvel is it, then, if John so consistently (28) mentions these particular points also in his Epistles, (29) saying about himself: 'What we have seen with our eyes (30) and heard with our ears and our hands (31) have handled, these things we have written to you'? [see 1 John 1.1–3] (32) For in this way he professes [himself] to be not only an eyewitness and hearer, (33) but also a writer of all the marvellous deeds of the Lord, in their order.

Despite the fact that the beginning of the document is missing, it is clear that the author believes the church accepts four and only four Gospels ('the third book of the Gospel . . .'; 'the fourth of the Gospels . . .'), the last two being Luke and John. No scholar seriously questions that the first two on his list were Matthew and Mark.[43] The controversy is only about the date of the fragment. Traditionally, the underlying document, of which the *Muratorian Fragment* is a badly executed copy, has been viewed as a product of the second half of the second century or the early third, probably from Rome or somewhere in Italy. But there has been strong criticism of this dating of the fragment from two scholars in particular, Albert Sundberg and Geoffrey Hahneman. They have argued at length that it is a fourth-century, eastern production and fits better alongside several other canon lists from the second half of the fourth century and later.[44] Detailed arguments cannot be undertaken here,[45] but the most straightforward way in which the document dates itself comes in its discussion of a work we have mentioned before, *The Shepherd* of Hermas. It says:

But Hermas wrote *The Shepherd* (74) very recently, in our times, in the city of Rome, (75) while bishop Pius, his brother, was occupying the [Episcopal] chair (76) of the church of the city of Rome. (77) And therefore it ought indeed to be read; but (78) it cannot be read publicly to the people in church either among (79) the prophets, whose number is complete, or among (80) the apostles, for it is after [their] time.

The author thus presents himself as a contemporary of Bishop Pius of Rome, who is known to have been bishop there in about 146–55 CE. This would seem to date the document to sometime in the second half of the second century, or possibly the early years of the third. Even if the author should happen to be wrong about when *The Shepherd* was written (Sundberg and Hahneman argue that it was sometime *before* Pius' episcopacy), the point remains that he sets the time of his own writing not long after Pius was bishop.

Sundberg and Hahneman also argue that when the author says the writing of *The Shepherd* and the episcopacy of Pius occurred 'most recently, in our time' (line 74), the words 'our time' here mean not 'our lifetime' but 'post-apostolic time' (see line 80) as opposed to 'apostolic time'. 'Post-apostolic time', of course, stretches into the fourth century and beyond. Yet, in all their studies the two scholars have not shown convincing parallels for phrases like 'in our time' meaning 'post-apostolic time', while there are, on the other hand, convincing parallels for the use of such language to speak of an author's own lifetime.[46] Joseph

Verheyden even argues that the full phrase used by the author should be understood to mean not 'most recently, that is, in our time', but 'most recently in our lifetime', as opposed to 'less recently in our lifetime'.[47] If so, then it would be hard to date the fragment much later than about 170, and this would be well before Irenaeus wrote about the 'fourfold Gospel' in *Against Heresies*, Book 3. While we may not be able to insist upon such precision, it is notable that Verheyden, author of the most thorough analysis of the Sundberg–Hahneman theory to date, concludes that 'the suggestion of a fourth-century, eastern origin for the Fragment should be put to rest not for a thousand years, but for eternity'![48]

In my view, the *Fragment* may be from the record of one of the councils to which Tertullian (writing *c*.210) alludes in *On Modesty* 10, councils which, he claims, judged *The Shepherd* to be 'among apocryphal and false (writings)'. This sounds like it could be Tertullian's polemical spin on a council's determination that the book's author was the brother of Pius of Rome and not a companion of apostles. We know from a comment made by Origen that some had accepted *The Shepherd* as written by the man named Hermas known to the apostle Paul, mentioned in Paul's epistle to the Romans 16.14. Therefore they had accepted *The Shepherd* at least partly on the supposition that it was penned by an apostolic companion. The *Muratorian Fragment*, however, bursts their bubble by identifying Hermas not as the companion of Paul but as the brother of Bishop Pius, who lived well after the time of the apostles. The *Fragment* appreciates the value of *The Shepherd*, but clearly denies that it can be considered in any sense apostolic, and disallows its reading in church along with the Scriptures.

Whether the *Fragment* originated as a council document or not, the determination that it belongs to the late second century rather than the late fourth ought to prevail as correct. This leads to the significant conclusion that we possess in the *Muratorian Fragment* another early witness, quite contemporary with Irenaeus, to the exclusivity of the four Gospels, and indeed to some notion of a fuller New Testament 'canon' of Scripture.

Conclusion

Bishop Irenaeus advocated a fourfold Gospels canon. On this everybody agrees, though many seem interested in depicting Irenaeus as isolated from the rest of Christianity in his 'choice' of Gospel literature. Yet the examples cited to prove Irenaeus' solitude only show that he had more friends than anticipated. In the last two or three decades of the second century Irenaeus in Gaul, Clement in Alexandria, Theophilus and Serapion in Antioch, and the author of the *Muratorian Fragment* in or near Rome, at points far distant from each another on the map, are all saying or implying that the church has the same four acknowledged Gospels. What might this striking unity, despite significant geographical diversity, imply for the many churches which lay in between?

We know that Christians read books besides the four Gospels and the other books now in the New Testament. At a point near the end of the second century the *Gospel of Peter* turned up in Rhossus and came to the attention of Serapion, visiting from Antioch. But this Gospel is never mentioned by Clement in Alexandria, Irenaeus in Gaul, or the author of the *Muratorian Fragment* in Italy. Clement, on the other hand, knows and even

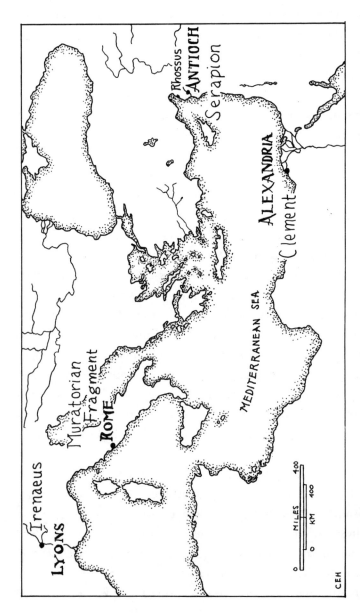

Illustration 4.2 Map. The four Gospels received in widely diverse geographical regions by the end of the second century.

quotes a few lines of the *Gospel of the Hebrews*. He also knows some who read the *Gospel of the Egyptians*. But neither of these Gospels is mentioned by Irenaeus, Serapion, or the author of the *Muratorian Fragment*. In his travels through Asia Minor, Rome, and Gaul Irenaeus has encountered the Valentinian *Gospel of Truth* and the Sethian gnostic *Gospel of Judas*. But neither of these is ever mentioned or used by Clement, Serapion, or the author of the *Muratorian Fragment*. Various Gospels popped up throughout the second century in various places, but the only Gospels known to all of these writers in common—and probably to the authors of the alternative Gospels too—are Matthew, Mark, Luke, and John. How is this possible, and how did they arrive at such a consensus?

A sensational, conspiratorial plotline could easily be concocted to explain it, perhaps with an intimidating Irenaeus in the starring role. Such fictionalizing might indeed be attractive to Hollywood producers, but it is hardly worthy of academics. The less sensational truth (though perhaps sensational in its own way) is that, even apart from the considerable efforts of Irenaeus, a four-Gospel canon appears to be secure in the church in the final decades of the second century. Irenaeus evidently had less to do with the further success of this four-Gospel canon than many have thought. This is because its acceptance must even have pre-dated him, a conclusion which follows from the wide geographical separation of the authors treated in this chapter. The testimony of these authors is that the four Gospels were not recently foisted on them, by Irenaeus or anyone else, but had been passed down to them from their forebears in their local Christian communities.

We have now heard about the Gospel Harmony compiled by Theophilus of Antioch in the decade or two before Irenaeus began to write. But his Gospel Harmony may not have been the first. We now move to a slightly earlier period, a period in which these popular Gospels have already achieved such a reputation and status that they are starting to be 'packaged' in different ways.

5

'PACKAGING' THE GOSPELS: OF HARMONIES, SYNOPSES, AND CODICES

Combining the Gospels: Harmonies and Disharmony

THOUGH the four New Testament Gospels have of course much in common, each has its own unique elements and its own personality, as it were, reflecting the aims, methods, and literary characteristics of those who wrote them. We know that all four were read individually, but at some point it occurred to someone to try combining all the common and unique aspects of each of the four Gospels into a single account. This is called a Gospel Harmony. In the following example, the Gospel sources for each phrase are noted in parentheses. Note the very exacting method of the compiler, taking words or phrases from the four individual Gospels and arranging them into a comprehensive, if somewhat cumbersome, narrative.

... the mother of the sons of Zebedee (Matt. 27.56) and Salome (Mark 15.40) and the wives of those who had followed him from Galilee to see the crucified (Luke 23.49b–c). And the day was Preparation: the Sabbath was dawning (Luke 23.54). And when it was evening (Matt. 27.57), on the Preparation, that is, the day before the Sabbath (Mark 15.42), there came up a man (Matt. 27.57), being a member of the council (Luke 23.50), from Arimathea (Matt. 27.57), a city of Judea (Luke 23.51b), by name Joseph (Matt. 27.57), good and righteous (Luke 23.50), being a disciple of Jesus, but secretly, for fear of the Jews (John 19.38). And he (Matt. 27.57) was looking for the kingdom of God (Luke 23.51c). This man had not consented to their purpose (Luke 23.51a).

As we saw in the last chapter, a Gospel Harmony was constructed by Theophilus of Antioch, probably in the 170s or early 180s, perhaps earlier. The most famous of the early Gospel Harmonies, however, was assembled by a man named Tatian. A Syrian by birth, Tatian had converted to Christianity in adulthood sometime around the middle of the second century and then moved to Rome, where he became a student of an eminent Christian teacher named Justin. During this period Tatian, like a number of other Christians of the time, wrote an apologetic work in defence of Christianity, entitled *Address to the Greeks*. After Justin's death in around 165, as the story is told by later Christians, Tatian veered away from the faith of his teacher and embraced a form of Christian asceticism called Encratism (from a Greek word meaning 'to hold it in'). Irenaeus charged that he even developed a speculative, theosophical system akin to Valentinianism (*AH* 1.28). Tatian eventually returned to Syria, and in about 170 or 175 composed his Harmony of the four Gospels. As Eusebius states, 'Tatian composed in some way a combination and collection of the gospels, and gave this the name of *The Diatessaron* and this is still extant in some places' (*EH* 4.29.6).

Most scholars nowadays think the *Diatessaron* was originally composed in Syriac and soon translated into Greek (though some have thought the opposite). In either case, this led to an interesting development in eastern Syria, where Greek was not much spoken. For the *Diatessaron* seems to have appeared in the

Syriac language before the four individual Gospels did. This meant that the first format in which people in parts of Syria came to know the four Gospels in their language was through the *Diatessaron*. While elsewhere Gospel Harmonies could function alongside the four separate Gospels, for these people the *Diatessaron* was their only Gospel book. Yet despite the eventual popularity of this work both in Syria and elsewhere, not a single copy of it survives today. This is partly due to the fact that Theodoret of Cyrus in the fourth century had some 200 copies destroyed and replaced by the separate Gospels. What we have of it exists only in much later and somewhat altered translations, a commentary on the Syriac version written by Ephraim of Syria in the mid-fourth century, and possibly a fourteen-line fragment of the Greek version of the *Diatessaron* written in the early third century.

Fighting Four on Four

All agree that the *Diatessaron* was based programmatically on the four Gospels. After all, *diatessaron* means 'through the four', not through the three, the five, or the innumerable.[1] All agree that Tatian finished his *Diatessaron* before Irenaeus wrote *Against Heresies* in the 180s. But here is where the fighting begins. Bruce Metzger considers that: 'The Diatessaron supplies proof that all four Gospels were regarded as authoritative, otherwise it is unlikely that Tatian would have dared to combine them into one gospel account. At a time when many gospels were competing for attention, it is certainly significant that Tatian selected just these four.'[2] This might seem reasonable, yet some scholars see it very differently. They look at Tatian's *Diatessaron* and see in it nothing but problems for the four Gospels. As mentioned earlier, McDonald uses the *Diatessaron* as evidence that Irenaeus was alone in his exclusive esteem for the four Gospels. How can this be?

First, McDonald claims that 'Tatian, appears to have accepted all four canonical Gospels equally, but he also included the *Gospel of Peter* and perhaps other traditions'.[3] Yet the authority McDonald cites for this information[4] concerns Justin, not Tatian. McDonald also says that Ephraem the Syrian 'points out that Tatian, like Justin and Clement of Alexandria, used more than the four canonical Gospels in his work'.[5] This too is inaccurate. Ephraem does not so much as mention Tatian and nowhere says how many Gospels Tatian used.

It is certainly the case that the late, versional manuscripts assumed to be based ultimately on the *Diatessaron* contain a handful of phrases or single-word substitutions which do not appear in any of our manuscripts of the four Gospels. But neither the *Gospel of Peter* nor any other known Gospel can be cited as providing any ample or consistent source for them. Almost certainly, at least some of these 'foreign' elements were added by Tatian himself. He is thought by scholars to have tweaked a few things in the *Diatessaron* in a way that supported the ascetical practices he became famous for. Some of the irregularities, on the other hand, seem to have entered into the textual tradition of the *Diatessaron* later, from the hand of someone other than Tatian. Whatever of them that might remain, which Tatian might have got from an alternative written source or sources, would amount to very little, and could hardly reveal the use of another source on anywhere near the level of one of the four Gospels.[6]

Others, however, who have reconciled themselves to Tatian's systematic use of the four and only the four canonical Gospels find different problems for these Gospels in the *Diatessaron*. Harry Gamble sees the eventual popularity enjoyed by the *Diatessaron* as 'a powerful indication that the fourfold Gospel contemporaneously sponsored by Irenaeus was not broadly, let alone universally, recognized'.[7] William Petersen even states (emphasis his) that '*the Diatessaron was an attempt to create a single, definitive gospel— a 'super-gospel'—superseding all other gospels. It was, in that sense, a frontal assault on the four-gospel canon.*'[8] He further asserts: 'A harmony is not just an acknowledgement of the fourfold gospel: it is, rather, a rejection of a multiple-gospel canon, and a battle-call to a single-gospel canon.'[9]

These comments are noteworthy because they mark a 'frontal assault' on something which many insist *did not exist* at the time, namely, a four-Gospel canon! If Petersen is correct and the *Diatessaron* is such an assault, then obviously the four-Gospel canon was in use in Rome before 170 or 175 and probably broadly recognized at that time. If not, surely Tatian would not have needed to assault it.

As Petersen sees it, the *Diatessaron* shows that 'the sources Tatian used [i.e. the four Gospels] were *not* endowed with such a sacrosanct status for him or his audience that he could not rip the sources apart, rearrange them and then present his new construction to an appreciative Christian audience'.[10] One wonders if there is a category somewhere between 'sacrosanct words' and 'rippable raw materials'. Literate people in antiquity made excerpts from books, even holy books, all the time and sometimes strung them together as 'testimonia' sources, from which they would then teach or compose their own works. Some examples using the inspired Hebrew words of the Old Testament are known from the caves of Qumran (the Dead Sea Scrolls), which pre-date the New Testament.[11] This did not mean the collators perceived their sources as 'rippable raw materials'.

In any event, it *could* be that Tatian's work reveals at least one person who was not happy with a four-Gospel canon, or who thought it could be improved upon. In that case, despite his forceful protest, Tatian would still be a witness, as Petersen's words concede, to the pre-existence of a four-Gospel canon by at least 170 or 175, before Irenaeus began writing, many miles away in Gaul. Again, one can choose to say that Tatian bucked the system, but this also means there was a system to buck.

But is it certain, after all, that a Gospel Harmony is 'a rejection of a multiple-gospel canon, and a battle-call to a single-gospel canon'? Reason to doubt that it is comes in Petersen's own acknowledgement that Theophilus of Antioch also created a Gospel Harmony.[12] This Harmony, as we saw in the last chapter, was constructed from the same four Gospels used by Tatian—a fact significant in itself—and was almost exactly contemporary with Tatian's *Diatessaron*.[13] Was Theophilus, by the mere act of constructing his Harmony, *rejecting* these four Gospels and issuing a battle-call to a single-gospel canon? Apparently not. Jerome tells us that Theophilus also wrote a commentary on Matthew which Jerome found useful. And as we saw in Chapter 4, Theophilus used Matthew, Luke, and John in his books *To Autolycus*, referring to them as the 'holy word' of God. He specifically cited John as inspired by the Holy Spirit. Did Theophilus then think he was 'ripping apart' John's inspired words as mere 'raw materials' for the construction of a replacement Gospel? To the contrary, the example of Theophilus demonstrates that at least not *every* attempt—perhaps not *any* attempt—to construct a Gospel Harmony in the early centuries had the intention of assaulting or supplanting the four Gospels.

On one of my shelves is a book entitled *A Harmony of the Gospels*,[14] kindly given to me by its author, Loraine Boettner, when some friends and I visited him at his home in Rockport, Missouri, in about 1980. He had first published the book in 1933 when he was a Bible instructor at Pikeville College in Kentucky. In the book's Introduction Boettner says that his Harmony 'proved to be a real help in class work'. He makes no claim of infallibility for his harmonic arrangement, but instead confesses: 'The four Gospels are the final authority.' He ends his Introduction with these words: 'It has been said that the greatest service that anyone can render is to make more available the riches of grace that are found in Christ our Saviour. The present arrangement is designed to make more readily available the material found in the Gospels, and so to make more interesting and rewarding the time spent in Bible study.'

It does not sound as though Mr Boettner ever intended either to mount an assault on the four Gospels or to supersede them with his Harmony. The fact is, some readers of the New Testament have always found it helpful to have the elements of all the individual Gospels laid out in a continuous narrative, as in one book. Throughout most of Christian history the use of Gospel Harmonies has not brought with it a rejection of the four individual Gospels.

Interestingly, in 1933, the same year in which Mr. Boettner published his *Harmony of the Gospels*, excavators working in Dura Europa, on the lower Euphrates in Syria, unearthed a four-inch-square parchment fragment of the *Diatessaron*.[15]

Illustration 5.1 P.Dura 10, the earliest-known fragment of Tatian's *Diatessaron*, in Greek. A parchment roll. Early third century. Used by permission of Beinecke Rare Book and Manuscript Library, Yale University.

Because the town of Dura was destroyed in 256–7 CE, we thus have a portion of a Greek translation of the *Diatessaron* that is probably no more than about fifty years later than Tatian's original. It is in fact the reconstructed translation of this fragment which was given at the beginning of this chapter (notice that it used all four Gospels).[16]

Many scholars at first assumed that the Dura Harmony must have functioned as Holy Scripture for a congregation of Christians which, archaeologists were able to discover, met in a house just two blocks away from where the fragment was found. But several decades after the discovery of the fragment, and after many other early Christian manuscripts had come to light, papyrologist C. H. Roberts made an interesting observation:

All Christian manuscripts of the Bible, whether of the Old Testament or the New Testament, attributable to the second or the earlier third century, are codices, all written on papyrus.[17]

With Christian manuscripts other than biblical, practice varies; some, possibly because they were candidates for the Canon, others more probably on the analogy of the biblical texts, are in codex form; others, and not only scholarly treatises when pagan practices might be expected to be followed, but texts such as Tatian's *Harmony of the Four Gospels* (found at Dura Europos and so written before the destruction of the city in A.D. 256) and one of the Logia papyri, are in roll form.[18]

The Dura fragment of the *Diatessaron*, as Roberts noted, is written on a parchment roll, while all other known Scriptural texts copied by Christian scribes from the second or third centuries are in (papyrus) codex form. This may not be infallible proof but it is significant *prima facie* evidence that this *Diatessaron* manuscript was not the congregation's 'sacred text' but perhaps a pastor's study tool. Eventually, as we know from later records, many congregations in Syria used the Syriac version of the *Diatessaron* as their only Gospel text; it was, after all, probably the first form of the four Gospels to have reached them in their vernacular and their reluctance to part with it is hardly surprising. But we do not know whether this was Tatian's intention for his Gospel Harmony or not. Perhaps, like Boettner's *Harmony*

constructed in 1933 for students at Pikeville College, it was intended
to facilitate the study of the Gospels and the life of Jesus.

Whatever Tatian's original motive, the main point here is that
his Gospel Harmony and that of Theophilus presuppose the use of a
four-Gospel collection in the 170s or earlier. This means that the
four were perceived, in comparison with other Gospels, as in a class
by themselves, and perhaps even suggests that Christians in Antioch
of Syria and Rome were by that time treating the four Gospels as
Scripture.

The Gospel Harmonies constructed by Tatian and Theophilus
(and perhaps others) represent one attempt at 'packaging' the four
Gospels so as to access their teaching more conveniently. But they
do not represent the only attempt.

Tabling the Gospels: The First Synopsis

There is another way of 'packaging' the words of the Gospels
together which can function as an aid to their study. It is called a
Synopsis. Because the four Gospels tell basically the same story of
Jesus, though each tells the story in its own way with episodes or
details or emphases not present in the others, it can be very helpful
to the student or preacher to have all four accounts laid out in
parallel columns to be easily compared. Table 5.1 shows an
example.

The first modern Synopsis of the four Gospels was produced
by J. J. Griesbach in 1776 to aid scholars in reconstructing the
most original forms of the accounts of Jesus. Since then many
others have been produced, and today Gospel Synopses are
regarded as indispensible tools for the detailed study of the
Gospels. But the first Gospel Synopsis was constructed long

Table 5.1. *Synopsis of Matthew 18.1–5; Mark 9.33–7; Luke 9.46–8; John 13.20*

Matthew 18.1:	Mark 9.33:	Luke 9.46:	John 13.20:

Matthew 18.1: At that time the disciples came to Jesus and asked, 'Who is the greatest in the kingdom of heaven?' ² He called a child, whom he put among them, ³ and said, 'Truly I tell you, unless you change and become like children, you will never enter the kingdom of heaven.⁴ Whoever becomes humble like this child is the greatest in the kingdom of heaven.⁵ Whoever welcomes one such child in my name welcomes me'.

Mark 9.33: Then they came to Capernaum; and when he was in the house he asked them, 'What were you arguing about on the way?' ³⁴ But they were silent, for on the way they had argued with one another who was the greatest.³⁵ He sat down, called the twelve, and said to them, 'Whoever wants to be first must be last of all and servant of all.' ³⁶ Then he took a little child and put it among them; and taking it in his arms, he said to them, ³⁷ 'Whoever welcomes one such child in my name welcomes me, and whoever welcomes me welcomes not me but the one who sent me'.

Luke 9.46: An argument arose among them as to which one of them was the greatest.⁴⁷ But Jesus, aware of their inner thoughts, took a little child and put it by his side, ⁴⁸ and said to them, 'Whoever welcomes this child in my name welcomes me, and whoever welcomes me welcomes the one who sent me; for the least among all of you is the greatest'.

John 13.20: 'Very truly, I tell you, whoever receives one whom I send receives me; and whoever receives me receives him who sent me'.

113

before Greiesbach, by an Alexandrian Christian named Ammonius in the early or middle third century. Eusebius, in his letter to Carpianus, says of him: 'Ammonius the Alexandrine, with the expense of much industry and zeal—as was proper—left us the Diatessaron Gospel, in which he had placed the similar pericopes [i.e. sections] of the rest of the Evangelists alongside Matthew, with the inevitable result that the coherent sequence of the three was destroyed inasmuch as regards the network of the readings.'[19]

We note that this Synopsis used all four canonical Gospels and only those four. Eusebius even calls it a 'Diatessaron Gospel', like that of Tatian, even though the format Ammonius employed was different from that of Tatian and Theophilus. As far as we can tell, Ammonius' experiment never became very popular. This may be partly because Eusebius himself used Ammonius's painstaking work and developed it in a way that enabled such comparisons as Ammonius had wanted to make, while not destroying 'the coherent sequence of the three'—in fact by preserving each Gospel in its intact form. By placing numbers in the margins of the Gospels, Eusebius devised a system whereby one could turn from a particular passage in one of the Gospels back to a table, affixed as a preface to the Gospels, which would tell the reader where to find the corresponding passage in one of the other Gospels. Thus were produced what have since been called the Eusebian canons or Eusebian tables, based on the Ammonian sections. To this day these Eusebian tables are printed in critical editions of the Greek New Testament.

For our purposes, the importance of Ammonius' work in the third century is that it is one more way of putting the four Gospels together for ease of study, and this presupposes their eminence and their separation from all other Gospels.

Binding the Gospels: A Convenient Four-pack

It is utterly commonplace for us to open a Bible and see all the books under one cover. In fact, in modern publishing, any kind of writing might be bound together with any other kind of writing to form an anthology. But this is not how things always were. Each book of the Bible, of course, began its life independent of the rest. In most, if not all, cases the original was written on a scroll, as virtually every other book in their day was. Whenever the transition began to be made from scroll to codex—and we know that with Christian documents this was very early—the codex, as a budding technological format for literary works, had a limited capacity. Many of our earliest examples, like the volume of John in the Bodmer collection called P^{66}, were probably 'single quire' volumes. That is, all the pages that make up the entire book were stacked in a single pile, then the whole pile was folded together (or perhaps the folding was done earlier) and bound in the middle. Anyone who tries this at home will find that only so many sheets can be put together this way before the volume gets very bulky and the middle pages stick out quite a bit further than the outside ones. Trimming the inside pages to acheive a more uniform look only narrows these pages, allowing less room for the contents. Thus, at some point it was discovered that dividing the whole into smaller stacks, called quires, folding each quire individually, and then attaching all the quires together at the folded end, could form a volume that was less cumbersome and with pages of more uniform size. This would also allow the codex to hold a greater volume of pages. And this meant that multiple books could now be more easily joined together.

But what happens to those separate books when you 'package' two or more of them together in a singe codex? Most likely you make a statement that, in *some* sense, these books belong together, and others don't belong. J. K. Elliott has said:

> Collecting the four chosen Gospels into one codex had the effect of according a special status to those four but, possibly more significant, helped to limit the number of Gospels to these four and no more! The fourfold Gospels could fit into one codex, but not onto one roll, so the adoption of the codex would itself have had the effect of enforcing the fourfold Gospel canon as a fixed entity.[20]

Beginning with the third-century codex P^{45} in the Chester Beatty collection, which contains all four Gospels plus the book of Acts, over 2,000 handwritten codices survive which contain the four Gospels bound together in a single codex.[21] In Chapter 2 we noted in passing, from the cases of Marinus of Caesarea and Euplus of Catania, that these four-Gospel codices must have been fairly commonplace already in the third century. An Italian-made, sixth-century Gospel book like these, but with illuminations, was brought to British shores by the monk Augustine in 597. It now resides in the Parker Library at Corpus Christi College, Cambridge (MS 286).

One might think that in the wild and woolly world of the early church (as often represented), when Gospels were 'multiplying like rabbits', Christians would certainly have produced codices containing an endless variety of Gospel combinations. It may, therefore, be surprising to learn that,

The Gospels that were rejected from that fourfold collection were never bound together with any or all of those four. There are no manuscripts that contain say Matthew, Luke and Peter, or John, Mark and Thomas. Only the Gospels of Matthew, Mark, Luke and John were considered as scriptural and then as canonical. It could be that the reason why the Christians adopted the codex long before anyone else was to safeguard the four Gospels from either addition or subtraction. This is in effect the operation of a 'canon'.[22]

So, when did the practice of binding these four Gospels together into a single codex, this tangible expression of a 'canon', begin? P^{66} (c.200) preserves most of the original codex of John, so we know it contained only that single Gospel. The papyrologist T. C. Skeat noted the possibility that P^{90}, a single-page fragment of John of the late second century, might have once belonged to a multiple Gospel codex, but, as with most of the rest of our fragmentary Gospel papyri, we have no way of knowing for certain. But in 1933 the great papyrologist Frederick G. Kenyon, remarking on the consequences of the discovery of codex P^{45}, dated to the first half of the third century, wrote: 'When, therefore, Irenaeus at the end of the second century writes of the four Gospels as the divinely provided evidence of Christianity, and the number four as almost axiomatic, it is now possible to believe that he may have been accustomed to the sight of volumes in which all four were contained.'[23] Later in the twentieth century other discoveries would make Kenyon's suggestion even more realistic.

In 1961 was published a two-Gospel codex from the Bodmer collection (Papyrus Bodmer XIV-XV), given the notation P^{75}, which contained the Gospels of Luke and John. P^{75} is dated by experts to around 200, and so it was possibly written before the end of the second century. It encloses Luke and John in a single quire and still contains the page on which Luke ends and John begins. Some 'subtle harmonizations' in the text, where the scribe conforms the wording to one of the other Gospels, seem to indicate the scribe's knowledge of Matthew and perhaps Mark.[24] Skeat suggested that this single-quire codex was originally connected to another which contained Matthew and Mark.[25] Certainly, if copied around 200, it is more likely than not that it had such a companion volume, whether attached or separated.

In 1979 C. H. Roberts concluded that the Gospel fragments given the names P[4] (a fragment of Luke), P[64], and P[67] (fragments of Matthew) had been written by the same hand and belonged originally to the same codex.[26] Because P[4] could be dated to the late second century, this would make these fragments the earliest example of a multiple Gospel codex known. Some years later Skeat, decided to subject Roberts's claim to his own scrutiny. Not only did he come to agree with Roberts, he believed he could also calculate from the fragments that in the codex from which they came Matthew was not followed immediately by Luke, but another work intervened. In other words, the codex contained at least three Gospels, and other features of the papyri indicated that this codex in fact originally contained four. Skeat concluded, 'we now have proof of a four-Gospel codex the ancestors of which must go back well into the second century'.[27]

Skeat's conclusions have indeed been accepted by a number of other papyrologists,[28] but they have not gone unchallenged.[29] The question, at the moment, remains under debate. It seems agreed, however, that the books of Matthew and Luke represented in P[4,64,67] were copied by the same scribe, whether bound together with Mark and John or not. And it seems that this scribe was commissioned to copy books that would function as one church's Scripture.

Pulpit Editions

The codex (or codices) produced by the scribe who copied Matthew and Luke in P[4,64,67] probably in the late second century, was handsomely and painstakingly executed. It was written in two very regular columns to a page, with punctuation marks and a system of text division, all features designed for easy public reading.[30] That is, we are looking at a codex which was not simply executed for the private reading of an individual Christian, but was a 'pulpit edition' made to be read out to the congregation during a service of worship. It is very unlikely that in P[4,64,67] we have stumbled upon something which was the first of its kind. 'This codex', Stanton says, 'does not look at all like an experiment by a scribe working out ways to include four gospels in one codex: it certainly had predecessors much earlier in the second century.'[31]

Similarly with the codex P[75], containing Luke and John. This manuscript is famous for its 'strict', meticulously copied text, and is generally considered the most accurate and mistake-free papyrus copy of New Testament writings we have. The scribe's relatively large letters form 'an attractive vertical uncial—elegant and well-crafted',[32] on large pages with generous margins. Like P[4,64,67], it too has sectional divisions which would make it easier to read aloud to a congregation.

Discoveries such as these have made it possible for a papyrologist of Skeat's stature and a veteran textual critic like Elliott to

Illustration 5.2 P⁴ (Bib. Natl., Supple. Gr. 1120), the earliest-known fragment of the Gospel according to Luke. A papyrus codex. Late second century. Used by permission of Bibliothèque nationale de France.

surmise that the codex form was adopted by the early Christians precisely because it, unlike the scroll, could accommodate all four Gospels together. Skeat thought this would have been done in the very early second century, shortly after the last of these Gospels

(John) was published. It must be said that our present state of knowledge cannot confirm this theory. But the evidence does nearly justify Kenyon's earlier surmise, that Irenaeus (and therefore others of his generation) may have been accustomed to the sight of four-Gospel codices.

Conclusion

In previous chapters literary evidence, not only from Irenaeus in Gaul but also from Clement in Alexandria, the *Muratorian Fragment* probably in Italy, and Serapion and Theophilus in Antioch, has made it clear that by the last decades of the second century the four Gospels were well established among churches distributed widely throughout the Roman empire. Now to this literary evidence we may add the material artefacts of multiple-Gospel codices (P^{45}, P^{75}, and possibly $P^{4,64,67}$), the four-Gospel Harmonies of Tatian and Theophilus (physically represented in the Dura fragment), and the slightly later Synopsis of Ammonius. Harmonies, Synopses, and multiple-Gospel Codices are all significant literary-technological 'packaging' projects which presuppose the primacy of the four. As far as we know, *none* of these projects was attempted with any Gospels but the four. All three forms of packaging also presuppose a notion of unity which 'binds' the four together, just the sort of unity which is evidenced in the writings of Irenaeus, Clement, and the *Muratorian Fragment*. Finally, the apparent liturgical design of the papyri P^{75} and $P^{4,64,67}$ also seems to confirm the Scriptural status of the Gospels they contained, the status they certainly held among the literary sources just named.

All of these witnesses, literary and literary-technological, suggest that the prominence of these Gospels, the perception of their overall unity, and even their sacred status must have originated from a time even earlier in the second century. The Gospel Harmony in particular gives us one lead. Though Tatian's was the most successful, it seems that he had at least one prototype to work from. Most scholars say that Tatian was building on work already done by his accomplished teacher in Rome. It is to that teacher, a man named Justin, that we now turn.

6

PREACHING AND TEACHING THE GOSPELS: JUSTIN MARTYR AND THE APOSTLES' MEMOIRS

A Philosopher's Spiritual Quest

LESS than a hundred years after Jesus' death his story captivated a young student of philosophy. Still unsettled after bouncing around the philosophical schools in his search for truth, the student was about to discard his philosopher's robe and give up his quest. Then an unexpected encounter with an old man changed his mind. The old man's arguments seemed to transcend those of the Neo-Platonists and Stoics with which the student had become so familiar. The old man introduced the young philosopher to the Jewish prophets, and then to the teachings of Jesus. The student walked away from the dialogue determined now to retain his philosopher's garb, believing he had found the only true philosophy, the one called Christian. The young philosopher's name was Justin. He has been dubbed 'Justin Martyr' by Christian tradition because he later surrendered his life for his new-found 'philosophy' (c.165 CE). Though he taught for many years in Rome and wrote several works, only three of his writings survive:

two traditionally called *Apologies*, written in the early 150s on behalf of the Christian religion and addressed to the secular authorities, and a *Dialogue with Trypho the Jew*, probably written between 155 and 160, though purporting to record an actual dialogue Justin and Trypho had about twenty years earlier.

Quatrophobia?

Due to Justin's early date and the reputation he gained even in his own day as a respected teacher of Christianity, attention has naturally focused on his use of Christian written sources. Which, if any, did he have? No doubt there are Christians today who would be disturbed to find out that someone of Justin's stature had more than four Gospels, or fewer than four, or even no Gospels at all that he considered to be Holy Scripture. But non-academic Christian laypeople are not the only ones who can get nervous about the number four.

At a recent academic conference, a paper was read arguing that Justin used the Gospel of John in his writings. Though the paper drew no explicit conclusion about the total number of Gospels Justin used, one scholar, in the discussion following the paper, pre-emptively protested, 'Who says we are talking about four Gospels used by Justin? Rather, six or seven!' The animated remark brought forth spontaneous head bobbles and grunts of approval from many in the room. Though none present volunteered any evidence for Justin's use of six or more Gospels, and the names of no non-canonical Gospels were put forward, the merest hint that Justin might have had all four (or only four) Gospels was all it took to tap into a mood which runs deep among many students of early Christianity. When it comes to Gospels, the number four, for some reason, just sounds oppressive and, well, anti-diverse. It does not seem to matter that 'four' is actually more diverse than 'one', 'two', or 'three'. The fact that some groups, like the Marcionites, used but one Gospel is entirely unobjectionable. The idea that others might have used five, six, or seven is, by its very nature, positively agreeable. But there is something about the number four which, when associated with the word 'Gospels', has the power to evoke feelings of repression, colonialism, and perhaps the Spanish Inquisition.

Visceral human reactions aside, however, the truth is that scholars who have studied the question of Justin's use of Gospels are today quite 'diverse' in their conclusions on the matter. It is true that some influential scholars, in keeping with the idea that a four-Gospel collection was the brainchild of Irenaeus, think that Justin either did not know or did not appreciate the Gospel of John, or that instead of the individual Gospels he knew only a three-Gospel Harmony, or that he held Gospels other than the four in equal or greater esteem. But a perhaps surprising number of experts are now of the opinion that Justin knew each one of the four canonical Gospels and held these Gospels to be the gold standard for Christian knowledge about Jesus.

And it is not only the number of Gospels Justin knew but the view he had of them which is disputed. Some argue that the Gospels contained what Justin considered true historical accounts of the life of Jesus, proving the fulfilment of Old Testament prophecies, but that he did not regard them as inspired or as Scripture.[1] One scholar even writes that Justin had 'misgivings about the emerging canonical status of the Gospels'[2] and accepted only the words of Jesus as authoritative. On the other hand, because Justin is the first Christian to mention the use of Christian

Gospels in Sunday-worship services, other scholars point to this liturgical use as a clear indication that Justin and the church in Rome in his day did indeed regard these Gospels as Scripture.

'Hoist with his Own Petard'

Answering the questions of which Gospels Justin had and how he regarded them is complicated by the fact that he never mentions any by name. Readers of Justin, including scholars, therefore sometimes ask: 'If Justin had the canonical Gospels (or any of the New Testament books for that matter) why didn't he simply tell us?' Since Justin seems more taciturn than Irenaeus about naming his Christian written authorities (the only New Testament author he mentions by name is the author of the book of Revelation, John, 'one of the apostles of Christ', *Dial.* 81.4), many conclude that he could not have held any Christian writings in particularly high regard.

But this largely ignores that in 'apologetic' or 'controversial' literature of the sort that Justin wrote there was often a principle involved that made explicit reference to one's own religious scriptures problematical. Perhaps we could call it the 'hoist with his own petard' principle. The phrase comes from Shakespeare's *Hamlet*, Act III, Scene iv, where the protagonist plans to intercept a letter carried by Rosencrantz and Guildenstern which he knows mandates his own death. So Hamlet will erase his own name and write in the names of his former companions instead. Hamlet takes some delight in his prank, 'For 'tis sport to have the engineer | Hoist with his own petard', that is, blown up by his own bomb.

How does this principle apply to Justin and his Christian sources? All of Justin's surviving treatises were written either to defend Christianity from accusations or to present it to those who were interested in adopting Judaism as opposed to Christianity. They were addressed ostensibly to outsiders and not to his fellow Christians. As works which relied heavily on the presentation of argument, they made use of rhetorical conventions and ideals of debate current in that day. One of those ideals was to defeat one's opponent by using the opponent's own religious or intellectual authorities—hoisting them with their own petard. Optimally, this could be done without even having to rely on one's own authorities, authorities which the opponent would not recognize anyway, apart from conversion or at least considerable defence. Some early Christian apologetic works, like Athenagoras' *Plea for the Christians*, contain no explicit reference to a New Testament text at all.

To illustrate the existence of this principle in antiquity, we take our first example from a non-Christian 'apologist'. The philosopher Celsus, writing sometime between 160 and 180, is the best-known, published opponent of Christianity from the second century. His great anti-Christian work, *The True Logos*, however, is only known today through the many quotations of it in a work Origen wrote against it several decades later. In the first part of his book Celsus speaks through a fictional Jewish opponent of Christianity who professes to have refuted the Christians 'from your own books, in addition to which we need no other witness; for ye fall upon your own swords' (*Contra Celsum* 2.74 cf. 2.77). Celsus calls it 'falling on your own swords', Shakespeare, being 'hoist with one's own petard'. Celsus saw that the most effective way to destroy Christianity would be to attack it from its own claimed source of truth, and indeed, Origen confirms that Celsus 'endeavours to cast reproach upon Him [Jesus] from the narratives in the

Gospel' (*Cels.* 2.34, cf. 2.37). Critics of Christianity today who use the New Testament to argue against Christianity are attempting nothing new; the effort has been going on at least since Celsus in the second century (clearly, with only limited results).

On the Christian side of things, Irenaeus professes the same ideal when he promises to write a treatise against Marcion: 'I purpose specially to refute him, convicting him out of his own writings; and with the help of God, I shall overthrow him out of those discourses of the Lord and the apostles which are of authority with him, and of which he makes use' (*AH* 1.27). Whether Irenaeus ever finished such a treatise we do not know, but he seems quite confident he can refute Marcion from the latter's own authorities, without having to call upon books like Matthew, John, Acts, or 1 Timothy, books which Irenaeus accepted but which Marcion rejected.

That Justin was given to this same ideal is evident in his debate with Trypho. There were certain passages which Justin believed some Jews had cut out of their copies of the Old Testament Scriptures because these passages provided too clear a witness to the Christ, that is, to Jesus. Regardless of whether or not there was any truth to this charge, Justin's words to Trypho are instructive: 'I have not attempted to establish proof about Christ from the passages of Scripture which are not confessed by you ... but from those which are even now confessed by you ...' (*Dial.* 120.5, cf. 71.5). Obviously, there were no New Testament writings 'confessed' by Trypho. Therefore it is not hard to see why Justin would be very circumspect about his use of such writings *as religious authorities* in the *Dialogue*.

This principle accounts for why Christian apologetic treatises addressed to Graeco-Roman officials or thinkers are often filled with arguments drawn from Homer, the Greek myths, or the philosophers, aiming either to convict critics of not living up to their own ideals, or to spotlight the immorality of their own gods, or in some other way to support the reasonableness of Christianity from sources these critics themselves accept. When Justin writes his *First Apology* to the Roman emperor and senate, he appeals to principles of reason, piety, justice, or philosophy to which he believes they want to submit: 'We presume that you who aim at [a reputation for] piety and philosophy will do nothing unreasonable' (1 *Apol.* 12). Justin then proceeds to plead the impiety and unreasonableness of the state's persecution of law-abiding Christians. In his *Dialogue with Trypho the Jew*, since Trypho's authority is the sacred Scriptures of the Law, the Prophets, and the Writings, Justin attempts to show the truth of Christianity from these books.

The principle we are talking about is, of course, not always adhered to perfectly. Some authors will find various ways of bringing in their own authorities through the back door, so to speak. It might be by using unattributed allusions rather than direct quotations; it might be by borrowing ideas, themes, and techniques used by those authorities without citing them. It might be by actually citing the authorities but presenting them as *historical* and not specifically *religious* or sacred documents. All of these ways of bringing in the witness of his written Christian authorities can be observed in Justin. One more way an apologist might justify invoking the testimony of his own religious authorities is if his opponent mentions them first, as when Justin tells Trypho, 'since you have read, O Trypho, as you yourself admitted, the doctrines taught by our Saviour, I do not think that I have done foolishly in adding some short utterances of his to the prophetic statements' (*Dial.* 18.1). Justin is thus able to justify a practice (citing some of

Jesus' sayings as indicators of Christian ethics) which otherwise might be deemed 'foolish' by his opponent in debate.

This principle also helps explain why Justin's preferred designation of the Gospels is not 'the Gospels', the name by which they were commonly known, but 'Memoirs of the Apostles', a title which might remind his educated readers of Xenophon's faithful reminiscences of his master, recorded in his *Memoirs of Socrates*. Justin even compares Jesus to Socrates (who, like Jesus and the Christians, was unjustly hounded to death), so the parallel with disciples of a great teacher writing memoirs of their master presented him with a model to exploit for his non-Christian readers.

In sum, this apologetic ideal of refuting one's opponent from the opponent's own authorities, and refraining from relying in the first instance upon one's own, is a major reason why it is often not clear just exactly what Justin's authorities were. But if we recognize this principle, Justin's failure to cite his Christian written authorities by name, appeal up front and often to their inspiration, or quote them with the kind of verbal accuracy of one who expects his citations to be checked by his opponent, is not surprising. Even with all this said, Justin still found ways of leaving us with many strong hints about his Christian authorities, as we'll soon see.

The Contents of the Apostolic Memoirs

What Were the Memoirs?

In his first *Apology*, addressed to the Roman emperor and senate, and in his *Dialogue with Trypho, the Jew*, he refers several times to certain books known as Gospels. His terminology is both interesting and important. He knows these books as 'Gospels', but his favourite way of referencing them is with the phrase, 'the Memoirs of the Apostles', or 'the Memoirs written by the apostles and those who followed them' (*Dial.* 103.8). First, there is the matter of just what Justin meant by these 'Gospels' or 'Memoirs of the Apostles'. Many have observed from examining his quotations of the sayings of Jesus that they often do not reflect the exact wording of a single one of our Gospels but look instead like amalgamated or 'harmonized' versions. Usually they show some combination of elements from Matthew and Luke, sometimes Mark. In other words, it looks as if he might have been using a Gospel Harmony, much like his student, Tatian, would later publish, except that we see in these harmonized accounts no evidence of his use of John. It has been suggested, then, that Justin did not even have the individual Gospels themselves but only this 'harmonized' Gospel.

Oskar Skarsaune, one of the premier living authorities on Justin's writings, has considered this question closely and has concluded that, whereas Justin used such a harmonized source in his *First Apology*, his quotations in his *Dialogue with Trypho* show that in this treatise Justin was using the individual Gospels themselves.[3] Some have assumed that if Justin used a Harmony at all, he could not have held the individual Gospels as authorities. But this simply does not follow. We have already seen that this was not the case with Tatian or Theophilus in the second century, or with any number of more recent compilers of Gospel Harmonies.

And while it is evident that Justin, either for convenience or for some other reason, sometimes blended together or harmonized Jesus' words, his ultimate authoritative source was what lay at the back of them. We know this because he actually mentions individual books called Gospels, or 'Memoirs of the Apostles', and even makes discriminating comments about them, as we'll soon see.

In fact, what is most impressive about the witness of Justin is that even in his apologetic works, where we would not expect him to call explicitly on his authoritative sources, he actually finds many ways of working in Jesus' teachings and the storyline of the Gospels, and even manages to tell us a few things about the Gospels themselves. Without ever naming the Gospels by title, he sometimes rather adroitly drops hints about them so that those who are 'in the know' will be able to figure out which Gospel(s) he is using.

Which Gospels Were They?

Justin's designation for the Gospels, 'Memoirs of the Apostles', was very useful for it allowed him to attribute the Gospels ultimately to the apostles without claiming that each Gospel was actually written personally by an apostle. In one place he says: 'For the apostles, in the memoirs which have come about by their agency, which are called Gospels, have thus delivered unto us...' (*1 Apol.* 66.3). The Gospels have come into being through the ultimate agency of the apostles, but not necessarily directly by their own authorial hands. In another place he testifies that the Gospels were composed by 'Jesus' apostles and their followers' (*Dial.* 103.8). Justin's use of the plurals here would seem to mean that he acknowledged at least four Gospels: at least two written by apostles and at least two by followers of apostles. Martin Hengel surmises, 'he is already thinking of the two "apostolic" Gospels of Matthew and John and of the two successors Mark and Luke'.[4]

It is worth noting that in Justin's day there were apparently no Gospels besides those of Mark and Luke which were attributed to *followers* of Jesus' apostles. Graham Stanton has remarked on the surprising lack of attention to this confession of Justin's in *Dial.* 103.8 among recent writers, and concludes: 'Since there is no clear evidence for Justin's knowledge of any gospels other than the canonical four, we can be all but certain that he had in mind Matthew, Mark, Luke, and John, no more, no less.'[5]

Other scholars, of course, instinctively recoil from such statements. 'Who says we are talking about four Gospels used by Justin? Rather, six or seven!' Since they think the eminence of these four did not pre-date Irenaeus and did not really catch on until much later, they naturally greet any suggestion that Justin knew a four-Gospel collection with the greatest scepticism. And yet, what we have seen from the evidence, not only from Irenaeus but also from Clement and even from Serapion, Theophilus, and Tatian, should encourage the historian to look to a time at least as early as Justin (*c.*150–65) for the first recognition of a special status for these four Gospels.

Scholars agree that Justin's Gospel allusions and citations favour the wording of Matthew and to a lesser degree Luke. But in one place Justin makes it clear that he also had Mark: 'And when it is said that he changed the name of one of the apostles to Peter; and when it is written in the memoirs of him that this so happened, as well as that he changed the names of two other brothers, the sons of Zebedee, to Boanerges, which means sons of thunder...' (*Dial.* 106.3). Jesus' renaming of Peter (from his original name Simon) is mentioned by Mark and Luke, but the nicknaming of the sons of Zebedee (the apostles James and John) as the 'sons of thunder' is mentioned only in Mark of all known Gospels (3.17).

What is more, Justin says that this account is contained in 'the memoirs of him', that is, the memoirs of Peter, one of the apostles. That the Gospel according to Mark was constructed from the testimony of the apostle Peter had been a part of Christian tradition at least since Papias of Hierapolis in Asia Minor, who had written some decades previously:

And the elder used to say this: 'Mark, having become Peter's interpreter, wrote down accurately everything he remembered, though not in order, of the things either said or done by Christ. For he neither heard the Lord nor followed him, but afterward, as I said, followed Peter, who adapted his teachings as needed but had no intention of giving an ordered account of the Lord's sayings . . . ' (Eusebius, *EH* 3.39.15)

Justin accepts this view of the origin of Mark's Gospel, and by referring to Peter's 'memoirs' subtly lets his Christian reader know he is using Mark as one of the 'Memoirs of the Apostles'.[6]

Justin's careful cluing-in of his Christian readers is evident again when he says, in the line mentioned above, that the Gospels were 'composed' by the apostles and those who followed them (*Dial.* 103.8). This notice marks the only time Justin uses such language, and, interestingly, it happens to be followed immediately by a reference to an incident recorded in only one Gospel, the Gospel according to Luke. Luke, of course, was not himself one of Jesus' apostles but was believed to be the companion of Paul and follower of the other apostles.

One final instance is worth noting. In *1 Apology* 33.5 Justin introduces a Gospel incident with the words, 'as they who have recounted all that concerns our Saviour Jesus Christ have taught, whom we have believed'. The plural 'they' here seems to show that he is aware that the information he is referring to is found in (at least) two authoritative sources. As it happens, these are Matthew 1.21 and Luke. 1.31–2. Here he does not say 'as the apostles wrote' but 'as they who have recounted all that concerns our Saviour Jesus Christ have taught', perhaps indicating his awareness that at least one of these writers was not an apostle but a follower of the apostles.

That Justin had all three synoptic Gospels, Matthew, Mark, and Luke, in mind when he spoke of the apostles' memoirs seems clear. But did Justin also use John, and was it among his apostolic memoirs or not?

Justin and John

Customarily, when Justin refers to Jesus' teaching his subject is Jesus' ethical teaching, for this was a point of contention between himself and others who were suspicious of the Christian faith. As we have seen earlier, slanders against Christians' allegedly immoral behaviour were rampant and sometimes led to prejudice and physical hostility towards them. But it is one of the distinctive characteristics of John's Gospel that it records little of Jesus' ethical instruction, such as occurs in Matthew's 'Sermon on the Mount' or Luke's 'Sermon on the Plain'. John focuses rather on Jesus' self-referential claims and the signs he performed, and on certain incidents which are not included in the other Gospels. Justin's familiarity with John thus tends to show when he is making theological statements about Jesus, or when reporting certain details from Jesus' life and work which are not contained in the Synoptics. Only once does Justin allude to something Jesus *said* in John's Gospel. But this single allusion is enough to make some scholars strongly suspect that Justin knew John's Gospel.

At one point in his *First Apology* Justin speaks of the Christian baptismal practice as he knows it in Rome:

Then they are brought by us where there is water, and are regenerated in the same manner in which we were ourselves regenerated. For, in the name of God, the Father and Lord of the universe, and of our Saviour Jesus Christ, and of the Holy Spirit, they then receive the washing with water. For Christ also said, 'Except ye be reborn, ye shall not enter into the kingdom of heaven'. (*1 Apol.* 61. 1)

Any readers who are familiar with the Gospel of John will recognize the resemblance to what Jesus said in John 3.3 and 5. 'Jesus answered him, "Very truly, I tell you, no one can see the kingdom of God without being born from above".... Jesus answered, "Very truly, I tell you, no one can enter the kingdom of God without being born of water and Spirit".' Even though Justin's quotation has 'kingdom of heaven' and John has 'kingdom of God', and though Justin uses a single compound word, 'reborn', instead of 'born from above', it seems obvious that Justin is simply paraphrasing these words from the Gospel according to John. Some scholars, however, noting the slight differences mentioned, prefer to attribute these words not to John's Gospel but to oral tradition or to a common baptismal formula that was allegedly known from a lost church liturgy.[7] Scholars who argue for these alternatives have a curious tendency to ignore the words which immediately follow in Justin's text. Justin continues: 'Now, that it is impossible for those who have once been born to enter into their mothers' wombs, is manifest to all.' These words echo very closely the reply of Nicodemus, according to John 3.4: 'Nicodemus said to him, "How can a man be born when he is old? Can he enter a second time into his mother's womb and be born?"' This would not have been in any alleged baptismal tract, and if it came from oral tradition it means that that tradition must have included the story of Nicodemus, which is unique to John of all known Gospels. It would be quite a coincidence indeed if Justin and the author of John's Gospel just happened to concoct independently the same objection about re-entering one's mother's womb! The simplest solution and the one that best satisfies the data appears to be that Justin was familiar with the account in John's Gospel.

This apparent use of the Gospel of John is, however, far from the only one we find in Justin. In *Dialogue* 105 Justin even seems to attribute a Johannine element to the apostolic memoirs when he writes: 'For I have proved he was Only-begotten to the Father of all things, begotten of him in a peculiar manner as Word and Power, and later having become man through the virgin, as we have learned from the Memoirs.' What Justin says he and other Christians had 'learned from the Memoirs' included that Jesus was 'Only-begotten to the Father'. Here it cannot be supposed that he derived this information merely from oral tradition because Justin explicitly attributes it to a written source, the Memoirs, which we know is a name for one or more of the Gospels. The only Gospel or Gospel-like source we know which teaches that Jesus is God's only begotten Son is the Gospel of John. Two of the best-known verses from this Gospel read, in the classic language of the King James Version, 'And the Word was made flesh, and dwelt among us, (and we beheld his glory, the glory as of the only begotten of the Father,) full of grace and truth' (John 1.14); and 'For God so loved the world, that he gave his only begotten Son, that whosoever believeth in him should not perish, but have everlasting life' (John 3.16).

Some have attempted to limit what Justin says he learned from the Memoirs to the single idea that Jesus was born through a virgin. This would imply only a reference to Matthew and Luke, for neither Mark nor John specifically speaks of his virgin birth. But Justin is not talking merely about the miracle of a virgin bearing a child. He is talking about a divine 'only-begotten of the Father' becoming man (cf. John 1.14, 'became flesh'), which happened through a virgin. Although one might draw the conclusion from Matthew and Luke by reading between the lines, neither of them, in their accounts of Jesus' birth, speaks of Jesus as existing prior to his birth from Mary. Only John does.[8]

We find that Justin also knows various details about Jesus' baptism, trial, and crucifixion contained only in John's Gospel. Some of these details have a particular interest because Justin mentions that they can be found in something he calls 'the acts which occurred under Pontius Pilate' (*1 Apol.* 35.9; 38.7). These 'acts' have nothing to do with the later apocryphal 'Pilate literature', such as the *Acts of Pilate*, now part of the fourth-century composition known as the *Gospel of Nicodemus*. Rather, this curious title, 'acts which occurred under Pontius Pilate', appears to be another way Justin has of bringing in the testimony of the Christian Gospels, which, up to this point in his *Apology*, he had not yet mentioned explicitly. Here Justin employs a Latin loan-word, *acta*, often used for official records or registers. The emperor and senate would have been quite familiar with the term. Julius Caesar had ordered that official *acta* of the proceedings of the senate be kept, and though Augustus temporarily suspended the practice, succeeding emperors made sure such records were kept by appointing certain senate members to the task.[9] By referring to information contained in the Gospels as belonging to the *acta* or 'register' of the things done under Pontius Pilate, Justin was able to emphasize the official or historical character of the information, and keep the religious aspect of the books out of the centre of debate at this point in his treatise.

Justin refers to these *acta* as something publicly accessible, as *acta* usually were, for he encourages the emperor to read them. 'And that these things did happen, you can learn from the registers (*acta*) of what happened under Pontius Pilate' (*1 Apol.* 35.9; cf. 48.7). One way of confirming that Justin is referring to the contents of the Gospels here is by observing that some of the things that he says in his *First Apology* (chs. 35 and 38) are found in these *acta*, he says in the *Dialogue* (chs. 101, 104) are found in the 'Memoirs of the Apostles'.[10]

Those who insist that Justin couldn't have used John's Gospel are forced to come up with alternative theories for how Justin might have obtained all the information he knows about Jesus which occurs in John's Gospel. If we add up Helmut Koester's proposals, for instance, we must suppose that Justin in Rome, in about 150–5, had somehow obtained at least four sources once used by the author(s) of John's Gospel: one used for John's Prologue, a baptismal liturgy expanded for John's story of Jesus' encounter with Nicodemus, another source used for John's account of Jesus' own baptism, and one used for John's account of Jesus' crucifixion—all of this without knowing the Gospel of John itself! On top of this, we would have to suppose that Justin independently developed sayings of both Nicodemus and John the Baptist along the same lines as did the author of John's Gospel. Compounding the unlikelihood of such an explanation is that Justin tells us that he possessed, not the supposed sources behind the Gospels, but the Gospels themselves, the 'Memoirs of the Apostles'.[11]

By far the most economical and comprehensive explanation of this data, and the one that accords best with the history of early Christian literature, is the simple admission that Justin knew and used John's Gospel, and that this Gospel was one of the apostolic memoirs. If Justin didn't have John, he must have had a Gospel that bore an amazing resemblance to it.

Six or Seven?

It seems clear, then, that Justin knew and used all four canonical Gospels in his writings and that it was these Gospels that he had in mind when he referred to the 'Memoirs of the Apostles' written by the apostles and their followers. But could he have had other Gospels in mind as well? Could there have been 'six or seven' of these apostolic memoirs?

It would be very surprising if Justin did not know any other Gospels. As a well-educated, well-travelled, and well-known teacher of Christianity living in Rome in the middle of the second century, who tells us he knew of a variety of groups who called themselves Christians, he was surely acquainted with all sorts of 'Christian' literature. And yet, oddly enough, more than one scholar has concluded that no clear evidence exists for Justin's knowledge or use of any Gospels besides the four.[12]

There are, it is true, three or four places where Justin, in passing, mentions details or sayings which are not contained in any of the four Gospels. For instance, he relates that on the night of Jesus' birth Joseph and Mary took refuge in a *cave* in Bethlehem (*Dial.* 78.7–8). Jesus' birth in a cave is not mentioned in the New Testament but is mentioned in a second-century book called the *Protevangelium of James* (18.1). But even Koester thinks it 'highly

unlikely' that Justin is dependent upon this source.[13] Most probably Justin is simply reliant upon local Palestinian tradition. Origen informs us that there was a cave near Bethlehem which had
attained local notoriety as the site of Jesus' birth.

With respect to the birth of Jesus in Bethlehem, if any one desires, after
the prophecy of Micah [4.1] and after the history recorded in the
Gospels by the disciples of Jesus, to have additional evidence from
other sources, let him know that, in conformity with the narrative in
the Gospel regarding his birth, there is shown at Bethlehem the cave
where He was born, and the manger in the cave where He was wrapped
in swaddling clothes. And this sight is greatly talked of in surrounding
places, even among the enemies of the faith, it being said that in this cave
was born that Jesus who is worshipped and reverenced by the Christians.
(CCels. 1.51)

The existence of the cave seems to have been common knowledge. Origen regards it as additional, confirmatory information,
but not information related by any of Jesus' disciples in a Gospel.
Justin also refers to the Greek version of Isaiah 33.16, which
speaks of a righteous one who will 'dwell in a high cave of a
strong rock'. That the worshippers of Mithras received initiation
in a cave Justin saw as a devilish counterfeiting of the truth of
Isaiah's prophecy, which was fulfilled by Jesus. All this simply
means that Justin's belief that Jesus was born in a cave is no firm
evidence of his acceptance of any alternative Gospel.

Justin's knowledge of the *Gospel of the Ebionites* has been argued
from one passage in particular. Justin says that when Jesus was
baptized, a fire was kindled in the Jordan, something no canonical
Gospel reports (*Dial.* 88.3). Contained in what Epiphanius in the
late fourth century called the *Gospel of the Ebionites* was the report
that 'a great light shone round about the place' when Jesus came

up from the water (*Panarion* 30.13.7–8). These two pieces of information are similar, though not the same. Justin speaks of a *fire* igniting *in* the Jordan as Jesus *enters* the water; the Ebionite Gospel speaks of a *light* shining *around* the place *after* the baptism. Many scholars think the two elaborations of the basic Gospel account are not actually related. The report of a fire igniting in the Jordan river as Jesus enters the water appears to be simply an expansion of the Gospel accounts, perhaps based on the prophecy of John the Baptist, that Jesus would baptize with the Holy Spirit 'and with fire' (Matt. 3.11/Luke 3.16). The light shining *after* Jesus' baptism in the *Gospel of the Ebionites*, Skarsaune and others think, is an outward, physical reflection of the inward illumination which was widely presumed to take place in baptism.[14] In any case, while we should not say it is impossible that Justin knew the *Gospel of the Ebionites*, the evidence for it is extremely thin and capable of other plausible explanations.

Finally, some have maintained that Justin used the *Gospel of Peter*, the same Gospel Serapion of Antioch discovered at Rhossus (assumed to be the Gospel discovered at Akhmim). But this oft-repeated assertion too has little to support it. Paul Foster concludes his study of the evidence with the statement: 'While there exist a couple of interesting shared elements, there is no extended verbatim agreement between the two authors that would be most convincingly explained through the theory of direct literary dependence.'[15] There are, in fact, only two passages in Justin from which the argument can be made, and in each case, interestingly enough, it appears that both Justin and the *Gospel of Peter* are paraphrasing and interpreting the same portions of the Gospel according to John. It is not at all impossible that Justin knew the contents of the *Gospel of Peter*. But even if he did, it seems that he and it simply reflect a common exegetical tradition based on the events reported in John's Gospel, which by this time must have been fairly widely known. As we shall see in a moment, Justin also reports that the 'Memoirs of the Apostles' were commented upon by preachers in Rome in their Sunday sermons. It is therefore only to be expected that certain elaborations of the contents of these Gospels would have come into the common Christian vocabulary.

It is helpful to recall that both the *Gospel of the Ebionites* and the *Gospel of Peter* (as well as several others) were themselves derivative documents based to a greater or lesser degree on the existing Gospels. Tjitze Baarda says:

It is very likely that such documents as *The Gospel of Peter* and *The Gospel of the Ebionites* were, to a certain extent, harmonies that combined materials from other sources including one or more of the 'canonical' Gospels. The main goal was probably not to create a 'scholarly' work, the result of a careful analysis of the sources, but rather to produce a 'popular' harmonization: a work which contained materials compiled from various sources so that readers would have more information about Jesus, his life and teaching than could be found [in] any single underlying source.[16]

Nor is it without significance that in none of these cases in which Justin relates information about Jesus not contained in one of the four Gospels does he refer that information to the apostolic memoirs. By far the best conclusion, then, is that Justin knew all four canonical Gospels and knew them as an already standard grouping. Almost as certainly, he attributed Matthew and John to apostles and Mark and Luke to followers of apostles.

The Character of the Apostolic Memoirs

Mere Historical Records?

Following Koester, many have argued that Justin regarded whatever Gospels he had as reliable historical documents, but no more. These Gospels provided the main facts of Jesus' life, words, and works, and showed how the prophecies of the Old Testament were fulfilled in Jesus, but as mere historical records they bore an authority far below the Scriptures of the prophets. But as we have noted already, Justin's predominant use of the Christian Gospels as historical documents instead of as explicitly religious authorities simply fits his design in the kind of literature he was writing.

There is also a logical problem with the 'reliable historical documents' view. It is that the Old Testament Scriptures themselves, agreed to be Scripture by both Justin and Trypho, were also perceived to be reliable historical documents! Thus, there is no reason to think that for Justin a writing which was a reliable historical document, something comparable on the one hand to official *acta* of the senate and on the other to Xenophon's *Memoirs of Socrates*, could not also be considered Scripture.

But now we'll see why one cannot really say that Justin's view of the Gospels was strictly confined to an appreciation of their historical value as providing the mere facts about Jesus.

Apostolic Authority

As we have seen, Justin characterizes the church's Gospels as apostolic memoirs, or as 'the memoirs which I say were drawn up by his apostles and those who followed them'. In one place they are called 'the memoirs which have come about by their [i.e.

the apostles'] agency, which are called Gospels' (*1 Apol.* 66.3).
This connection with the apostles is important to keep in mind
when assessing claims about the type of authority Justin recognized these Gospels to bear.

The apostles of Jesus, of course, were authorities 'confessed'
neither by Trypho, a non-Christian, Jewish thinker, nor by the
Roman officials addressed in Justin's apologies. The Scriptures of
the Old Testament, on the other hand, were acknowledged by
Trypho and Justin in common, and were universally known as the
sacred books of the Jews. Throughout his *First Apology*, and more
especially in his *Dialogue*, Justin tries to show that these Jewish
Scriptures predicted the coming of Jesus and the salvation that he
brought. But Justin does not simply argue that these ancient
Scriptures spoke of Jesus. He also argues that these same Scriptures
spoke of Jesus' apostles, foretelling their mission and their message. This meant that, according to Justin, the apostles of Jesus and
the message they brought were authorized by Scripture. He
interprets the popular prophecy in Isaiah 2.3, 'For out of Zion
shall go forth the law, and the word of the LORD from Jerusalem ... ' to mean: 'For from Jerusalem there went out into the
world men, twelve in number, and these illiterate, of no ability in
speaking: but by the power of God they proclaimed to every race
of men that they were sent by Christ to teach to all the word of
God' (*1 Apol.* 39.3; cf. *Dial.* 24.1, 3). What the apostles taught was
the word of God. Expositing Psalm 110.2, 'The LORD sends
forth from Zion your mighty sceptre. Rule in the midst of your
foes!', Justin explains that this 'is predictive of the mighty word,
which his apostles, going forth from Jerusalem, preached every-
where' (*1 Apol.* 45.5). The word of the apostles is God's mighty
sceptre by which Christ rules. As Abraham believed God's voice

and it was credited to him as righteousness (Gen. 15.6), 'in like manner we, having believed God's voice spoken by the apostles of Christ, and promulgated to us by the prophets, have renounced even to death all the things of the world' (*Dial.* 119.6). What was spoken by these apostles of Christ is God's very voice.

It will do no good to argue that Justin is talking only about the apostles' 'speaking' or 'preaching' and not their writings as carrying God's own authority. For in just the same way Justin also talks about the Old Testament prophets speaking or preaching God's word to the people, and this authority clearly pertains to the prophets' writings as well. Thus, when Justin characterizes the Gospels as the memoirs of the apostles, written by the apostles and their followers, this very designation shows that these are no mere historical records that he has in mind. The apostles of Jesus spoke with God's own voice. And whether it was they or their assistants who wrote down their message, that written message, like the messages of the prophets, was the voice of God too.

Liturgical Use as Scripture

This indeed seems to be borne out when Justin informs the emperor and senate that Christians read these Gospels and expound them in their services of worship on Sundays: 'And on the day called Sunday, all who live in cities or in the country gather together to one place, and the memoirs of the apostles or the writings of the prophets are read, as long as time permits; then, when the reader has ceased, the president verbally instructs, and exhorts to the imitation of these good things' (*1 Apology* 67). Someone may object that not everything ever read in a Christian meeting in the second century was considered Scripture. And

this, I believe, is certainly true. For instance, Dionysius of Corinth, in a letter preserved by Eusebius, says that the letter called
1 Clement was read from time to time in the church at Corinth
in the 170s (*EH* 4.23). Does this mean that the Corinthians
considered *1 Clement* to be Scripture? There is no shortage of
scholars who will say yes,[17] and who will do so while at the same
time denying that the reading of the Gospels in worship services
in Rome in the 150s means that they were considered to be
Scripture. But there are reasons why we should say that the
reverse is true.

Here is what Dionysius writes to the Roman church: 'Today
we observed the holy day of the Lord, and read out your letter
[i.e. Bishop Soter's recent letter, written perhaps only weeks
earlier], which we shall continue to read from time to time for
our admonition, as we do with that which was formerly sent to us
through Clement.'[18] If this means the Corinthians thought Clement's letter was Scripture, it means they thought Soter's was
Scripture as well! Dionysius simply seems to be speaking of the
occasional reading of epistolary correspondence between
churches in Christian meetings for mutual encouragement.
Clement's letter, now seventy or more years old, was widely
respected, but Clement, like Irenaeus' esteemed teacher Polycarp,
was not an apostle and not one of the apostles' mission assistants.
Clement does not even write in own name but on behalf of the
church, and, fittingly, Dionysius speaks of the letter as written
'through Clement'. This is probably why Dionysius classes the
ecclesiastical letter of Clement with that of Soter written so
recently.

By contrast, when Justin speaks about the reading of the
Gospels in the worship services in Rome he is talking about a

liturgical reading of Scripture. How do we know this? We know this because he reports that these Memoirs were read alternatively with the Old Testament prophetical books, and that they were then expounded by the preacher. Justin's account parallels the long-standing Jewish custom of reading Scripture and then expounding it in the synagogues. The Jewish writer Philo describes meetings on the Sabbath in first-century Alexandria: 'And then some priest who is present, or some one of the elders, reads the sacred laws to them, and interprets each of them separately till eventide; and then when separate they depart, having gained some skill in the sacred laws, and having made great advances towards piety' (*Hypothetica* 7.13). Describing the worship of the Jewish sect of the Essenes, he says:

Then one, indeed, takes up the holy volume and reads it, and another of the men of the greatest experience comes forward and explains what is not very intelligible . . . and thus the people are taught piety, and holiness, and justice, and economy, and the science of regulating the state, and the knowledge of such things as are naturally good, or bad, or indifferent, and to choose what is right and to avoid what is wrong . . . (*That Every Good Man is Free* 12.82–3)

An example of this practice in the New Testament is contained in the Gospel according to Luke, when Jesus in his home synagogue in Nazareth first reads and then interprets a text from the prophet Isaiah (Luke 4.16–21). Jesus interprets the passage as speaking of himself:

When he came to Nazareth, where he had been brought up, he went to the synagogue on the sabbath day, as was his custom. He stood up to read, [17] and the scroll of the prophet Isaiah was given to him. He unrolled the scroll and found the place where it was written: [18] 'The Spirit of the Lord is upon me, because he has anointed me to bring good news to the poor. He has sent me to proclaim release to the captives and recovery of sight to the blind, to let the oppressed go free, [19] to proclaim the year of the Lord's favour.' [20] And he rolled up the scroll, gave it back to the attendant, and sat down. The eyes of all in the synagogue were fixed on him. [21] Then he began to say to them, 'Today this scripture has been fulfilled in your hearing.'

Justin's report in *1 Apology* 67 shows an essential continuity with this liturgical practice evident in the first-century accounts of Luke and Philo. The import is that what was being read in church services in Justin's day in Rome was not a collection of mere historical records, nor a harmonized fusion of written and oral traditions from various sources, but real, publicly known and acknowledged books called Gospels, which Justin characterizes as apostolic memoirs. Mary Ann Donovan has it right when she says, 'Justin ... gives evidence that by the mid-second century the worshiping community used the gospels liturgically (thus as Scripture)'.[19] All our evidence suggests that (as queasy as this may make some people feel) these Gospels were none other than Matthew, Mark, Luke, and John.

We noted in a previous chapter Fredrick Kenyon's remark about Irenaeus possibly being accustomed to the sight of four-Gospel codices in his day. It is interesting, then, to read Skarsaune laying out the following possibility: 'It is likely, but not absolutely certain, that Justin already had a complete four-Gospel codex at his disposal.'[20]

Conclusion

One thing which stands out about the four Gospels in Rome in the middle of the second century is their impressive versatility. They were being used as records of the historical fulfilment of the prophetic Hebrew Scriptures in controversial, apologetic contexts. At least the first three, those known today as the Synoptic Gospels, had probably been 'harmonized' as an aid to teaching and writing. But the four Gospels were not simply being used for research or didactic purposes, they were also functioning as religious authorities, as Scripture, in the worship services of Christians.

This is one-and-three-quarter centuries before the Council of Nicaea, and more than two centuries before Bishop Athanasius would write his Easter letter listing the 'canonical' books. How long had it been the custom of the church in Rome to treat these books as Christian Scripture? Was it a practice only recently introduced? And was Justin's church exceptional, as isolated as some say Irenaeus was? Or did he possibly have 'co-conspirators' too? In the next chapter we explore this latter, enticing possibility.

7

JUSTIN'S 'CO-CONSPIRATORS': THE GOSPELS AS PUBLIC DOCUMENTS

IN an earlier chapter we noted that the approach of many leading scholars of early Christianity today depends on the acceptance of a sort of conspiratorial mindset. There is a tendency to view the prevalence of one form of Christianity (the one these scholars like to call 'proto-orthodox') in the early period as only apparent, the illusory product of post-Constantinian Christianity's largely successful attempt to destroy contrary evidence and rewrite history. One might say that this tendency is fittingly embodied in Dan Brown's *The Da Vinci Code*, and other books and films of this genre. Accepting this approach, one could envision another Hollywood thriller, this one set in the late second century, with Clement, Serapion, Theophilus, and the author of the *Muratorian Fragment* acting as Irenaeus' co-conspirators in an earlier plot to impose an unwanted four-Gospel canon on the church. Indulging the thought for a moment longer, we might now even propose a 'prequel', featuring Justin and an earlier cabal of 'co-conspirators'. For the Irenaeus movie, the screenwriters' job, and the plot's credibility, would be helped by the fact that the fellow plotters all shared Irenaeus' basic theological convictions (or his desire to put other people under his authoritarian control, as the case may be). In the case of the Justin prequel, however, the task of suspending the viewers' sense of reality would present a greater challenge. For Justin will have recruited his co-conspirators from the ranks of unbelievers.

Trypho

The first of his unwitting partners would have to be Trypho, Justin's non-compliant opponent in debate. This is because Trypho, though he is a non-Christian Jew of the Diaspora whom Justin meets in the city of Ephesus, acknowledges his familiarity with 'the Gospel' of the Christians. 'Moreover, I am aware that your precepts in your so-called Gospel are so wonderful and so great, that I suspect no one can keep them; for I have carefully read them' (*Dial.* 10). From Trypho's appellation, 'your so-called Gospel', we cannot tell if Trypho had read just one Gospel or more, since sometimes the singular 'Gospel' was used indiscriminately to refer to any of the church's acknowledged Gospels or to a plurality of them collectively (see below on Celsus). Theoretically, it could be that what he had read was another, unknown Gospel. But when Justin later recounts the teaching of Jesus by borrowing from Matthew and Luke, he assumes that Trypho, who has admitted to reading 'your so-called Gospel', had read these teachings: 'since you have read, O Trypho, as you yourself admitted, the doctrines taught by our Saviour, I do not think that I have done foolishly in adding some short utterances of his to the prophetic statements' (*Dial.* 18.1). Whatever it was that Trypho in his investigation of Christianity had read, Justin assumes it bore a very close resemblance to at least the Gospels of Matthew and Luke, which Justin held to be apostolic memoirs. Trypho's familiarity with 'your so-called Gospel' implies that 'the Gospel' was accessible enough that a well-educated, philosophically minded, but Torah-keeping Jew had little problem finding one.

Now, since all of this comes in a dialogue written by Justin, it is of course impossible to be sure that the historical Trypho (assuming he was historical) really knew any of the Christian Gospels or not. While most scholars seem to think the character of Trypho is based on a real person, Justin, of course, was free to reconstruct the dialogue as he wished. All we can really say is that Justin thought it would be believable to his intended readers, a large proportion of whom were probably Jews or Jewish-leaning Gentiles in Rome, that an educated and philosophically minded Jew should have read the Christian Gospels, the same ones which were familiar to the Christians in Rome. But there are other signs from the writings of Justin and from other works quite contemporary with him that the Christian Gospels must have gained this kind of notoriety outside the church.

The Emperor and Senate

True, the emperor Antoninus Pius (138–61) and the Roman senate have to be considered most unlikely co-conspirators. But in a sense they could be made to play the part. For Justin invites the emperor and the senate of Rome to learn about Christianity 'by looking into our writings' (1 *Apol.* 28.1), later informs them of the existence of written records, 'acts', documenting the events that took place under Pontius Pilate (35.9; 48.3 and alluded to in 38.7), and finally mentions explicitly 'memoirs' originating with the apostles 'which are called Gospels' (66.3). Justin's words, of course, do not imply that any of his august addressees were already familiar with the Christian Gospels. Justin's words do legitimately suggest, however, that these Gospels were not so hard to obtain. And this suggestion receives further support from what he says about a man named Crescens.

Crescens

In what is known as Justin's *Second Apology* we are introduced to the name of Crescens, a self-professed philosopher and opponent of Christianity in Rome who pursued a public and personal campaign against Justin. Crescens' antagonism to Justin was public enough that even Justin's one-time student Tatian mentioned the feud, and Crescens' efforts to get Justin and himself killed (Tatian, *Oration* 19). Justin even wrote that he expected that such aggression would eventually lead to his own arrest and burning at the stake (*2 Apol.* 3). Justin turned out to be wrong, however. He was not burned at the stake but beheaded.[1]

Now here is where the mention of Crescens matters for our investigation. Justin criticizes Crescens for charging Christians with atheism and impiety, as Justin says, either 'without having read the teachings of Christ' or, 'if he has read them . . . [he] does not understand the majesty that is in them' (*2 Apol.* 3.3). But where, we must ask, was Crescens expected to read the teachings of Christ? Would just any Gospel do? Obviously not. Justin's criticism of Crescens hardly makes sense unless the teachings of Christ were readily obtainable in some kind of generally acknowledged, *written* form. This in itself implies that the sources commonly associated with the Christian church in Rome, and the Gospels in particular, those 'apostolic memoirs' which contained Christ's teachings, must have been fairly well known. And this is confirmed more extensively by the next co-conspirator.

Celsus

What Justin invites the emperor and senate to do, and what he criticizes Crescens for probably not doing, was done by the critic Celsus, at least to a degree. Celsus took the time to give the books of his opponents at least a cursory reading. In fact, many scholars have thought that Celsus, who wrote his *True Logos* sometime between about 160 and 180, was responding directly to some of the challenges posed in the writings of Justin.

Robert Grant finds the significance of Celsus' work to lie in the fact 'that he has investigated second-century Christianity and knows a good deal about it'.[2] For one thing, Celsus is aware of the common notion that the disciples of Jesus wrote accounts regarding him which portrayed his suffering and death. Indeed, he accepts this as true (*Against Celsus* 2.16). And, somehow, he has procured copies of these accounts. As was noted earlier, he has his fictional Jewish opponent of Christianity professing to have refuted the Christians 'from your own books' (2.74 cf. 2.77). Which books would those have been?

Origen says that Celsus 'endeavours to cast reproach' upon Jesus 'from the narratives in the Gospel' (*Cels.* 2.34) and 'extracts from the Gospel narrative those statements on which he thinks he can found an accusation' (*Cels.* 2.37). Though Origen uses the singular, 'the Gospel', he clearly means the four Gospels collectively. He attests specifically that Celsus 'makes numerous quotations from the

Gospel according to Matthew' (*Cels.* 1.34). Origen notes that Celsus 'extracts from the Gospel' (this time it is John) 'even passages which are incorrectly interpreted' (*Cels.* 2.36). One of Celsus' assertions was that the 'framers of the genealogies, from a feeling of pride, made Jesus to be descended from the first man, and from the kings of the Jews' (*Cels.* 2.32). The only known Gospels, canonical or non-canonical, which contain genealogies of Jesus are Matthew and Luke. Matthew traces Jesus' lineage to 'the kings of the Jews', Luke back to Adam 'the first man'. Celsus must have seen both these Gospels. In one place Celsus refers to Jesus as a carpenter (*Cels.* 6.36). Though Matthew relates that Jesus' putative father Joseph was a carpenter, only Mark's Gospel relates that Jesus himself was a carpenter (Mark 6.3). Thus, Celsus apparently used all four canonical Gospels in his attempt to argue against Christianity 'from your own books'.

There is even one text which some believe indicates Celsus' awareness of a fourfold Gospel canon (*Cels.* 2.27).[3] When Celsus complains about the 'threefold, and fourfold, and many-fold' form of the Gospel, this sounds like a reference to the three Synoptic Gospels and then the four (adding John). Others have thought that it is instead a charge that Christians have altered the original text of the Gospel, three, four, and many more times.[4] But even the last interpretation of Celsus' words could be taken to imply Celsus' familiarity with a fourfold Gospel, which Celsus would have seen as successive attempts by Christians to modify the original Gospel into a form which would allow them to escape criticism. Though there is no way to know for certain, the possibility that Celsus had even obtained a four-Gospel codex would not be out of the question.

But whether or not Celsus knew a definite fourfold Gospel collection, or codex, his use of the four Gospels in his broadside against Christianity is apparent. So, how is it that Celsus came up with just these four when many want to assure us that these were but four among many? It would appear that these four were the Gospels that had standing in the churches which Celsus took to be the majority or mainline of Christianity, what he called 'the Great Church' (*Cels.* 5.59, cf. 5.61, 'those of the multitude'). These books were so well known that an outsider had no problem ascertaining which ones they were and then finding copies of them. Celsus confirms the usage of Justin and the practice of the church in Rome as Justin describes it.

The *Gospel of Truth*

Among the Nag Hammadi discoveries in 1945 were two Coptic versions of the *Gospel of Truth*, a moderate Valentinian document which probably originated around the middle of the second century. Though it went under the name of 'Gospel of Truth'—apparently simply because these were the first words of the document—it does not belong to the same genre as the canonical Gospels, the *Gospel of Peter*, and a few others. That is, it is not a narrative biography of Jesus but is rather a theological treatise or, as Bentley Layton argues, 'a sermon on the theme of salvation by acquaintance with god (*gnosis*)'.[5] Several scholars have concluded that this work was authored by Valentinus himself. If it was, then it originated in Rome around the midpoint of the second century and would be quite contemporary with the work of Justin. We have no good evidence that Justin knew of this particular 'Gospel', though he did know of the Valentinians, but it was known to Irenaeus (*AH* 3.11.9). Even if Valentinus was not the author, scholars seem to agree that this is one of the earliest expressions of Valentinian thought we possess.

Harold Attridge, I think rightly, sees this work as an attempt by its author to attract non-Valentinian Christians to the Valentinian point of view. The more radical Valentinian elements are played down 'so that the author may make an appeal to ordinary Christians, inviting them to share the basic insights of Valentinianism'.[6] It is interesting, then, to note which authorities the author seems to invoke in his appeal to 'ordinary Christians'. It has long been recognized that, while it never quotes another text verbatim, the *Gospel of Truth* shows its familiarity with virtually the whole New Testament.[7] Of the Gospels, its knowledge of Matthew and John is quite clear; evidence for the knowledge of Mark and Luke is more debatable. The author's awareness or probable awareness of writings that now form the New Testament does not, of course, mean that he or she considered any of these works to be Scripture or as bearing final authority. But, just like the other evidence we have considered in this chapter, the evidence from *The Gospel of Truth* does seem to confirm that such writings were widely known and acceptable to the Christians it was attempting to reach. Its use of at least Matthew and John, and perhaps all four Gospels, and, as far as we can tell, no others,[8] confirms the evidence provided by Justin.

Justin seems to have recruited his co-conspirators from the strangest of places. And there is one more, perhaps even stranger, ally to consider here.

The *Gospel of Judas*

It seems to be universally recognized that the value of this newly famous Gospel in providing independent, historical information about Jesus, Judas, or the first-century situation in Palestine is nil. For what historical knowledge it does reflect, Frank Williams argues that the *Gospel of Judas* 'seems to be based on clues or hints in the four gospels which it is possible for us to identify. This is not to say that Gos. Judas spells these hints out or refers explicitly to the four gospels; for this school their authority is not more than relative, and to name or emphasize them would be counter-productive. Still, it is not difficult to see how they have been used as sources.'[9]

The *Gospel of Judas* is also familiar with the canonical book of Acts (*GJ* 36.1–4). 'Thus it seems clear that, at least for the portions of our work which are meant to be historical, the four catholic gospels and the Book of Acts were the chief literary sources.'[10] The *Gospel of Judas*, of course, rejects the four Gospels and the book of Acts as its own religious authorities. As noted earlier, it seeks to rewrite the Gospels and to cast aspersions on the apostles of Jesus.[11] But by doing so the author attests to the acknowledged authority of these very Gospels in the church that he despised. By the time the *Gospel of Judas* was written one was not going to get very far without somehow dealing with them.

With the publication of the *Gospel of Judas* in 2006 many were excited about its potential to prove to an assumedly uninformed public, once and for all, something scholars have known about for a very long time: the wide diversity that existed among claimants of the name 'Christian' in the second century. It is something of an irony, then, that one of the most telling contributions of the *Gospel of Judas* to our knowledge of early Christianity, besides showing us a group who voiced its opposition to apostolic Christianity with particular vigour and vulgarity, just might be its witness to the existence and authority of the canonical Gospels before Irenaeus.

In a general way we see a similar dependence on the four Gospels in other second- and third-century literary productions from gnostic circles. While we cannot say, regarding each gnostic document, that it knows all four canonical Gospels, it is at least the framework of Jesus' life provided by these Gospels that is assumed in the several attempts to supplement or supersede them. Speaking of the somewhat later *Gospel of Mary*, Pheme Perkins says: 'Its incorporation of kingdom sayings of Jesus into the canonical framework of resurrection appearances suggests that the canonical Gospels played a crucial role in determining what could be credibly attributed to the Lord.'[12] Speaking more generally, she says: 'What is to count as revelation must be recognizably associated with canonical texts.'[13]

This is certainly the case already by the time Justin began writing and would remain so thereafter. In the next chapter we'll see that it was the case even earlier.

SOME
'PROTO-CONSPIRATORS':
TWO FORGERS AND
AN APOLOGIST

Two Popular Scholarly Myths

WHOEVER thought of inviting all the authors or co-authors of books on the *Gospel of Judas* to speak at a session of the 2007 Society of Biblical Literature meeting in San Diego underestimated the attractiveness of the idea. The large meeting room at the San Diego Convention Center was packed beyond capacity and the line of scholars who couldn't find a seat spilled out well into the hallway. During his presentation, one well-known scholar of early Christianity tweaked his colleagues with what he thought, in the wake of the recent discovery of the *Gospel of Judas*, was a provocative question. If the 'proto-orthodox' texts were so abundant in the early period, he queried, why is it that among the important archaeological finds in recent decades proto-orthodox texts are so rarely discovered? Why is it that instead, virtually everything discovered nowadays is heterodox? As we saw in Chapter 1, this scholar's question signals that he is a bit out-of-touch with the actual state of the manuscript discoveries. Almost as if to point up the irony in his words, from 2007 to the present (the summer of 2009, as I write), six new fragments of New Testament manuscripts have been published from the Oxyrhynchus discoveries.[1] In the same period the number of new manuscripts of heterodox writings to be published is zero.

In the discussion that followed the papers that night, a questioner politely reminded this scholar about the many New Testament papyri that have been discovered, which are obviously 'proto-orthodox' in their theological orientations. The reply bristled with self-assurance, as if delighted that the questioner had just walked into a trap. The scholar announced to the crowd that one of best-attested New Testament books among the papyri, the Gospel of John, is not a proto-orthodox work! Instead, John was widely used by gnostics, and the Valentinians loved it.

Our famous scholar's comments about John reflect a long-held scholarly theory. For a long time, and in many quarters, the theory has been treated as historical fact. The theory is that that John's Gospel, arising from questionable beginnings, was popular first among gnostics and other heterodox Christians while it was greeted with scepticism and distrust by the orthodox. In fact, according to this point of view, John finally had to be 'rescued' for the orthodox by Irenaeus and a few others. Once again, however, this scholar's ideas are behind the times. This scholarly theory about the early fortunes of John's Gospel is now recognized by many to be not a fact but a scholarly myth. Several studies have shown that John was used earlier and rather more often by orthodox Christians than has been reported.[2] Not only this, but, perhaps even more unexpectedly, John's reception by the gnostics was frequently something less than friendly.[3]

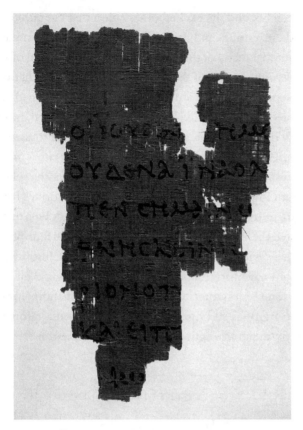

Illustration 8.1 P⁵² (J. Rylands Univ. Libr., Gr.P. 457), the earliest-known fragment of the Gospel according to John. A papyrus codex. Probably early to middle second century. Reproduced by courtesy of the University Librarian and Director, the John Rylands University Library, University of Manchester.

It is quite true that many of the second-century gnostic writings show a knowledge and use of John (as do many of the orthodox ones). But this proves no more than that John was a popular Gospel all around. It has only been relatively recently that scholars have gotten beyond the excited observation that the gnostics used John in their writings and have started to ask *how* they used John. It turns out that many of these writers were quite critical of—even hostile towards—some of the leading ideas taught in that Gospel and even antagonistic towards the apostle John, its alleged author.

The three writings treated in this chapter are featured, however, not simply because of their attestation of and attitude towards John, but because they are three separate pieces of literature from the period before 150 which show visible intimations of the popularity of the four Gospels in the church. In none of these do we have any explicit mention, as in Irenaeus, of the four Gospels by name. Nor do we have the clear statement of a four-and-only-four principle. Still, each provides evidence for recognizing that Justin and Irenaeus might have had real precursors. One could say they provide producers and scriptwriters with the possibility of another prequel, furnishing Irenaeus and Justin with some 'pre-conspirators' or, to use a prefix much in vogue today, 'proto-conspirators'.

A Pair of Forgers

The Apocryphon of James

One of those 'gnostic' works which shows a less-than-cordial reception of the Gospel according to John is a work preserved only among the Nag Hammadi collection called the *Apocryphon of James*. To see the 'anti-Johannine' sentiment of this book, we need to glance back for a moment at one aspect of John's Gospel, its emphasis on the importance of authorized, eyewitness testimony to Jesus' true humanity and true human suffering on the one hand, and to his divinity on the other.

The Gospel according to John claims to have been written by an eyewitness of Jesus (21.24). It presents itself as the testimony of one of those disciples who has seen Jesus and beheld his glory: 'And the Word became flesh and lived among us, and we have seen his glory, the glory as of a father's only son, full of grace and truth' (1.14). This same high appreciation of personal, eyewitness testimony is reflected in the closely associated letter known as 1 John, which begins: 'We declare to you what was from the beginning, what we have heard, what we have seen with our eyes, what we have looked at and touched with our hands, concerning the word of life.' The testimony of those who actually saw, heard, and touched Jesus, a person who was 'in the beginning...with God' and who 'was God' (John 1.1), and yet came with a real human body, was undoubtedly important in the context in which the Gospel and 1 John were written. A key, and dramatic, narrative presentation of this is in John's account of the resurrection of Jesus. When Jesus appeared to a group of his disciples after his resurrection, 'he showed them his hands and his side. Then the disciples rejoiced when they saw the Lord' (20.20). But Thomas, one of the twelve, was not present. His remark to his companions was: 'Unless I see the mark of the nails in his hands, and put my finger in the mark of the nails and my hand in his side, I will not believe' (20.25). Jesus later appeared to Thomas and invited the doubting disciple to see and touch the wounds, and to believe. In the face of such proof, now 'believing Thomas' exclaims, 'My Lord and my God' (20.29). After offering this proof by sight and touch, Jesus pronounces a blessing upon those who, like the readers of the Gospel, will come to such faith as Thomas had without the sort of sensory experience Thomas and the others were given: 'Jesus said to him, "Have you believed because you have seen me? Blessed are those who have not seen and yet have come to believe"' (John 20.29).

The *Apocryphon of James*, as scholarship in general has observed, is familiar with John's Gospel.[4] But how does it receive the testimony of John? Does it identify with John's conceptions of Jesus, and defend them? One place where its attitude becomes conspicuous is in the way it uses the saying of Jesus just quoted from John's Gospel. Not content with repeating the blessing on those who believe without seeing, it gives that saying a twist. That twist comes in the form of a *curse* on those who did perceive Jesus with their senses! Jesus is portrayed as saying: 'Woe to those who have seen the Son [of] Man; blessed will they be who have not seen the man, and they who have not consorted with him, and they who have not spoken with him, and they who have not listened to anything from him; yours is life!' (3.17–25).[5] It takes little deciphering to see that those being disparaged are Jesus' original disciples, like the one assumedly responsible for the Gospel of John. Later in *ApocJas* Jesus reproves the disciples because 'when I was with you, you did not know me...Blessed will they be who have not seen, [yet have believed]!' (12.36–13.1). In decided contrast to John and 1 John, which put great stock in the testimony of those who saw, heard, and touched Jesus even after the resurrection, the *ApocJas* encourages pity for such people. For they only saw 'the man' and did not recognize the transcendent being who somehow stood behind or within him and who acts as a guide for readers of the *ApocJas* to surpass even Jesus himself: 'Become better than I!...be eager of your own accord and, if possible, arrive even before me!' (6.19; 7. 13–14).

A view like this was known to Origen in the third century, who found it necessary to criticize any who say that, those who have not seen and have believed are more blessed than those who have seen and believed, because they have misconstrued what the Lord said to Thomas at the end of John's Gospel: 'Blessed are those who have not seen, and have believed.' For [it is] not [possible] that those who have not seen and have believed are more blessed than those who have seen and believed. According to their interpretation at least then, those who come after the apostles are more blessed than the apostles, which is the most ridiculous of all things.[6]

In these and other places it is clear that the *ApocJas* is well aware of John's Gospel, but just as clear that it opposes some of John's central claims. But John is not the only Gospel it knows. The opening scene of the book's narrative relates an incident said to have occurred 550 days after the resurrection, when the disciples were gathered and Jesus appeared to them: '... the twelve disciples [were] all sitting together and recalling what the Saviour had said to each one of them, whether secretly or openly, and [putting it] in books. [But I] was writing that which was in [my book] ... ' (*ApocJas* 2.7–16). This is most interesting for its tacit admission that Jesus' disciples wrote books which contained his teaching. And the mention of the disciples 'recalling what the Saviour had said' and putting these recollections or remembrances in books reflects the same understanding which lies behind Justin's favourite characterization of the Gospels as 'apostolic memoirs'. It parallels how Papias of Hierapolis had earlier spoken of the Gospel of Mark as the apostle Peter's recollections of Jesus. The author of *ApocJas*, of course, is not so interested in those existing Gospels[7] but in the new revelations which James is about to receive from the risen Jesus. The passage is nonetheless important for showing how commonplace was the notion that there were Gospels which went back to Jesus' own disciples.

Further indication of this author's awareness of the previously existing Gospels comes when Jesus mentions by title certain parables which the author presumes the reader already knows from the canonical Gospels: 'it was enough for some <to listen> to the teaching and understand "The Shepherds" and "The Seed" and "The Building" and "The Lamps of the Virgins" and "The Wage of the Workmen" and "the Didrachmae" and "The Woman"' (*ApocJas.* 8.5–10). Koester identifies these known parables as those contained in Matthew, Mark, and Luke:[8]

The Shepherds	Luke 15.4–6
The Seed	Mark 4.3–9 or 4.26–9 or 4.30–2
The Building	Matthew 7.24–7; Luke 6.47–9
The Lamps of the Virgins	Matthew 25.1–12
The Wage of the Workmen	Matthew 20.1–15
The Didrachmae	Luke 15.8–9
The Woman	Luke 18.2–8

The author's intent is clear: it was enough for *some* people to understand these well-known parables from the well-known Gospels, but not for others. For these others there is now the *Apocryphon of James*. The hope of the author is to persuade the reader that the new revelations in this book offer something spiritually superior to what is contained in the apostolic Gospels already available. Still, in so doing, the authority of the well-known Gospels had to be invoked.[9] It was no use denying that Jesus' disciples had heard him, seen him, touched him, or that some of them had handed down their records of Jesus' words and ministry to the church. These things were not in dispute. The approach taken by this author, and by other gnostics and

Valentinians as well, was to try to go the church one better with contrary revelations that surpassed the apostolic testimony.[10]

It is thus not without reason that Perkins sees the *Apocryphon of James* as an example 'of the growing influence of the canonical Gospels'.[11] It assumes the previous acceptance of probably all four of these Gospels and does not contest the tradition that they go ultimately back to Jesus' original disciples. It simply treats those Gospels as inadequate.

A fictional work like this seems bound to have provoked a reaction from Christians in the 'apostolic' church. Some think that a reaction came in the form of another fictional work written to counteract it, a book known as the *Epistula Apostolorum*.

The Epistle of the Apostles

As we noted in an earlier chapter, pseudepigraphal works may have been written for widely different purposes. Often, as in the *Apocryphon of James*, the aim was to present a point of view the author believed was under-appreciated or maligned, and to gain sanction for that point of view by placing it under the name of some respected authority. At other times the device was apparently used in a half-serious or entirely facetious way, for what was regarded as harmless or edifying enjoyment. The *Epistula Apostolorum*, or *Epistle of the Apostles* (existing in Coptic and Ethiopic versions), is one of a number of second-century pseudepigraphal works which uses a false authorship for another purpose: to defend the orthodox faith from attacks. Some readers might recoil from the idea that right-thinking, professedly honest believers might ever have resorted to such tactics. Other readers might assume that it was their everyday *modus operandi*. In this instance, anyway, it appears that the author assumed a false name (in fact, several names) in order to respond to an opponent who had assumed a false name. Fighting fire with fire, so to speak, or, 'hoisting him with his own petard'.[12]

Like the *Apocryphon of James*, this pseudepigraphon borrows the form of the 'post-resurrection dialogue' between Jesus and his disciples. This form was popular with gnostics, who needed an occasion on which Jesus could give his advanced teaching not recorded in the acknowledged Gospels, which mostly deliver Jesus' pre-resurrection teaching. While the *ApocJas* is presented as Jesus' secret revelation to two disciples, Peter and James, who only partly understood what Jesus had to reveal to them, the *EpApost* purports to be a letter written by *all* the apostles to the entire church after a revelatory session with Jesus. Whereas *Apoc-Jas* presents itself as gnostic teaching that is superior to that represented in the commonly known sources of Christianity, the *EpApost* reaffirms orthodox teaching and in so doing affirms the traditional sources like the Gospels, and specifically endorses the role to be played by the apostle Paul. The *ApocJas* is fictively addressed to someone whose name ends in '-thus'. We don't know the full name because the manuscript is damaged and the first part of the name is lost. There were not that many Greek names that did end in '-thus'. Interestingly enough, the *EpApost* is addressed 'to the Catholics' in opposition to 'the false apostles Simon and *Cerinthus*'.

John and the Synoptic Gospels

One sign of the author's knowledge of John's Gospel, and of his opposition to *ApocJas*, is his treatment of Jesus' apostles and their eyewitness knowledge of Jesus. We have seen how the *ApocJas* tried to turn Jesus' words to 'believing Thomas' in John 20.29 against the apostolic Christians by saying that those who saw and heard and touched the mere physical body of the risen Jesus were not blessed, but set for woe. The author of *EpApost* reacts to such a teaching much like Origen later would. In chapter 2 the apostles unashamedly confess, 'we have heard and felt him after he had risen from the dead'. In chapter 29 they say to the risen Jesus: ' "Blessed are we, for we see and hear you as you speak to us, and our eyes have seen such mighty deeds that you have done." And he answered and said to us, "But much more blessed will they be who do not see me and (yet) believe in me ... " ' (Ethiopic). Here is a return to the emphasis of the Gospel of John and 1 John. The eyewitness apostles are blessed, though more blessed are those who will believe their testimony in the absence of sight. The testimony of these eyewitnesses, rejected in *ApocJas*, is reaffirmed in *EpApost*.

It is admitted on all sides that the *EpApost* makes heavy use of the Gospel according to John. For example, it mentions Jesus' presence at the wedding feast at Cana of Galilee (5.1–3) a story recorded only in John (John 2.1–12); it mentions the disciple Nathanael (2.1), who is mentioned only in John (John 1.45–51; 21.2); it repeats Jesus' 'new commandment ... that you love one another' (18.5), which is recorded only in John (John 13.34). Many other instances could be cited, but they are unnecessary. Besides the abundant evidence of high respect for John, one can see in this book allusions to each of the Synoptic Gospels as well, Matthew and Luke quite heavily, Mark more sparingly.[13]

And despite their diametrically opposed approaches, *EpApost* shares with *ApocJas* a common assumption of the existence of well-known Gospels believed to go back to the apostles. In the very first chapter 'the apostles' remind the readers that they had heard 'the word of the Gospel', and then continue: 'As we have heard (it), kept (it), and have written (it) for the whole world, so we entrust (it) to you, our sons and daughters' (1.3). Many have simply assumed that the writing mentioned here is the *Epistle of the Apostles* itself. But it seems instead that this refers to apostolic responsibility for the writing of the Gospels. The idea is repeated in chapter 31, where the *EpApost* has Jesus referring to 'every word which I have spoken to you and which you [the apostles] have written concerning me, that I am the word of the Father and the Father is in me . . . '. What he says that they have written concerning him, 'that I am the word of the Father' and that 'the Father is in me', are straight from the Gospel according to John: 'And the Word became flesh and dwelt among us, full of grace and truth; we have beheld his glory, glory as of the only Son from the Father' (John 1.14); 'that you may know and understand that the Father is in me and I am in the Father' (John 10.38); 'In that day you will know that I am in my Father, and you in me, and I in you' (John 14.20). The author cannot be referring here to the *EpApost* itself, for, as Jesus is at that moment in the narrative still speaking, the *EpApost* has not yet been written!

Other Apostolic Sources? Jesus Incognito and Jesus the Child Prodigy

The upshot of this is that for the author there already existed some recognized, standard Gospels believed to have originated with Jesus' apostles. They certainly included John, Matthew, and Luke, and apparently Mark as well. But did they also include others? This is at least possible, on the surface, since the *EpApost* repeats two stories about Jesus before his resurrection which are not contained in any of the canonical Gospels. Yet it cannot simply be assumed that these came from written 'apostolic' Gospels, for it is possible (in fact, overwhelmingly probable) that they are unwritten, extra-canonical traditions that the author felt were useful to his or her cause.

The first of these is the story of how Jesus, before his birth to Mary, descended to her from the seventh heaven. As he descended he took on the likeness of the angelic beings in each of the seven heavens so that they would not recognize him (*EpApost* 13). As odd and 'unorthodox' as this might sound, someone as orthodox as Irenaeus also knew this story and even accepted it as true (*Proof* 9, 84). However, neither he nor the *EpApost* attributes it to, or associates it with, a written source. Instead it seems to be related to exegetical traditions that were intended to illuminate two activities that are recorded in the Gospels: Jesus' descent from heaven to be incarnated and his subsequent return to heaven after his resurrection.[14]

The second of these 'non-canonical' stories is a cryptic one about the boy Jesus, 'who was delivered by Joseph and Mary his mother to where he might learn letters. And he who taught him said to him as he taught him, "Say Alpha." He answered and said to him, "First you tell me what Beta is." And truly (it was) a real thing which was done' (*EpApost* 4.1–3). Where did the author come up with such a tale?

A version of it was at some time incorporated into what is now called the *Infancy Gospel of Thomas*, a work which apparently was originally anonymous.[15] Despite its modern title, the *IGT* is not a Gospel but a series of peculiar stories about Jesus from age 5 to 12, designed to 'fill in the blank' of Jesus' childhood, leading up to his appearance in the Temple at the age of 12, as recorded in Luke 2. It follows a popular genre of fictional biographies about the prodigious childhoods of famous men. In the *IGT* a mischievous and somewhat bad-tempered boy Jesus brings clay pigeons to life, corrects and teaches his elders, and curses people who bother him. In the most thorough analysis of the work to date, Reidar Aasgaard argues that it originates from a rural Christian setting and that its 'purpose was to serve as both entertainment and edification for early Christians'.[16] He argues that it is perhaps the earliest piece of Christian 'children's literature' ever written, penned to teach faith and values to children through fictitious stories from the childhood of Jesus. 'IGT, then, can be regarded as comparable to other ancient children's stories, and as a supplement or an alternative to the contemporary pagan canon.'[17]

Irenaeus was familiar with a slightly different version of the same story. He called it 'false and wicked' and said it was contained in an unnamed writing forged by the followers of Marcus the Valentinian (*AH* 1.21.1). The writing known to Irenaeus may or may not have been an early version of the *Infancy Gospel of Thomas* (there is no good evidence of Valentinianism in the *IGT*), but it is most likely that the author of the *EpApost* simply knew an isolated story about Jesus teaching his teachers. The story as told in the *IGT* is much elaborated and spread out into three different narrative episodes. Noting the fluctuations in the accounts of second-century writers who share something in common with the *IGT*, Aasgaard says: 'The fluidity and variation can imply that *Ep. Apost.* and Justin, and probably also *Gos. Truth*, can be dependent on oral rather than written tradition.'[18] In any case, given the contents of the *IGT* and its original anonymity, it is highly unlikely that the author of the *EpApost*, if he knew the *IGT*, would have conceived of this example of popular 'children's literature' as an apostolic source of 'the word of the Gospel'! So what could have induced this author, so concerned to affirm and establish the true humanity and bodily resurrection of Jesus, to include a story such as this with no backing in a known, apostolic writing at this time?

Writing in the late fourth century, Epiphanius gives us a reason. Epiphanius, with a version of the same story in mind, says that Jesus 'ought to have childhood miracles too, to deprive the other sects of an excuse for saying that "[the] Christ," meaning the dove, "came to him after [his baptism in] the Jordan" . . . ' (*Panar.* 51.20.3). That is, these 'sects' taught a docetic view of the man Jesus being temporarily adopted or possessed by a heavenly Christ only from the time of his baptism until the cross. Stories of Jesus' childhood miracles or supernatural wisdom, therefore, would help confirm the orthodox view of him as fully human and fully divine from the time of his conception. As with the story of Jesus' incognito descent through the seven heavens, this story too supports the unity of the divine and human in Jesus from the time of his conception in the womb of Mary.

Like the *ApocJas*, which opens with a notice of the disciples of Jesus 'remembering' what he had taught them and writing those things in books, this pseudepigraphon too opens with the apostles referring to their writing of the word of the Gospel for the whole world and entrusting it to the church. Very much like Irenaeus, it knows the four Gospels, Acts, a corpus of Paul's letters, 1 Peter, 1 John, and Revelation. When Jesus tells the disciples that a man named Paul will come one day, he says that upon Paul 'will come the completion of the testimony to me' (*EpApost* 31 Eth.). Paul is also called 'the last of the last'. This seems to indicate the author's belief that approved apostolic testimony to Jesus had reached a state of closure by the time he wrote.

And just when was that? The *EpApost* helps us somewhat in answering this question because of its daring to set a date for the return of Jesus. The Coptic version says the blessed event will happen in 120 years, 'when the hundredth part and the twentieth part is completed'. Most scholars agree that the figure of 150 years used by the Ethiopic version reflects a modification. What they are not so sure about is whether the author meant the count to start at the birth of Jesus or with his resurrection some thirty-three years later. In either case, this would mean that the book must have been authored sometime before about 120 CE or, at the latest, sometime before about 150. As it happens, dates either in the 110s or the 140s would work well with the historical record of earthquakes, plagues, and famines which are mentioned in the book.[19] Many students of the work have in fact argued for a date before 120, though the trend more recently is towards accepting a somewhat later origin. But even if we accept the most probable later date, sometime in the 140s,[20] this is still well before Justin wrote. And if the *EpApost* was written partially in response to the *Apocalypse of James*, the latter, with its presupposition of the canonical Gospels, is earlier still.

Marcion the Inventor of the Canon?

Both of these forgeries, then, were written well before Justin published his *First Apology*. A very important consequence of this has to do with Marcion, probably the most famous Christian teacher of the second century outside the mainstream or apostolic church. Marcion was expelled from the church in Rome in about 144 CE and then founded a movement which apparently caught on quickly in several regions. The church had two basic problems with Marcion's teaching. First, he taught that the God of the Old Testament was a lower deity and that his Scriptures, with their laws and their promises of a Messiah, were strictly for the Jews and not for Christians. Jesus, on the other hand, had come to preach a higher, supreme, but previously unknown God. This God had no laws and threatened no punishments. Salvation was for the soul only and not the body. Marcion's book *Antitheses* laid out what he considered to be the irreconcilable contradictions between the god of the Jews (and of ordinary Christians) and the God introduced to the world by Jesus. To the theologians of the Great Church this meant not only a blasphemy of the Creator, as Justin would say, but a salvation that pertained to only half the human being.

The second complaint against Marcion levelled by later writers such as Irenaeus, and in great detail by Tertullian, was that in order to support his novel doctrines the heretic had to reject a number of the church's holy books in favour of his own shortlist. That list consisted of a modified version of Luke and a curtailed corpus of Paul's letters. As Irenaeus put it: 'Wherefore also Marcion and his followers have betaken themselves to mutilating the Scriptures, not acknowledging some books at all; and curtailing the Gospel according to Luke and the Epistles of Paul, they assert that these are alone authentic, which they have themselves thus shortened' (*AH* 3.12.12). Tertullian accused Marcion of taking a knife to the Scriptures. Since the very earliest reports (Justin and Polycarp in the 150s) do not seem to know about Marcion's 'editorial' work, it would appear that it may not have been one of his earlier achievements.

Because nothing of Marcion's own writings survives and we cannot hear his side of the story, many scholars have approached the charges of his opponents with grave suspicion. Some suppose that Marcion, instead of selecting from a pre-existing corpus of sacred writings, as Irenaeus and Tertullian charge, was in fact the first to assemble any Christian writings together and treat them as Scripture. Thus they would credit Marcion, even before Irenaeus, with being the first to hatch the idea of a closed 'canon' of Christian books.

Though always debated, this portrait of Marcion as in some sense the father of the New Testament canon has remained a staple of scholarship for many decades. In his recent investigation of the issues surrounding Marcion, however, John Barton concludes, on the contrary, that Marcion 'was not assembling a collection of Christian books, but making a (very restricted) selection from the corpus of texts which already existed and which must already have been recognized as sacred by many in the church—otherwise he would not have needed to insist on abolishing them'.[21] We may now observe that our look at the *Apocryphon of James* and the *Epistle of the Apostles* substantiates Barton's conclusion. Both pseudepigraphons pre-date Marcion's canonical activities. One of them endorses, the other seeks to supersede, a set of writings already acknowledged as apostolic and authoritative in the larger church. Justin, Marcion's contemporary in Rome, reports that the Gospels, the 'Memoirs of the Apostles', were read and preached on in Roman Christian services of worship. The earlier fictional works, the *Apocryphon of James* and the *Epistle of the Apostles*, strongly support our earlier impression that the liturgical practice reported by Justin was not new.

The Apologist Aristides of Athens[22]

According to the historian Eusebius, the emperor Hadrian was presented with two petitions in the form of Apologies on behalf of the Christians, one by a man named Quadratus, one by Aristides (*EH* 4.3.3). The *Apology* of Quadratus, all but a few lines preserved by Eusebius, is lost. But the *Apology* of Aristides has been recovered. While Aristides might have written at any time during Hadrian's reign (117–38 CE),[23] Robert Grant thinks it most likely that he wrote it before 132, and some have suggested that the work was presented to Hadrian on the occasion of his visit to Athens in 124–5. The original text can only be pieced together by a meticulous comparison of fragments of the original Greek discovered at Oxyrhynchus, a later Greek 'metaphrase' which was incorporated into a longer medieval romance called the *Life of Barlaam and Joasaph* (26–7), and translations made in Syriac and Armenian.

What is germane to our discussion is that in his *Apology* Aristides entreats the emperor to read 'the Gospel'. Below is the passage as translated from both the Greek and the Syriac versions:

Greek of *Barlaam*[24]

15.1. And if you would read, O King, you may judge the glory of his presence from the holy gospel writing, as it is called among themselves.

Syriac

2.4. This is taught in the gospel, as it is called, which a short time ago was preached among them; and you also if you will read therein, may perceive the power which belongs to it.

Aristides' use of the singular, 'Gospel', could mean that he had just one Gospel book in mind, but this is not likely. We know that often in the second century, even with Justin and Irenaeus, a reference to 'the Gospel' can be a reference to a plurality of individual written expressions of the gospel, or to any of the Gospels in such a collection.[25] This usage probably reflects the idea that there is in reality but one true Christian Gospel, 'according to' a plurality of authoritative sources. When we look at what Aristides implies can be read in 'the Gospel' we see, in fact, that this must have been the case with him as well. For what he seems to have derived from 'the Gospel' cannot be derived from any one Gospel alone. Rather, there are indications of his knowledge of Luke, John, and perhaps Matthew and Mark.

He mentions that Jesus was confessed as 'Son of God Most High'. This is a title for Jesus found only in Mark 5.7 and Luke 1.32, 8.28, and not in Matthew or John. He then mentions Jesus' descent from heaven and his incarnation through a Hebrew virgin. The descent from heaven is explicit only in John (3.13, 6.38), as is the statement about his incarnation or taking on flesh (John 1.14). His birth from a Hebrew virgin is recounted only by Matthew and Luke. Then come references to the piercing of Jesus' body on the cross, the burial, the resurrection after three days, and the ascension to heaven. The 'piercing' could only have come from John and the burial, resurrection, and ascension could have come from any of the four. At minimum this seems to require Luke and John, but it is hard to exclude Matthew, and even Mark cannot be ruled out.

Some scholars, aware of the early date of Aristides' *Apology*, would like to attribute and restrict Aristides' information about Jesus to an oral transmission which would require no knowledge of a written source of any kind. But while it is true that much or all of it could have been part of the common story about Jesus known from oral preaching and teaching, such an explanation will not do here. This is because Aristides explicitly says that this information about Jesus is contained in 'the Gospel, as it is called', which he invites Hadrian to *read*.

Once more, in chapter 16, Aristides repeats his bold challenge to the emperor.

Greek of *Barlaam*	Syriac
And that you may know, O King, that in saying these things I do not speak at my own instance, if you deign to look into the writings of the Christians, you will find that I state nothing beyond the truth.	Take, then, their writings, and read therein, and lo! you will find that I have not put forth these things on my own authority, nor spoken thus as their advocate; but since I read in their writings I was fully assured of these things as also of things which are to come.

Chapters 15–17 in the Syriac version (which are absent from the Greek of *Barlaam*) preserve three more references to the Christians' writings, including one reference to their 'other writings', probably a reference to apostolic letters, in which are 'things which are hard to utter and difficult for one to narrate' (cf. 2 Peter 3.15–16). This is corroborated by the several times he borrows phrases from Paul's letters.

Whether Aristides wrote in 125 CE or at another point in Hadrian's reign, his early statements about Christian writings, though often ignored, are very worthy of note. Even if written at the end of Hadrian's reign (138), his testimony, like those of the *ApocJas* and the *EpApost*, pre-dates the 'canonizing' work of Marcion. Since Aristides' reference to 'the Gospel' apparently signals the existence of a collection of individual written expressions of the gospel, it is perhaps less likely that this collection contained only Luke and John than that it included all four. The main point here is that he is not simply referring to loose, free-floating, 'oral tradition' about Jesus. Nor is he getting his information from written 'sayings collections', which have sometimes been postulated as being still in circulation at this time. For the 'Gospel' to which he refers contains narrative material as well. What is more, his recommendation that the emperor read the written Gospel—anticipating and perhaps motivating Justin's later attempt to do the same—carries at least the rhetorical implication that the Christian Gospel in some standard, recognizable form was readily accessible, enough so that the emperor might be expected to be able to obtain a copy for himself.

As surprisingly early 'proto-conspirators' who reflect in the first half of the second century something of the normative influence already being exercised by the four canonical Gospels both inside and outside the mainstream church, the two forgers and one apologist treated in this chapter surely stand out. But as I hope now to show, they do not quite stand alone.

9

SOME 'CO-PROTO-CONSPIRATORS': THE APOSTOLIC FATHERS

Present Even While Absent

As most readers will know, the state of Florida, where I now live, regularly receives more than its share of high and destructive winds. Floridians do not look back with 'undiluted pleasure' (to borrow a phrase) on the year 2004, our own, local *annus horribilis*, in which five named storms, four of them bona fide hurricanes, made landfall in the state. Let me paint an imaginary Florida scenario which I hope might illustrate a main point of the present chapter.

Suppose a tropical-force wind has blown through the vicinity, scattering small tree branches and the contents of unsecured rubbish bins throughout the neighbourhood. While pondering the debris in my lawn my eyes light upon a smattering of papers, among which are some recent receipts of a young couple who live a few houses down. I see that these include records of the purchase of an expensive crib, loads of disposable nappies (diapers, as we call them in this country), and other assorted baby items. Now I think I know something about the couple I didn't know before.

As I make my way to their house I see that out of their bin has also tumbled an empty can which, I cannot help but observe, once contained light pink paint. Now I think I can even deduce the baby's sex. Mind you, I have not actually seen the newborn yet. Perhaps the baby has already been born and brought home without any neighbourhood fanfare. But perhaps not. The blessed event may still be weeks or months away. And perhaps the partial records I hold in my hands (for I surely don't have them all) are the expenses for not just one baby but triplets or quadruplets! But if the occupants of the house in question have not already increased, it seems clear that they will relatively soon. In a sense, even if she or they have not yet been born, the new baby or babies have already had many effects on the couple and their home.

It is something akin to this which we see with regard to many of the group of writers known as the 'Apostolic Fathers'. And in this sense, these writers might be called 'co-proto-conspirators' with the authors mentioned in Chapter 8, for many of the Apostolic Fathers too played a foundational role in bequeathing to the church the four canonical Gospels.

Mining for Gospel Nuggets: Some of What Glitters May Be Gold

'The Apostolic Fathers' is a name given to a set of early Christian authors who are traditionally thought to have succeeded the apostles of Jesus and, conceivably at least, might have known those apostles. The boundaries of the traditional collection of Apostolic Fathers have shifted somewhat over the years. The two most recent and most authoritative collections in English each include the same eleven authors.[1]

The writings of the Apostolic Fathers have been mined closely over the years in a search for what sources they might have used. Did they use any of the New Testament writings? Did they use other books? Did they only know oral traditions? In 1905 a landmark study of these questions was published by a committee of scholars at Oxford University.[2] For a full century, *The New Testament in the Apostolic Fathers* was a mainstay for scholars interested in the subject of the rise of the New Testament canon. To commemorate the centenary of that famous volume and to test and update its work, a new, two-volume set was published in 2005 under the editorship of Andrew Gregory and Christopher Tuckett.[3] Repeating the aims of the older Oxford tome, Volume 1 restricts itself for the most part to the question of the possible use of 'writings that later formed the New Testament' in seven of the Apostolic Fathers. Volume 2 contains related studies of a somewhat wider focus. To relieve the reader's curiosity (though not by any means intending to depress sales!), I'll reveal that the findings of 2005 do not differ substantially from those of 1905. One thing, however, which does distinguish the later study is its greater attention to the investigative methods and standards employed by its contributors. The writers consistently aim at 'minimal but assured results that can be achieved on the basis of methodologically rigorous close readings of particular texts'.[4] Because the issue has been a sticking-point in recent decades, and does have important implications, I have chosen to give the reader some background on it.

Perhaps the single most significant cause for the 2005 emphasis on methodological rigorism was the publication in 1957 of a book by Helmut Koester.[5] Koester's book itself has been seen as a landmark. Influenced by Walter Bauer's approach to the history of early Christianity, which repudiated the idea that 'orthodox'

Christianity and its texts predominated in the early period, Koester proposed a new standard for determining whether an Apostolic Father actually knew or used one of the Synoptic Gospels. (He and his students would later develop similar standards for John's Gospel and the rest of the New Testament writings.) In effect, Koester argued that one could not claim knowledge of one of the Gospels by an Apostolic Father unless one could show that the parallels in question could not be attributed to any other source—even if that source no longer exists (and even if we have no proof that it ever existed). Such would include any source theoretically used by one of the Gospels,[6] even a hypothetical earlier form of one of the same Gospels. In other words, one had to demonstrate the use of what is called 'redactional' material, that is, words peculiar to (what Koester or some other 'redaction critic' determined was) the 'final stage' of the particular Gospel, after it left the hands of the presumed last 'editor'. Otherwise, the possibility exists that the Apostolic Father did not actually get the words from one of the Synoptic Gospels.

In addition, Koester, like many both before and after him, requires a rather high standard of verbal precision before anything can be claimed as a quotation of or allusion to one of the canonical Gospels. For some scholars, any but the most minor deviation from the text of one of the Gospels can be grounds for denying that the writer knew that Gospel. We saw in Chapter 6 an example of the complex and improbable results this approach can sometimes produce. One has to posit that Justin used at least three or four independent, hypothetical sources allegedly used by the writer(s) of John in order to maintain the evidently much-cherished position that Justin did not know the Gospel of John. Koester's approach has been a useful corrective to others which seemed to assume too quickly the presence of one of the known Gospels without testing other alternatives first. Yet the list of alternatives it sometimes requires us to manufacture can stretch credulity as well.

The presence of 'Synoptic-sounding materials' or 'Johannine-sounding materials' in an ancient writer does not necessarily denote that writer's knowledge of the Synoptic or Johannine Gospels. Ancient Mediterranean culture was an oral culture, very much given to storytelling, memorization, and oral performances of every kind. People were more apt to reproduce words, sayings, and narratives from memory (accurately or not) than we are today, who are trained not to trust to our memories but to go to our books to check for accurate and contextual use. But recognizing ancient culture as an 'oral culture' cuts both ways. On the one hand, people might be more prone to reproduce from memory what they had *heard* and not *read* in a book. On the other hand, people used to the oral retelling of stories, each time with certain nuances of change, would feel less inhibited about 'retelling' or 'rewriting' with minor modifications even what they had *read*, or heard someone else read, in a book. This is well noted by John Barton:

The often inaccurate quotations in the Fathers, it is argued, show that they were drawing on 'synoptic tradition' but not actually on the Synoptic Gospels. Such a theory cannot be ruled out absolutely, but it is not the only or, probably, the best explanation for loose quotation. We should remember instead how loose are quotations from the *Old* Testament in many patristic texts, even though the Old Testament was unquestionably already fixed in writing. The explanation is to be found not in oral transmission in the strict sense, but in the oral *use* of texts which were already available in written form.[7]

Even quite literate and literary persons might readily reproduce from memory rather than look something up. Not only this, but recent studies have shown that ancient authors, when quoting or alluding, were also more likely to change intentionally the wording of a source than we are, who fear being caught misquoting.[8] Quotation standards, or better, methods of borrowing pre-existing material, in the early second century were not so strict as they are today, even when borrowing sacred materials (as Barton noted above). Unless there was a particular reason for quoting verbatim, as when you expected an opponent to check your citation, or when you were expounding particular words in a sermon or commentary, the rather more cumbersome practice of quoting precisely from open books was often deemed unnecessary. It was sometimes even seen as more sophisticated and less boorish to one's informed reader to adapt the words of one's source rather than repeat them verbatim. The typical style of Clement of Rome, Polycarp, Ignatius, and others mentioned in this chapter, for instance, very often was not to quote, in our sense of the word, but to work the words or phrases of their sources (which their readers were assumed to know) into their own statements, or to mix sources together.

The 2005 Oxford volume mentioned above tries to steer a judicious course between the exacting but not well-defined standards of 1905 and the more self-conscious but sometimes nearly unworkable ones of Koester, while definitely still working in the latter's shadow. Its aim at 'minimal but assured results that can be achieved on the basis of methodologically rigorous close readings of particular texts' means its authors intentionally set out to err on the 'safe' side. That is, to err on the side of *not* claiming a knowledge of a New Testament book unless it can be demonstrated beyond reasonable doubt. This method assuredly has its place in scholarship, and it is always helpful to have a collection of 'minimal but assured results'. These should simply not be confused with final, concrete, or definitive results, lest a *lack of certainty* about what an Apostolic Father *did* know slide imperceptibly into a *certainty* about what he *didn't* know.

Greeting the New Arrivals

We cannot treat all eleven of the Apostolic Fathers in this chapter. And it is not easy to draw generalized conclusions about all of them. A few of them show awareness of oral or written sources other than our four Gospels. Nearly all seem to show knowledge of one, and sometimes more than one, of the four Gospels—or at least of something that looks like one of these Gospels. Some of this evidence will be briefly touched on in this section. But what I also hope to show in the selection of authors below is that even in cases where we cannot be sure of a particular author's familiarity with one of the four Gospels, sometimes the 'trappings' of their imminent reception, so to speak, are already present. Like the accommodations already made by the expectant couple in our opening illustration, there may be signs which would tempt us to consider the authors mentioned below 'co-proto-conspirators' of the four-Gospel canon.

The Epistle to Diognetus

Though given the title of 'epistle' by modern editors, this interesting work reads more like the transcript of a speech given by a Christian apologist before an upper-class individual, a 'most excellent' hearer named Diognetus, and possibly some of his entourage.[9] It is anonymous, and while no suggested author has yet gained wide recognition, it is quite possible that it is the work of the celebrated bishop Polycarp of Smyrna,[10] probably from sometime between about 140 and 150 CE. There is some disagreement about the last two chapters (11 and 12), which have been claimed as part of an unrelated and perhaps slightly later work. It appears that somewhere along the line some pages were lost at the end of chapter 10, accounting for the rough transition to chapters 11 and 12, which, in my opinion, do constitute the true ending of the original speech.[11]

Addressing a non-Christian audience, the speaker tends to refrain from mentioning his textual authorities, until the final chapter, when he begins to contemplate Diognetus' conversion to Christianity. Still, his familiarity with at least the Gospel of John[12] and probably Matthew[13] has been widely noted. In chapter 11 he tells Diognetus: 'I am not talking about strange things, nor am I engaged in irrational speculation, but having been a disciple of apostles, I am now becoming a teacher of the Gentiles. To those who are becoming disciples of the truth I try to minister in a worthy manner the teachings that have been handed down' (11.1).

The word 'teachings' in the last sentence is actually not in the text. 'The things handed down' is literally what the author is claiming to minister in a worthy manner, and, having been a disciple of apostles, it is surely their handed-down things that he is ministering. This is familiar language. We have seen it applied by Irenaeus and Clement of Alexandria to the four Gospels and by Serapion to apostolic writings perhaps more generally. It is not unreasonable to suppose, then, that what the speaker was so concerned to hand down worthily included the church's authoritative, written accounts of the life of Jesus, and other apostolic materials. The author goes on to speak of the public teaching which 'the Word' (the distinctive title used in the Gospel of John for Jesus) delivered to his disciples (11.2). Likely he is contrasting this public teaching to the alleged secret teaching of works like the *Gospel of Thomas*. When the grace given through Jesus, the Son of God, flourishes, he says: 'Then the reverence of the law is praised in song, and the grace of the prophets is recognized, and the faith of the gospels is established, and the tradition of the apostles is preserved, and the joy of the church exults' (11.6).

This author, whether Polycarp or not, places the Law, the Prophets, the Gospels, and the 'things handed down' of the apostles together, and thus seems to have a complete corpus of Scriptures. Though he does not use the terminology, he has an Old and a New Testament. He sees it as his calling to pass down faithfully what was delivered by the apostles.

The Letter of (Pseudo) Barnabas

The so-called *Letter of Barnabas* was probably written between the mid-90s and the 130s.[14] There are a few possible indications of the author's knowledge of Matthew and perhaps Luke, but one might see these instead as 'what one might loosely call synoptic passion traditions'.[15] Yet there is one reference in particular which stands out: '. . . let us be on our guard lest we should be found to be, as it is written, "many called, but few chosen"' (4.14). It is a very short citation, but the author here explicitly cites from a written source and does so in just the same way one would cite from the Old Testament ('as it is written'). Despite attempts by some to find a better alternative, James Carleton-Paget shrewdly observes, 'it still remains the case that the closest existing text to *Barn.* 4. 14 in all known literature is Matt. 22.14 ['For many are called, but few are chosen'], and one senses that attempts to argue for independence from Matthew are partly motivated by a desire to avoid the implication . . . that the author of *Barnabas* regarded Matthew as scriptural'.[16]

Was the apparently Scriptural quotation from Matthew? Practically all scholars would say that Matthew's finished Gospel existed by the time this author wrote. Or shall we conjecture the existence of a written, Matthew-like source which this author treated as Scripture but which has not survived? Whatever the answer, the existence of some Matthew-like book functioning as Scripture may throw further light on the ultimate source of 'what one might loosely call synoptic passion traditions' which appear elsewhere in the book.

But even on the most cautious and 'minimalist' reading of the evidence for Gospel knowledge, *Barnabas* offers us something more that may put him in the camp of the 'proto-conspirators'. He shows an unambiguous understanding of the source of the Christian faith.

And when he chose his own apostles who were destined to preach his gospel . . . (5.9)

. . . those who preached to us the good news about the forgiveness of sins and the purification of the heart, those to whom he gave the authority to proclaim the gospel (there were twelve of them as a witness to the tribes, because there are twelve tribes of Israel). (8.3)

Along with at least one reference to something which is written in Matthew, a Gospel attributed by Papias of Hierapolis to an apostle of Jesus,[17] as Scripture, the author believes the authority to proclaim the gospel (literally, 'the authority of the gospel') was delivered first of all not to all Christians in common, but to the twelve apostles of Jesus. He holds an idea of the apostles as the authoritative transmitters of the message about Jesus. This is the same idea held by Irenaeus several decades later, an idea which Irenaeus regarded as the foundation for the reception of the Gospels and other books as Christian Scripture.

Polycarp of Smyrna

I mentioned above the possibility that Polycarp was the original orator behind the anonymous *Epistle to Diognetus*. But the only writing we have which has survived under his name is his early letter to the Philippian church. Polycarp was the teacher of Irenaeus, and Irenaeus claims that his teacher as a younger man had known some of the apostles of Jesus, John in particular.[18]

From the concepts and phrases that he employs in this single letter to the Philippians, written probably around 110 or slightly later, many scholars, including Koester, think it probable that Polycarp reflects knowledge of the Gospels of Matthew and Luke (see 2.3; 7.2, etc.).[19] Michael Holmes, maintaining an even more resolute neutrality than Koester at this point, prefers to say: 'It is possible that Polycarp made use of one or more of the gospels of Matthew, Mark, and/or Luke; but there is no evidence to demonstrate that he did, nor is it possible to demonstrate that he did not know or use any of these three writings.'[20] Nonetheless, Holmes cannot avoid speaking several times of the presence of 'parallel(s) to synoptic tradition'.[21] In the opinion of some (not Koester or Holmes), it is likely that Polycarp knew the Gospel of John too,[22] making it at least possible, though far from proven, that he had all four Gospels. Though he never mentions any Gospel by name, he knows many of Jesus' sayings, for besides 'parallels to synoptic tradition', he also has dire words of warning for anyone who 'twists the sayings of the Lord to suit his own sinful desires' (7.1). While he makes fairly heavy use of I Peter, which claims to be written by an apostle, and he almost certainly knows I or 2 John (7.1), the only apostle Polycarp mentions by name is Paul. He also refers to something Paul wrote in Ephesians as Scripture (12.1).

But it is another statement Polycarp makes which now draws our attention. Very much like the author of *Barnabas*, he refers to 'the apostles who preached the gospel to us, and the prophets who announced in advance the coming of our Lord' (*Philippians* 6.3).

Polycarp views the apostles as the ones who delivered the gospel to his generation. By 'preached the gospel' Polycarp must have primarily in mind the oral preaching of the good news. If we may believe Irenaeus, Polycarp would have heard this oral preaching personally; perhaps the 'us' in 'preached the gospel to us' is meant not only collectively of all Christians, but personally, to him as well.[23] But it certainly cannot be ruled out that Polycarp also knew writings containing the 'sayings of Jesus' which he held to be part of that apostolic gospel deposit. This is particularly the case since he here in 6.3 places the apostles in a position next to the prophets, whose *writings* were accepted Scripture. As we'll see in the next chapter, some of Polycarp's contemporaries in Asia Minor knew at least Matthew as the work of that apostle, and Mark as the record of Peter's preaching.

But even if we should take a stand for strict neutrality about Polycarp's possible knowledge of written Gospels, or even contend that he knew only a *preached* gospel, he still shows us something critically important. Polycarp regards the delivery of that gospel message as the special work of Jesus' apostles and places that authoritative, apostolic gospel message alongside the prophets who announced it beforehand. It is but a small and instinctive step to apply the apostolic preached gospel to apostolic written Gospels. Whether Polycarp has left enough evidence in his single epistle for us to conclude that he had already taken that step is a question upon which competent scholars may disagree. In any case he shows that the step, which others around him took and which his disciple Irenaeus took, is quite prepared for.

Ignatius of Antioch

The theological apparatus for receiving the Gospels as Scripture is even more abundantly visible in the seven letters of Ignatius, an early bishop of Antioch in Syria, a predecessor of both Theophilus and Serapion. Though the circumstances which provoked the incident are quite unclear, Ignatius was arrested in Antioch probably in about 107 or 108 CE as a leader of the Christians there.[24] He was transported under Roman guard across Asia Minor to Rome, where he was executed. On his journey in Roman custody Ignatius wrote five letters to churches in Asia Minor, one to Polycarp, and one to the church in Rome.

As with the other Apostolic Fathers, scholars have warmly debated Ignatius' possible knowledge of written Gospels and other New Testament sources. Some have explicitly sought for 'proof', 'conclusive proof', or 'really conclusive proof' of such knowledge, holding him to the standard of exact verbal precision for a protracted amount of text before they will allow that they have found it. They are certainly free to do this, but such scholars usually take no account of the fact that, as a prisoner in Roman custody on his way to Rome, it is unlikely that Ignatius would have had all his books with him to copy from as he wrote his letters! Hence, a tendency towards more oblique or 'sloppy' references to earlier materials, and the blending of words, phrases, and ideas from any earlier sources he might have known into his own sentences is what we might expect to find in the writings of Ignatius. And this is just what we do find.

As to written Gospels, even Koester in his 1957 book admitted that the letters of Ignatius presuppose the finished Gospel of Matthew. Koester proposed, however, that Ignatius did not know this Gospel first-hand, but only knew a phrase from Matthew at second- or third-hand, through an oral source which was dependent upon Matthew. How he was able to divine this I will not pretend that I know. In 1963 Robert Grant could still write that 'there is no reason to suppose that Ignatius did not know the Pauline epistles and the gospels of Matthew and John'.[25] But in more recent years scholars have tended to be stingier. Paul Foster proposes the 'meagre' finding that Ignatius knew Matthew and four epistles attribute to Paul.[26] My own assessment is more like Grant's (with the addition of Luke), but let's not for the moment insist on this. There are still two issues that should not be ignored.

Ignatius and the Apostles

Ignatius is well known for his developed view of the hierarchy of the church, its offices of deacon, presbyter, and a presiding local presbyter increasingly singled out as 'bishop'. So lofty is his view of this ecclesiastical hierarchy that he compared it to the hierarchy in heaven. 'Be zealous to do all things in harmony with God, with the bishop presiding in the place of God and the presbyters in the place of the council of the apostles, and the deacons, who are most dear to me, entrusted with the service of Jesus Christ . . . ' (*Magnesians* 6.1).

Most interesting for our purposes is that the apostles of Jesus occupy for Ignatius a place not on the *earthly* side of the analogy, but the *heavenly*. The apostles, as a group, are of so eminent a stature that they can function alongside God the Father and the Lord Jesus Christ as permanent and heavenly archetypes of authority to which the local church's presbyters can only be compared (see also *Smyrnaeans* 8.1).

In their historical ministries on earth the apostles functioned as the unique personal agents of Jesus Christ, such that Christ's actions can be described as done 'by himself' or done 'through the apostles' (*Magnesians* 7.1). But now the apostles occupy a permanent place in the transcendent, heavenly hierarchy on which the earthly is modelled. Such highly elevated ideas about the apostles and their authority are, at least, in harmony with the practice of treating apostolic writings (or writings originating with them) as Scripture.[27]

Ignatius and the Gospels

Koester and others have insisted that Ignatius never used the term 'gospel' for a written work but only for the preached good news. In all but one instance (*Philadelphians* 5.2), however, it appears that Ignatius' use of the term gospel is more nuanced than that. In his seven other uses of the word it seems to function, if not exactly as a title, as a reference to the content of a written work or works.[28]

For Ignatius, 'the gospel' is defined by its contents, Jesus Christ and the major events in Jesus' life. When detractors at a meeting in Philadelphia of Asia Minor refuse to believe something that is 'in the gospel' and refer instead to 'the archives' (the Old Testament), Ignatius retorts: 'But to me the archives are Jesus Christ, the inviolable archives are his cross, and his death and resurrection, and the faith which is through him' (*Philadelphians* 8.2). These things which constitute the 'inviolable archives' and which define the gospel in *Philadelphians* 8.2 correspond to the things he says are contained 'in' the gospel in *Philadelphians* 9.2 ('the coming of the Saviour, our Lord Jesus Christ, his suffering, and the resurrection') and in *Smyrnaeans* 7. 2 ('the passion . . . and the resurrection'). The physical realities of Jesus' life, his suffering, death, and resurrection, as well as 'faith through him', the things Ignatius says are 'in' the gospel, are at least contained 'in' the written canonical Gospels—though they are not in Gospels like the *Gospel of Thomas*, the *Gospel of Judas*, nor even in the hypothetical Gospel source 'Q'.

It is also notable how naturally and how often Ignatius lays whatever it is he calls 'the gospel' alongside the Old Testament or categories of Old Testament writings, much as we have seen in the *Epistle to Diognetus* and Polycarp above. His eight uses of the term 'gospel' appear in the following combinations:

Philadelphians 5.1–2: gospel . . . apostles . . . prophets . . . gospel . . . gospel
Philadelphians 8.2: archives . . . gospel

Philadelphians 9.1–2: prophets ... apostles ... gospel ... gospel
Smyrnaeans 5.1: the prophecies ... the law of Moses ... the gospel
Smyrnaeans 7.2: prophets ... gospel

Five categories of religious authority are used: the archives (apparently the entire Jewish Scriptures), the law of Moses, the prophets or prophecies, the gospel, and the apostles.[29] Each Ignatian passage contains at least one designation for the Old Testament Scriptures, and at least one which pertains to the new Christian revelation, always 'the gospel', and in two passages 'the apostles' as well. All of these (except 'the archives') are terms used by other second-century writers to denote well-known groupings of their sacred writings. 'The gospel' thus too looks like one of these 'canonical' categories. What is more, Ignatius' admonition to pay attention 'especially' to the gospel, in preference even to the prophets (*Smyrnaeans* 7.2), and his statement that the gospel has something 'exceptional', in relation to the prophets (*Philadelphians* 9.2), show that what is contained in the gospel is in Ignatius' mind even more important than what is in the Old Testament.

Ignatius' use of the term 'gospel' as a 'canonical' category should help provide the context for evaluating the parallels he has with materials in the known Gospels. But even if there were no traces of New Testament writings in his letters (and by everyone's count, there are), we would still have to say that he already knows very well the structure of religious authority, the categories of 'gospel' and 'apostles', which inevitably led to a recognition of a canon of writings to supplement the Old Testament. Clearly, this makes Ignatius a 'proto-conspirator' as well.

The Didache

Citing the early writing known as the *Didache* ('The Teaching', in Greek) is a bit tricky today because of renewed debate about just when and how it was put together. As recently as 1992 Graham Stanton could write, 'few scholars doubt that the Didache is dependent on Matthew'.[30] That has since changed.[31] Almost any conclusions we draw about its relationship to Matthew (though, I believe, not the one drawn below) will step on somebody's tightly held theories. Most agree that the document we have now was not all written at one time but was reshaped, perhaps more than once, by more than one writer. Many argue that its earliest form (or at least the earliest material it incorporates) goes back to sometime in the first century, and most regard it as finding its final form sometime in the first half of the second century.

I mention the *Didache* briefly here for three reasons. First, it shows clear and unmistakable use of a good deal of pre-existing 'Matthean-sounding' tradition (perhaps also use of 'Lukan-sounding' tradition), including a prayer whose wording is extremely close to that of the Lord's Prayer of Matthew 6.9–13 (*Did.* 8.2). This is the case whether one argues that the author was dependent (directly or indirectly) on Matthew, whether the two are entirely independent, or even whether Matthew is dependent upon the *Didache*.

Second, in four places the writer attributes his 'Matthean-sounding tradition' to something called 'the gospel' (see 8.2; 11.3; 15.3–4). These instances seem to presuppose the existence of a written document under the name of Gospel, though some scholars hold that these passages are from a point relatively 'late' in the history of the *Didache*'s composition. While he stresses that the author was not writing with Matthew 'open in front of him or her as he or she wrote', Christopher Tuckett thinks, 'the *Didache* is primarily a witness to the post-redactional history of the synoptic tradition'.[32] That is, the *Didache* presupposes the finished Gospel of Matthew (possibly Luke also), not simply any postulated, earlier forms, and not simply oral tradition.

Third, the writer seems to have a notion of apostolic authority. An early stratum of the *Didache* was written at a time when either the original apostles of Jesus were still travelling, or when local churches were sending their own apostles on preaching missions. In one passage the writer exhorts: 'Now concerning the apostles and prophets, deal with them as follows in accordance with the rule of the gospel. Let every apostle who comes to you be welcomed as if he were the Lord' (11.3–4). The writer seems to be referring to what is written in the Gospel of Matthew 10.40, where Jesus tells his apostles: 'Whoever welcomes you welcomes me, and whoever welcomes me welcomes the one who sent me.' Irenaeus held this same view of the apostles as the representatives of Jesus, and it was this statement of Jesus which for him established the authority of apostolic Gospels and other writings.

Clement of Rome

Ehrman is probably right in saying that *1 Clement*, written sometime in the 90s CE, is 'the oldest Christian writing outside of the New Testament'.[33] *1 Clement* is so early that the Gospel of John may not even have been written yet, or had hardly begun to circulate. There is no good reason to think Clement knew this Gospel. And because of the stylistic arrangement of the 'synoptic-sounding material' he used,[34] we do not know which if any of the Synoptic Gospels he possessed. Some think Clement used 'a collection of sayings that is independent of and earlier than the broadly similar sayings of Jesus that are preserved also in Matthew and/or Luke'.[35] This is entirely possible. After all, Irenaeus says that Clement 'might be said to have the preaching of the apostles still echoing [in his ears] and their traditions before his eyes' (*AH* 3.3.3). After his own detailed consideration of the evidence, Gregory even-handedly concludes, 'while it is not possible to demonstrate that Clement did not know or use any of the synoptics, there is insufficient evidence to demonstrate that he did'.[36] In either case, Clement relies on some information about Jesus that is now contained in the Synoptic Gospels. If any of it comes from written Gospels, Clement did not copy from them but wrote from what he held in mind, giving what amounts to *summaries* of Jesus' teaching and not 'quotations' from texts as we think of them.

Deciding just how and where Clement acquired his 'synoptic-sounding' material is not so crucial for us here. For what Clement says elsewhere shows that he believes the gospel material he has—whether still 'echoing in his ears', or whether in part or in whole written on papyrus—was authoritatively delivered to the church by the apostles, who received it from Jesus.

The apostles received the gospel for us from the Lord Jesus Christ; Jesus the Christ was sent forth from God. 2 So then Christ is from God, and the apostles are from Christ . . . 3. Having therefore received their orders and being fully assured by the resurrection of our Lord Jesus Christ and full of faith in the word of God, they went forth with the firm assurance that the Holy Spirit gives, preaching the good news that the kingdom of God was about to come. (*1 Clement* 42.1–3)

Here, in the oldest Christian writing outside the New Testament, a letter written before the end of the first century, is the view Irenaeus would espouse some ninety years later. Even if by 'gospel' Clement understood *only* the oral good news (which contained a lot of 'synoptic-sounding material'), this still exhibits exactly the pattern of religious authority accepted in the church from here to Irenaeus, and beyond. In this sense, though we cannot say he knew the four written Gospels, Clement is a true 'proto-conspirator' for Irenaeus and his cause. The gospel which the apostles received 'for us' would soon be perceived, if it was not already perceived, as authoritatively represented by certain writings known as Gospels. It seems clear that *if* Clement knew any writings left by Jesus' apostles—even if he never quoted them accurately or never quoted them *at all*—he would have viewed them not only as 'inspired' (as he in fact attests in 47.1–3 of Paul's letter to the Corinthians) but as authoritative, as Scripture.

Drinking from a Common Well

In my opinion, all the writers reviewed above (excepting possibly Clement) show sufficient evidence for us to believe that they knew at least one of the four Gospels. Others may prefer a more reserved position. Yet, even if one insists on such reservations, I think one will have to agree that the Synoptic and Johannine Gospels—or at least 'synoptic-sounding materials' and 'Johannine-sounding materials'—like the babies in the illustration which opened this chapter, were already making themselves felt before we can tell with certainty that they had received visible or official welcome. And like the parents in the illustration, Clement of Rome and his 'co–proto–conspirators' show that the family and the home were well prepared for new arrivals. The religious apparatus, so to speak, the view of the rightful location and transmission of religious authority which made the reception of the four Gospels, as well as the rest of the New Testament, possible (if not inevitable), was in place already in the late first century.

One may devise tests as rigorous as one likes for determining the use of canonical Gospels in the Apostolic Fathers. One may accept only the most 'minimal assured results'. It will not matter. Even the occasional discovery of some alleged saying of Jesus not contained in the canonical Gospels (as in *2 Clement* 12.2, but even already in Acts 20.35) does not really affect this point. For, from as early as we have records, Clement of Rome, followed by the *Didache*, Ignatius of Antioch, Polycarp of Smyrna, the author of *Ps. Barnabas*, and the orator who urged Diognetus to convert to Christianity, all hold to the belief that the saving gospel of Jesus Christ had been authoritatively delivered to Jesus' apostles, whose responsibility it was to teach and hand down that gospel to the continuing church. The mechanism for receiving those Gospels which were received was in place. But it is not a mechanism these church leaders would have derived from writings such as the *Apocryphon of James*, the *Gospel of Judas*, or even from the *Gospel of Thomas*, writings which emphasized secret, higher teaching than was available in these Gospels and, with more or less gusto, belittled, marginalized, or (in the case of *Judas*) literally demonized the apostles of Jesus. So where did they get it?

Of course, for any, like Clement of Rome or Polycarp, who might have known or heard one or more of Jesus' apostles personally, one can imagine that their understanding of the role of these apostles could have been gained at first-hand. And for these and for others, the mechanism was also available in the four Gospels or the tradition that they embodied (it makes little difference which, as both follow the same trajectory). In Book 3 of *Against Heresies* Irenaeus finds the source of apostolic authority in Jesus' words to his apostles contained in Luke 10.16: 'He who hears you hears me, and he who rejects you rejects me, and he who rejects me rejects him who sent me' (*AH* 3.praef.). He could have quoted the similar words in Matthew 10.40 or John 13.20. At the end of Luke's Gospel (24.46–9) Jesus appoints his apostles to be his official 'witnesses', and throughout the book of Acts these apostles and Paul, who later joined their ranks, are portrayed as being quite conscious of this appointment. As we just saw, the author of the *Didache* seems to have this teaching in mind when he says: 'Now concerning the apostles and prophets, deal with them as follows in accordance with the rule of the gospel. Let every apostle who comes to you be welcomed as if he were the Lord' (*Didache* 11.3–4).

Irenaeus laboured hard to demonstrate that a continuity existed between himself, some of these same Apostolic Fathers, and the writings of the New Testament, in their views about God, Jesus Christ, and salvation. The same kind of continuity is visible on the subject of religious authority. We find this continuity when we observe that these Apostolic Fathers are using what look like some of the same sources Irenaeus used for the words and deeds of Jesus Christ. But beyond that, we see this continuity also in their answer to the question: where does the church and the Christian go to find the last word? It is found, they all agree, in the collective, public teaching of Jesus' authorized apostles, who received this authority from Jesus to pass on to the church.

There remains one more conduit of this continuous trajectory, one of the Apostolic Fathers, an early source known to Irenaeus, which we have yet to consider. I have saved it for last because of the possibility that this source holds the answer to the major question of this book: who chose the Gospels?

THE SEARCH FOR AN 'ARCH-CONSPIRATOR': A BISHOP, AN ELDER, AND AN ELDERLY APOSTLE

An Anonymous Tip

IN the last chapters we considered several early witnesses who might be considered 'proto-conspirators' for an imaginary plot to fit the church with four Gospels. But was there, dare we ask, an 'arch-conspirator', an actual originator before Irenaeus, before Tatian, and before Justin, of the idea that the church ought to regard four (and only four) accounts of the life of Jesus as authoritative?

There is one important, early testimony to the four Gospels that I have not yet dealt with in this book. Not very many do deal with it, perhaps because it is not so apparent quite what to do with it or where, chronologically, to place it. This testimony is preserved by Eusebius in Book 3, chapter 24 of his *Ecclesiastical History*. Its endorsement of the four Gospels, Matthew, Mark, Luke, and John, is clear and unmistakable. But, unfortunately, and to the chagrin of all modern interpreters, Eusebius fails to name the written source of his report. The reason I am treating the account here is because of the possibility—I stress here, only the possibility, though in my opinion it is a high probability—that the report relied on by Eusebius in Book 3, chapter 24 is very early indeed and that it discloses an extremely early proponent of the four Gospels.

There are various levels of testimony involved here. We have Eusebius, writing a draft of his *Ecclesiastical History* in the early years of the fourth century. But he is paraphrasing a much earlier report. How much earlier? I shall argue that it may be traced to the writings of Papias of Hierapolis in Asia Minor, who wrote his five books titled *Exposition of the Lord's Oracles* perhaps as early as 110 CE and not later than the early 130s. But the report in question may not have Papias as its ultimate source. If I am correct, it is part of a report which Papias years earlier had learnt by heart from an older churchman whom he simply called 'the elder', probably an elder named John.

We'll come to this tantalizing report in due time. First we must introduce Papias, who is a significant witness in his own right.

The Bishop: Papias the Story Collector

Papias, bishop of Hierapolis in Asia Minor, was probably born sometime around 70 CE, the year the Temple in Jerusalem was destroyed. As he was growing up, some of Jesus' original apostles were still alive. Living in Asia Minor at this early time makes it possible that Papias could have had contact with primitive, Palestinian Christians who emigrated to or travelled through his region. His only known writing, *Exposition of the Lord's Oracles*, was largely a collection of stories about Jesus, evidently mostly stories elaborating the contents of written Gospels, and possibly new stories and sayings he picked up from oral sources. Not a single manuscript of this work survives; we only know fragments of it from quotations in later writers. Papias sought his information about the Lord particularly from any who might have known one of Jesus' apostles or their followers and who had learnt the 'traditions of the elders'. In Hierapolis he personally heard stories from the 'daughters of Philip', either Philip the apostle mentioned in the Gospels or Philip the evangelist from the book of Acts, who settled there in later life (Eusebius, *EH* 3.39.9). Eusebius says Papias knew a story 'about a woman accused of many sins before the Lord'. According to Eusebius, a version of this story was also told in the *Gospel according to the Hebrews* (*EH* 3.39.17). At some point another version of it was incorporated into some manuscripts of the Gospel according to John and has been printed in most modern translations (John 7.53–8.11).[1]

Papias has long been an important source of information about early Christianity, but a controversial one, because at least some of the information he provides seems to breathe the air of legend. Eusebius himself had a very conflicted impression of Papias. He obviously valued much of the tradition Papias preserves, but described him as 'a man of very little intelligence, as is clear from his books' (*EH* 3.3913)! This surprising disparagement is made partly because Papias imbibed so uncritically a doctrine Eusebius rejected, that Christ at his second coming would set up a material kingdom of plenty for a thousand years on a fabulously renovated earth. It is perhaps because Eusebius only wanted to draw attention to the report itself, and not particularly to the man who reported it, that he was not concerned to name Papias in 3.24 in his account of the four Gospels, which we shall examine below.

There is no reason to doubt that Papias is a faithful reporter of what he heard and memorized, though there may be very good reason to doubt the historical factuality of much of what he reported. His reports should not be treated as automatically true, but neither as automatically legendary. They are early testimonies to what was known or believed at that time, no matter how much actual truth they contained. In any case, what he reported about the origins of two Gospels, Mark and Matthew, is still treated with a high degree of respect by the majority of New Testament scholars today.

The Elder: John the Elder on Mark and Matthew

The part of Papias' testimony to written Gospels which everyone agrees is genuinely his consists of two fragments Eusebius gives in *EH* 3.39.14–16 about Mark and Matthew. Eusebius reports:

14. In his writing he also passes along other accounts of the sayings of the Lord belonging to Aristion, who has been mentioned above, and the traditions of John the Elder, to which we refer those interested. For our present purpose we must add to his statements already quoted above a tradition concerning Mark, who wrote the Gospel, that has been set forth in these words:

15. 'And the elder used to say this: "Mark, having become Peter's interpreter, wrote down accurately everything he remembered, though not in order, of the things either said or done by Christ. For he neither heard the Lord nor followed him, but afterward, as I said, followed Peter, who adapted his teachings as needed but had no intention of giving an ordered account of the Lord's sayings. Consequently Mark did nothing wrong in writing down some things as he remembered them, for he made it his one concern not to omit anything that he heard or to make any false statement in them".'

Such, then, is the account given by Papias with respect to Mark. 16 But with respect to Matthew the following is said: 'So Matthew composed the oracles in the Hebrew language [or, in Hebrew style][2] and each person interpreted them as best he could' (*EH* 3.39.15–16).[3]

We may mention four points here. First, when Papias was collecting his traditions, probably sometime near 100 CE, attention was already being given to the origins of written Gospels which churches in Asia Minor were using. Whoever he was, this elder, evidently the 'John the Elder' mentioned above in 3.39.14, was very interested in Mark and Matthew.

Second, the fact that the elder knows these Gospels *by name* is important. We saw in Chapter 9 that many early Christian leaders often used 'synoptic-sounding' or 'Johannine-sounding' materials in their letters, but in such a way that leaves scholars unsure of whether the writers knew or had ever seen actual written Gospels or not. But here, indisputably, is reflected a very early knowledge of at least two written accounts of Jesus' words and deeds which went under the names of Mark and Matthew. This establishes the existence and circulation of these Gospels at a time when most of the other Apostolic Fathers wrote, and actualizes the possibility that they might have known the same writings. Also, as has been noted, Mark was not quoted very often by second-century writers, perhaps because most of what it contained could also be read in the more comprehensive Gospels of Matthew and Luke. But the elder shows us that Mark was indeed known, and treated as an authoritative source (ultimately deriving from the apostle Peter), from a very early time, just as Justin demonstrates about half-a-century later.

Third, there was already at this time a concern for 'order' in the Gospels of Mark and Matthew. The Greek word translated 'order' in the account above is not restricted to the idea of

Illustration 10.1 P⁴⁵ (P.Chester Beatty I), the earliest-known fragment of the Gospel according to Mark. A papyrus codex. Early to middle third century. Used by permission of the Chester Beatty Library, Dublin.

chronological order, though it may include that. It refers more properly to literary arrangement, skill in composition. It seems as if someone had already made some observations about what were regarded as deficiencies in Mark's 'order' or arrangement of his material. The elder defends the evangelist on the basis that it was not Mark's intention to produce a sophisticated (possibly chrono- logically correct) literary account, but simply to record accurately and without omission the gospel story preached by Peter.

Fourth, this very early testimony is also the first indication we have of the belief that one of the church's Gospels, Matthew, was attributed to an apostle of Jesus and another, Mark, had been written by a follower of an apostle, preserving the apostle's teach- ing. As we saw earlier, this is exactly the way Justin spoke about the four Gospels as 'Memoirs of the Apostles', written by apostles and their followers, and even of Mark's Gospel as the 'Memoirs' of Peter. It is, of course, the way Irenaeus speaks about them too.

But the burning question left by this testimony is: why doesn't Eusebius record here anything Papias said about John or Luke— or about any other Gospel for that matter? One possible answer is that Papias knew no other Gospel. Yet, as we'll now see, it has become evident to many scholars that Papias did use Luke and John and did regard them as authoritative accounts of the life of Christ.

From the order and identities of the disciples named in an introductory section of Papias' book, the great nineteenth-century scholar J. B. Lightfoot, along with many recent experts, including Hengel, Culpepper, Grant, and Bauckham,[4] have all concluded that Papias knew and accepted John's Gospel. 'And if by chance someone who had been a follower of the elders should come my way, I inquired about the words of the elders—what Andrew or

Peter said, or Philip or Thomas or James or John or Matthew, or any other of the Lord's disciples . . . '(*EH* 3.39.4). Three of the disciples listed, Andrew, Philip, and Thomas, have speaking roles in John but are barely mentioned in the Synoptics. And apart from the mention of Matthew, who was probably added at the end of the list because he was the author of another Gospel, the first six names listed by Papias are mentioned in the exact order in which these disciples appear in the narrative in John's Gospel. The odds of this happening independently have to be pretty low.

Moreover, Irenaeus cites a tradition of certain 'elders, the disciples of the apostles', which there is good reason to think he got from Papias' book. This tradition of the elders referred to one of Jesus' distinctive sayings recorded only in John 14.2: 'In my Father's house are many mansions' (*AH* 5.36.2).[5]

As far as Luke goes, the situation changed in 1981 when F. Siegert published a quotation of Papias contained in Andrew of Caesarea's fifth- or sixth-century *Commentary on the Apocalypse*.[6] Andrew cites a comment Papias made on Revelation 12.9, which describes in visionary language the casting out of Satan from heaven.[7] Papias is quoted as saying: 'As this occurred, the victory of Michael and his legions, the guardians of humankind, became completed, and the dragon could resist no more, because the death of Christ exposed him to ridicule and threw him to the earth—concerning which Christ said, "I saw Satan fallen from heaven like a lightning bolt".' This saying of Christ's is recorded only in Luke's Gospel (Luke 10.18). While it is possible to suggest that there was an unknown source used by Luke still circulating in Asia Minor at this time, the simplest explanation, and the one which requires the least dependence on supposition, is that Papias here reflects a familiarity with Luke's Gospel.

All this points to the conclusion that Papias in Hierapolis, writing probably in the 120s, knew all four Gospels, Matthew, Mark, Luke, and John. This would make him the earliest person we can name who knew them all. So far.

John the Elder on the Elderly John (and Matthew, Mark, and Luke)

Since it appears that Papias knew all four Gospels, we return to our question. Why doesn't Eusebius report anything Papias said about John or Luke when he records what Papias said about Mark and Matthew? Here is a 'silence' which seems to cry out for a conspiracy theory to fill it, and scholarship has not disappointed.

Walter Bauer, for instance, divined that Papias either 'expressed himself in an unfavorable manner [about John], or he kept silent also with respect to this gospel'. If he kept silent it was because John's Gospel 'apparently belonged to the long-winded prattle in which the great masses took pleasure ... the Fourth Gospel [was suspect], no doubt, because of its content, origin, and the friends it had made.'[8] Bauer is the main source of the popular but recently debunked theory mentioned at the beginning of Chapter 8, which states that the Gospel of John was for a long time avoided or rejected by the orthodox (who suffered from what we might call 'orthodox Johannophobia') but was loved by the heretics ('heterodox Johannophilia'). Bauer thus leaves us with a choice of two possible conspiracies: either it was Papias who suppressed the Gospel according to John, because it was entirely suspect and was popular with the wrong sorts of people; or Papias said something negative about John and it was Eusebius who edited out Papias' embarrassing testimony.

It is the second of these conspiracy theories which has been preferred by a few more recent scholars. In contrast to Bauer, these scholars suppose that Papias had a quite positive view of John, but they still propose that Eusebius purposely censored Papias' testimony because Papias had, as Bauer suggested, 'expressed himself in an unfavorable manner' about it. What these scholars believe Papias said about John that was unfavourable was that its author was not the apostle John but the mysterious 'Elder John' mentioned above (yes, John was a quite common Jewish name). This would mean that Eusebius was intentionally concealing from his readers a very crucial fact. Now, I have to say, a lot of people are quite prepared to believe that Eusebius was fully capable of this kind of duplicitous censorship. It would certainly not be the only time Eusebius could be accused of reporting things in a way most favourable to his own position. Yet, it should not be forgotten that copies of Papias' writings were in existence when Eusebius wrote, and he seems not the least threatened by the possibility that others will read Papias' books and learn the 'truth' themselves. In fact, he recommends it (*EH* 3.39.14, 'to which [i.e. Papias' books] we refer those interested'). Moreover, the deception in this case cannot be confined to Eusebius. Other 'interested' people clearly *had* read Papias' books, including Irenaeus and a number of other second- and third-century writers, yet neither they nor any one else ever reports the opinion that the Gospel according to John had been written by John the Elder. If Papias reported that the true author of the Fourth Gospel was not John the apostle but John the Elder, this would mean that a host of people in different times and places were involved in the same cover-up. In my opinion, this conspiracy theory more than stretches credulity.

There is, however, no need to posit a conspiracy of any extent. For there is no reason to think that Eusebius has included at 3.39.15–16 (the section on Mark and Matthew) *everything* Papias said about the Gospels and therefore no reason to come up with a conspiratorial explanation of why his testimony to other Gospels was suppressed by Eusebius. Eusebius' topic at this point in his *History* was not 'The Origins of the Four Gospels', or even 'Everything Papias of Hierapolis Said About the Gospels'. He was simply reporting on Papias and his times, and before closing his report decided to append some of what Papias had received from the elder about the authors of Mark and Matthew.

There is, in fact, a much simpler and non-conspiratorial explanation for why Eusebius did not give Papias' tradition about Luke and John when reporting on Mark and Matthew in 3.39.15–16. That explanation is that he had already given Papias' tradition about Luke, and particularly about John, earlier in 3.24.5–16, in a chapter entitled 'On the Order of the Gospels'.[9]

In the long quotation from that chapter which follows, notice Eusebius' careful mention of the 'record' which preserves this information, and his references to 'they say' as referring back to that record[10] (these references are italicized). The use of the plural, 'they say', in this case would fit well with the idea that Eusebius is quoting Papias, who is himself quoting someone else, namely, the same Elder John who gave him the information about Matthew and Mark.[11] Here is how Eusebius introduces, then paraphrases and interacts with, his early source in *EH* 3.24.5–13:

5. Yet nevertheless of all the disciples of the Lord, only Matthew and John have left us their recollections. *A (written) record preserves* that they took to writing out of necessity. 6. Matthew, having first preached to Hebrews, and when he was on the point of going to others, supplied to

those from whom he was sent, through his writing, the lack of his presence by handing down the Gospel according to himself, written in his native tongue. 7. And after Mark and Luke had already made the publication of the Gospels according to them, John, *they say*, used all the time a proclamation which was not written down, and at last came to writing for the following cause. After the three Gospels which had been previously written had already been distributed to all, and even to himself, *they say* that he welcomed them and testified to their truth,[12] but that there was therefore only lacking to the Scripture (or writing) the account concerning things which had been done by Christ at first and at the beginning of the proclamation. 8. *The record* is certainly true. It is at least possible to see that the three evangelists had written down only the things done by the Saviour during one year after John the Baptist had been put in prison and that they stated this at the beginning of their narratives. [Eusebius then produces the testimonies of Matt. 4.12, Mark 1.14, Luke 3.19–20 to show that they begin their accounts of the commencement of Jesus' public ministry after John was imprisoned.] 11. Now *they say* that on account of these things, the apostle John was exhorted to hand down in the Gospel according to himself the time passed over in silence by the first evangelists and the things which had been done by the Saviour at this time (that is, things before the imprisonment of the Baptist), and that he signified this when saying 'this beginning of marvels did Jesus' [John 2.11], and then by calling to mind the Baptist in the midst of the acts of Jesus as still then baptizing at Aenon near Salem, plainly indicating this when he says 'for John was not yet cast into prison' [John 3.24]. 12. Thus John in the Scripture (or writing) of the Gospel according to him hands down the things done by Christ when the Baptist had not yet been cast into prison, but the other three evangelists record the things after the Baptist had been shut up in prison. 13. If this be understood, no longer do the Gospels seem to disagree with one another, because that according to John contains the first things of the acts of Christ, but the rest the narrative of what happened to him at the end of the period. And fittingly John passed over the genealogy of our Saviour according to the flesh, because it had been already written out by Matthew and Luke, and began with the description of his divinity since this had been reserved for him by the Divine Spirit as for one greater than they.[13]

After thus relating what he calls the 'cause' for the origins of Matthew and John, Eusebius reminds his readers that he had earlier given the cause for the Gospel according to Mark. He is referring to what he had written in 2.15.1–2, where he had explicitly stated that his sources of information were Clement of Alexandria and 'the bishop of Hierapolis, named Papias'. It is plausible to think, then, that Eusebius expected his readers to connect the dots and conclude that one or the other of these sources had just been paraphrased in his traditions on Matthew and John. But the source cited in 3.24 was apparently not Clement, for Eusebius later gives Clement's tradition on the origin of John's Gospel (*EH* 6.14.7), and it is not the same as this one.

To round out this section, Eusebius then includes a shorter notice on the origin of the Gospel according to Luke (3.24.14–15). This he takes largely from Luke's own preface but includes a detail or two which could well have come from the same early source.

This early source, I believe, was Papias, quoting the teaching of the 'elder'. The full case for this has been made elsewhere and cannot be repeated here.[14] The two lines of evidence on which the case is based, however, may at least be mentioned. The first comes from the fact that this passage on Matthew and John (3.24.5–13) shares several elements or concerns in common with the two passages where Eusebius explicitly mentions something Papias said about the Gospels (2.15.1–2 on Mark; 3.39.15–16 on Mark and Matthew). These commonalities may be briefly stated:

(a) A concern to maintain that each of the Gospels had its origin in the preaching of one or more of the apostles of Jesus.

(b) A further idea that the apostles, who were first of all preachers and teachers of the gospel of Jesus Christ, did not simply take it upon themselves to write but they, or their associates, wrote at the request of others.

(c) A prevalent use of some form of the words 'remember' (cf. John 14.26) or 'remembrances' to describe these Gospels as first-hand reports of the Lord's disciples who knew him personally. We have seen how Justin would later use this concept, designating the Gospels as 'Memoirs of the Apostles', and even how the *Epistle of the Apostles* emphasized, like John's Gospel and 1 John do, the sensory experience of Jesus by those who bore their witness of him.

(d) A concern with the 'order' or 'literary arrangement' of the contents of the Gospels, with undertones of a desire to defend from criticism. This concern is repeated in the *Muratorian Fragment* (see below).

(e) An attempt to find an 'endorsement' for each Gospel from another accepted, apostolic source.[15]

It is hard for me to believe that an independent source on the origins of the four Gospels (*EH* 3.24.5–13) would share all of these characteristics with the account of the origins of Matthew and Mark explicitly attributed to Papias and his elder.

The second line of evidence which supports the idea that Eusebius' source in *EH* 3.24.5–13 is Papias comes from the similarities shared by this fragment and by writers who seem to know Papias' testimony about Mark and Matthew recorded in

EH 3.39.15–16. Irenaeus tells us he had read Papias' words, and we have seen that Justin knows the tradition about Mark that Papias cites. Some scholars have pointed to similarities in the *Muratorian Fragment*, Clement of Alexandria, Origen, and Victorinus of Pettau which suggest their familiarity, either at first- or second-hand, with the tradition Papias gives about Matthew and Mark. This familiarity means that if Papias *did* say something about John and Luke, something like what Eusebius preserves in *EH* 3.24, then we would expect that certain elements in 3.24 might turn up in these same authors who seem familiar with Papias' tradition about Mark and Matthew. This is in fact what we do find. Here are three things which the source used in 3.24 has in common with one or more of these authors, all having to do with the Gospel according to John:[16]

(a) The notion that John wrote his Gospel at the request of others (*Muratorian Fragment*, Clement, and Victorinus).

(b) Mention of the 'order' of the events in John's Gospel is also present in the *Muratorian Fragment*, where the order of Jesus' miracles in particular is also noted: 'For in this way he [i.e., John] professes [himself] to be not only an eyewitness and hearer, but also a writer of all the marvellous deeds of the Lord, in their order.'[17] This mention of John as a writer of 'all the marvelous deeds of the Lord, in their order' is a reference to John's specifying 'the first of his signs' in John 2.11, and then the second in John 4.54. Both sources, then, specifically cite John's 'ordering' of Jesus' marvellous deeds. Both sources, too, refer to those deeds in the same unusual way. That is, John uses a word that means 'signs', for he emphasizes that the purpose for Jesus' mighty works was not only to help those who benefited from them, but also to serve as signs which revealed something about Jesus' true identity. But when Eusebius relates the information of his source in 3.24.11, instead of using the word for 'sign' he uses a Greek word which means 'marvel'. In the same manner, the *Muratorian Fragment* uses the Latin word for 'marvel', not John's word for 'sign'.

(c) Concern for the number and order of the Gospels (Irenaeus, *Muratorian Fragment*, Clement, Origen). All these writers appear to consider Matthew the first, and all consider John the last of the Gospels written.

We may also note that all of the authors whom scholars have suggested might have been familiar with Papias' account of the elder's traditions about Mark and Matthew also held to the authority of John and Luke. None lists alongside these any other Gospels, such as the Gospels of Thomas, Peter, Mary, Philip, or the *Gospel of the Hebrews*.

Conclusion: The Bishop, the Elder, or the Elderly Apostle?

Where does all this leave us? At a minimum, it seems best to conclude that Papias, writing probably in the 120s, knew all four of our Gospels, for there are sound reasons for acknowledging his use of them in the fragments of his writings that have survived. This would make Papias the earliest first-hand source for a recognition of all four Gospels. Was it he, then, who chose the Gospels?

But Papias also reports earlier tradition. We cannot be sure exactly how early this tradition goes, but a reasonable assumption is that the information he derived from 'the elder' was learned sometime around the year 100 and in any case not very many years thereafter. All agree that the information he imparted included tradition about Mark and Matthew, and if Eusebius' source in *EH* 3.24 indeed goes back to the same person, it would mean that all four Gospels were known to Papias' elder at around the turn of the second century, very near the time when, according to most scholars, John's Gospel was first released for circulation.

The implications of this identification would be even more significant. For the source referenced by Eusebius in *EH* 3.24 already accepted these four Gospels (and only these four, as John is perceived as the last) as textual authorities for the life of Christ. These Gospels were held to be the direct or indirect record of the preaching of Jesus' eyewitness apostles. It is in any case certain that attempts were being made in the generation before Papias wrote to explain the origins of at least two named Gospels which were obviously of some importance to some churches in Asia Minor. And if *EH* 3.24 goes back to the elder too, we can affirm that fairly sophisticated efforts were being made even then to account for the origins of, to exposit the meaning of, and even to deal with some of the difficulties posed by, the four Gospels. The four even then were seen as belonging together. Was it, then, an Asian elder named John who chose the Gospels?[18]

The report in *EH* 3.24.7, on the other hand, allows for an even earlier endorsement of the four Gospels. For it says that the apostle John 'welcomed' or 'received' the three previous Gospels and 'testified to their truth'. He is said to have observed that they only lacked 'the account of what was done by Christ at first and at the beginning of the preaching', which he then supplied in his own

Gospel. This would make the aged apostle John the earliest 'chooser', endorser, or 'canonizer' of the four Gospels.[19] This is not to claim, of course, that this testimony about John 'choosing the Gospels' is historically factual, only that it is an extremely early tradition.

Origen, in the third century, knew a similar tradition. In his *Homilies on the Gospel of Luke* he mentions in passing that he had read in an older writing (it is a pity he doesn't name it) that 'John collected the written Gospels in his own lifetime in the reign of Nero (54–68 CE), and approved of and recognized those of which the deceit of the devil had not taken possession; but refused and rejected those which he perceived were not truthful' (*Hom. Lk.* 1, fr. 9). These two traditions have a few things in common. Both assign the 'canonization' to John; both say John 'welcomed' or 'recognized' (the same Greek word is used by each author) the other three; and both say John made some assertion of the 'truth' of the three previous Gospels (the elder positively, Origen by way of denying the truthfulness of others). Was Origen condensing the same written source used by Euesbius? Was it a later tradition based on Eusebius' source? Were the two accounts entirely independent? Unfortunately we cannot be sure, but the coincidence is interesting.

More importantly, may we now say that we possess in the combined accounts in Eusebius' *Ecclesiastical History* the earliest witness to the acceptance of the four Gospels, a witness going back to near the beginning of the second century, or even slightly earlier? Unfortunately, barring some new manuscript discovery, we will probably never know with certainty, since Eusebius, here as occasionally elsewhere, was not thoughtful enough to distinguish all his sources by name. What we can say is that the testimony he reports in *EH* 3.24 fits very well with what we know of the elder's report in 3.39.15–16 (cf. also 2.15.1–2) and that no other alternative for identifying the source shows anything near the promise of this one. Moreover, the identification of Papias as the source would explain why the tradition concerning the four Gospels is as consistent as it is from his time on. The material preserved in *EH* 3.24.5–16 could just be the missing link.

We have noted before Skeat's conjecture that the Christians, perhaps around 100 CE, adopted the codex for the transmission of their sacred texts because it, and not the scroll, could contain all four Gospels. Our present knowledge, however, does not allow us to confirm that the newly developing technology of the codex could have accommodated the text of all four Gospels until sometime later in the second century. And yet Skeat's instincts might not be far wrong. For it was around the year 100, when Papias was collecting stories about Jesus, and stories about the *books* about Jesus, when some may already have held the seeds of the idea which would eventually produce the four-Gospel codex.

WHO CHOSE THE GOSPELS?

Natural Selection: The Gospels that Imposed Themselves

W E began this book by noticing how the selection of the four Christian Gospels is portrayed today as (in Darwinian terms) anything but 'natural'. It is not just popular media, novels, films, and the work of journalists which depict an 'unnatural' process, attended with coercive ecclesiastical and even imperial pressures. In certain academic circles as well the triumph of these Gospels is tied inseparably to the 'conquest' by one particular branch of Christianity over its many rivals, each perceived to be equally deserving (or undeserving). That victory for both the 'orthodox' and their Gospels is portrayed as the result of a great and protracted struggle, aided by conspiratorial designs on the part of certain powerful bishops, like Irenaeus and Athanasius.

Those who describe the process in this way place the victory for the orthodox and their four Gospels sometime in the fourth century. It was late in the fourth century when the church, through councils and the work of individual bishops and scholars, achieved virtual unanimity about the *entire* contents of its New Testament Scriptures, including some of the less-often-cited epistles in the collection. But this fact is rather carelessly interpreted to imply that even the four Gospels did not achieve wide recognition until roughly the same time. The present book, I hope, has shown the emptiness, sometimes bordering on disingenuousness, of that claim. Whoever it was who made the first or definitive choice of the four Gospels, it wasn't the emperor Constantine, the bishop Athanasius, the Councils of Nicaea, Laodicea, or any other council of the fourth century. At the dawn of the fourth century the four Gospels, unlike a few other books in the New Testament, were not inconvenienced by any real dissent in what was recognized almost universally as the Christian church. They had long been functioning as the church's acknowledged sources for the life and teaching of Jesus; individual copies were stored in the book cupboards of countless churches; they had been transmitted as a unit in four-Gospel codices, even in languages other than their original Greek.

Who, then, first chose the Gospels, if it wasn't anybody in the fourth century? It wasn't Origen, Tertullian, or Hippolytus in the first half of the third century, or Clement of Alexandria or Serapion at the end of the second. It wasn't even Irenaeus or anyone writing in the last quarter of the second century. All these had inherited the same four Gospels from previous generations.

It wasn't Tatian in Rome or Syria or Theophilus in Antioch. Despite the odd extraneous detail which might have occurred in Tatian's original *Diatessaron*, both men in the 170s 'packaged' the *same* four Gospels in a Gospel Harmony. Neither could have been the first to choose these Gospels, which were already prominent and perceived as a cohesive unit in ecclesiastical circles in Rome and Antioch. It was perhaps at about this time that codices packaging all four of the Gospels between two covers began to be produced. By the early part of the third century one more way of 'packaging' the contents of the four Gospels for study purposes was attempted with the first Gospel synopsis.

Who first chose the Gospels? It wasn't Justin Martyr, who by the early 150s in Rome was using the same four Gospels, and treating evidently only these four as 'Memoirs of the Apostles', composed by the apostles and their followers; as official registers of the things which took place under Pontius Pilate. The church in Rome was at that time using these Gospels as Scripture in worship, and the prominence befitting such a use is reflected in rival or adversarial works such as the Valentinian *Gospel of Truth*, the Gnostic *Gospel of Judas*, or Celsus' *True Logos*.

The evidence brings us, then, to an earlier time. But how much earlier? While the data prior to 150 are not quite so clear, the four Gospels are known as authoritative sources in the *Epistle of the Apostles* and the *Apocryphon of James* in the 140s. Papias, probably in the 120s, knows all four; Aristides, at about the same time, knows 'the Gospel' in multiple individual written expressions, including Luke and John, and a decade earlier Ignatius knows at least Matthew and John. And sometime around the year 100 Papias' elder discusses the origins of Matthew and Mark, and, if the argument summarized in Chapter 10 is near the mark, Luke and John as well.

How is it that these four Gospels came to be known so widely from such an early time? There was certainly no great council of Christian churches before 150 which laid down the law on which Gospels to use. No single bishop, not even the bishop of Rome, should he ever have made such a proclamation (and there is no reason to think he did), had the clout to make it stick. If there was any authoritative figure who endorsed the four Gospels, the most viable option would have to be, as a tradition known to Origen and possibly Papias' elder said, the aged apostle John. Such a story is a long, long way from historical verification, though that fact in itself does not make it impossible.

But if we set aside that story as likely to be legendary, our search appears to have reached a dead-end. We cannot find who chose the Gospels. It looks like nobody did. They almost seem to have chosen themselves through some sort of 'natural selection'. And this at least concurs with the conclusion of Bruce Metzger, one of the last generation's premier scholars of the New Testament canon, who wrote, 'neither individuals nor councils created the canon; instead they came to recognize and acknowledge the self-authenticating quality of these writings, which imposed themselves as canonical upon the church'.[1]

Wherefore Four?

The mystery resulting from our faltering quest to find the original chooser of the four Gospels (unless he be the apostle John) combines with another big question. Why four? Other options existed.

Marcion took one of the existing Gospels, edited it down to what he alleged was its original form, and made it his only Gospel. The authors of the *Gospel of Peter*, the *Gospel of the Ebionites*, the Gospel represented by P.Oxy. 840, and perhaps others borrowed the overall structure and many details from the existing Gospels, added in some interpretative traditions and some new materials of various kinds, and wove them into a new narrative. The more scholarly Tatian painstakingly combined all four of the church's Gospels into one continuous and harmonized narrative. Any of these three options—a single remodelled Gospel, a single new Gospel, or a single, unified Gospel Harmony—would have made life less complicated for the church. Each offered simplicity, greater convenience, and an easier defence against critics like Celsus who saw the existence of four authoritative Gospels as a concession of weakness and sought to expose the differences between them. Why, then, didn't the church take any of these options? Why did it persist in holding before insiders and outsiders four separate Gospels, four Gospels which in their commonalities could seem repetitious, and in their peculiarities always held the seeds of conflict for opponents to exploit?

This question, combined with our inconclusive search for a primal chooser, may help us come to grips with what seems to be the key realization. Many treatments of this subject assume or assert that the church made a conscious choice not to take one of the three options mentioned above and instead decided to allow a degree of diversity in permitting four. Such an explanation is certainly attractive. Picturing the church of the second and third centuries taking a principled stand for the hearing of a plurality of voices in the face of sectarian calls for narrow uniformity would be happily in keeping with our current sensibilities. But it also forces the question: 'why only four?' There was, after all, 'a sea of Gospels' out there. Gospels were 'multiplying like rabbits', and all that. This in turn raises the question of criteria, what standards might the church have used to apply to the candidates for inclusion in its new set of Scriptures? And although people have written lots of more-or-less plausible speculation on this (naming apostolicity, antiquity, orthodoxy, liturgical suitability, etc. as the criteria), real evidence for it is embarrassingly lacking. That is, we simply know of no councils or synods from this period which deliberated on the matter. Nor is there evidence of a flurry of inter-ecclesiastical correspondence on the subject (as there was, for instance, on the late second-century controversy about the observance of Easter). Nor have disinterested archaeologists unearthed any examples of the experimental binding together of five, six, or seven Gospels into a single codex; no attempts at harmonizing a greater number of Gospels—no Diapentes,[2] Diahexes, or Diaheptas. Only Diatessarons.

In short, we have no evidence that the church ever sat down collectively or as individual churches and composed criteria for judging which Gospels (or other literature) it thought best suited its needs. On the contrary, the key realization which best explains our inability to find an ultimate 'chooser', which best explains why the church didn't take the easy way out with some kind of singular Gospel and why it never cobbled together a set of criteria to apply to all the Gospel candidates, is that the church essentially did not believe it had a choice in the matter! The question 'why did you choose these Gospels?' would not have made sense to many Christians in the second century, for the question assumes that the church, or someone in it, had the authority to make the choice. To many, it would be like the question, 'why did you choose your parents?'

External Properties: 'Handed Down from the Apostles'

Handed Down . . .

As we noted in Chapters 1 and 3, Christian writers often spoke of their Gospels (and other books) as handed down to them. Christian writers of the second century do not speak of choosing the Gospels, or of the criteria they might have created for making such choices. This is not the way they thought. When speaking of the church's part in the process they instead use words like 'receive', 'recognize', 'confess', 'acknowledge', and their opposites. Just like the faith itself, which had been 'received from the apostles and transmitted to its children' (Irenaeus, *AH* 3.1.praef.;

231

cf. 1.10.1), so the Gospels themselves were 'handed down' to the church by the same apostles (*AH* 3.1. praef.; 3.1.1, 2). Irenaeus contrasts the *Gospel of Truth* to 'those [Gospels] which have been handed down to us from the apostles' (3.11.9). He criticizes Marcion and his followers for not 'recognizing' some books of the New Testament (3.12.12), and others because they do not 'confess' the Scriptures but pervert them with their interpretations (3.12.12). Others, again, 'do not admit' John's Gospel . . . but 'set aside . . . both the Gospel and the prophetic Spirit' (3.11.9).

The *Muratorian Fragment*, too, speaks of certain books which cannot be 'received' into the catholic Church (lines 66–7; cf. l. 82), and includes a story about the apostle Andrew and others 'receiving' or 'recognizing' (l. 14) the Gospel which John wrote. Serapion tells the church at Rhossus: 'For our part, brethren, we receive both Peter and the other apostles as Christ but the pseudepigrapha written in their name we reject, as men of experience, knowing that we did not receive such by tradition' (*EH* 6.12.3–6). Clement of Alexandria speaks of the 'acknowledged' Gospels and calls them 'the four Gospels that have been handed down to us'. Justin distinguishes between those books which the Jews 'confess' and those they do not 'confess' (*Dial.* 120.5; cf. 71.5), and has a notion of what the church has 'received' from the apostles (here specifically a tradition of Jesus' words instituting the Eucharist). The *Epistle of the Apostles* depicts the apostles 'entrusting' the 'word of the gospel' to their sons and daughters in the church. In the view of these Christians the church is not in a position to choose the books it wants but rather to receive, confess, or acknowledge what has been given.

Implicit to the 'handed down' nature of the Gospels is that each church leader seems to know not only what had been passed down but also somebody—more likely, many people—who had done the passing down. It was, in other words, not just a *doctrine* of succession but an experience of personal history, like the passing down of family photographs or other heirlooms from an older family member to a younger.

But it is not that each 'family', one in Gaul and others in Rome, Alexandria, Antioch, and Ephesus, simply passed down its own exclusive collection of family photographs. They all had the same 'photographs', the same ancestors. Their family histories were the same. At least by the second half of the second century churches throughout the empire had received the same four Gospels, which each would say had been in the family as long as anyone could remember, back to the time of the earliest common ancestors: in this case, the apostles of Jesus.

... *From the Apostles*

There is, of course, a problem here. Their opponents, their rivals for the title 'Christian', also claimed descent from the same apostles. The *Gospel of Thomas* claims to be the words recorded by the apostle Thomas, the *Apocryphon of James* a revelation of the resurrected Jesus to two disciples. Nearly all of the pseudepigraphal documents originating in heterodox circles claimed authorship by one or another of the apostles. The Great or 'apostolic' Church did not own a monopoly on the claim to be apostolic, so, don't we have a stalemate? Many assert that we do and then want to leave the matter there. But leaving the matter there would seem to involve some sleight of hand.

That is, we can declare a stalemate only if we are pre-committed to the proposition that all Gospels are created equal, and are compelled to ignore their origins, early histories, and contents.

It may be a well-guarded secret, but serious historians do not really believe that the teachings of the historical Jesus are better traced through the *Gospel of Judas*, the *Gospel of Mary*, the *Gospel of Philip*, or even the *Gospel of Thomas* than through Matthew, Mark, Luke, and John. Undoubtedly, some people in antiquity preferred the gnostic Gospels to the canonical ones, just as some do today. But the reasons for doing so, whatever they might have been and might be, do not justifiably include a better and truer access to the historical Jesus and his authentic Palestinian life situation.

And not to be forgotten is the fact that opponents of 'apostolic Christianity' generally conceded that its faith was indeed 'apostolic'. 'The *Gospel of Judas*', for instance, writes DeConick, 'attempts to harpoon apostolic Christianity for its blind reliance on the authority of the twelve apostles for its teachings.'[3] Nor did opponents typically dispute even the idea that the four Gospels ultimately went back to the apostles of Jesus. As we saw in Chapters 7 and 8, some of the most striking testimony on behalf of the four Gospels, and other parts of the New Testament, comes from outside of apostolic Christianity. Most, if not all, of the known rival Gospels, and other pseudepigraphal works as well, actually presuppose to one extent or another the witness of the canonical Gospels. Pagan critics of Christianity like Celsus, when they took the time to read the Christian sources, went to the same canonical Gospels, which Celsus, at least, accepted as written by Jesus' disciples.

The opponents of what Celsus called the Great Church claimed the apostles too, but usually in a different way. As Perkins says, the author of the *Apocryphon of James* appears 'to recognize that the Gospel canon and apostolic authority must be claimed for gnostic exegesis'.[4] The names of the apostles had to be invoked, and in a couple of cases a succession from the apostles was even claimed.[5] But by and large, the apostles of Jesus could simply be treated as spiritual novices, or something much less complimentary. For the highest appeal among such groups as these was typically to a professed 'secret knowledge', superior to the commonly received, public teaching of the apostles (cf. Irenaeus, *AH* 3.2.1). The *Gospel of Thomas* begins: 'These are the secret sayings that the living Jesus spoke and Didymos Judas Thomas recorded.' The *Gospel of* Judas begins: 'The secret revelatory discourse in which Jesus spoke with Judas Iscariot.' The persistent appeal to *secret* teachings of Jesus given to one or another of the apostles is a tacit admission that not very much support could be gained from his acknowledged *public* teachings. It was only the Valentinians, in the late second century, who seemed to have the exegetical creativity (to run the risk of over-using an earlier metaphor) to 'pull a rabbit out of the hat' of the existing Gospels.

Internal Properties: The Contents of the Gospels

Differences Without a Difference

But what set the four Gospels apart for most was not simply their 'apostolic credentials', widely recognized inside and outside the church. It was not even simply that churches scattered throughout the empire knew these four as the ones that had been passed down to them from their elders. It was also, and ultimately, the contents of these Gospels that commended them.

Readers of the four canonical Gospels today, particularly those who have little or no acquaintance with the other Gospels, are often impressed with the differences in form and expression between them. Already sometime near the year 100, not long after the Gospel of John was put into circulation, Papias' elder had taken notice of differences in 'order' between the Gospels. He excused the author of Mark in particular, saying it was not his intention to put everything into literary 'order', and, if I am right, he also defended the 'order' of John's Gospel and tried to reconcile it with the Synoptics.

The author of the *Muratorian Fragment* was aware of differences between the four, and for him too they did not seem to constitute a deep spiritual crisis:

And so, though various elements [or beginnings] may be taught in the individual books of the Gospels, nevertheless this makes no difference to the faith of believers, since by the one sovereign Spirit all things have been declared in all [the Gospels]: concerning the nativity, concerning the passion, concerning the resurrection, concerning life with his disciples, and concerning his twofold coming; the first in lowliness when he was despised, which has taken place, the second glorious in royal power, which is still in the future.

Clement of Alexandria wrote of the acknowledged Gospels, 'although perchance the expressions vary slightly in each, yet all show identical agreement in meaning' (*Who is the Rich Man?* 5). Thus, while the differences between the four canonical Gospels seem wide and scandalous to some, they seem less so to others (who are usually able to find some path of reconciliation between them). Let me suggest two reasons for this.

Unity in Diversity

Both Clement and the *Muratorian Fragment* point to the unity between the four Gospels as overriding any of their mutual differences. This unity was only set in greater contrast when certain of the 'non-apostolic' Gospels were placed alongside them. As we have seen, some of the alternative Gospels, such as the *Gospel of the Hebrews*, the *Gospel of Peter*, or the Egerton Gospel, were basically a blend of two or more of the canonical ones, with elements of various kinds added or subtracted. Gospels such as these offered to some an initial plausibility such that a Clement, an Origen, or a Jerome could take some of their 'extra-canonical' contents seriously. But as regards the 'gnostic Gospels', like the *Gospel of Judas*, and the gnostic post-resurrection dialogues, like the *Apocryphon of James*, even the casual observer was likely to see that in doctrine, tone, and spirit these were quite foreign to the four. They made any discrepancies between the four look pale and insignificant by comparison. Irenaeus only slightly exaggerates the obvious when saying that the 'comparatively recent writing "The Gospel of Truth"' . . . agrees in nothing with the Gospels of the Apostles'. He invites any who might wish to do so to compare them and learn how the *Gospel of Truth* is 'totally unlike those which have been handed down to us from the apostles' (*AH* 3.11.9). While the *Gospel of Truth* has its own poetic beauty and has been hailed as the jewel of Valentinianism, I imagine that few who take up Irenaeus' challenge could possibly disagree.

The handed-down Gospels were unified in many ways, and one of them goes back to something mentioned in Chapter 2. The four Gospels assumed and promoted belief in the one, monotheistic God Almighty, maker of heaven and earth. The gnostic Gospels assumed a plurality of gods (from two to 365), with the creator of the material universe occupying a spot at the bottom of the hierarchy, as the one who made the cause of gnostic, spiritual reclamation necessary by his dreadful cosmic blunder.

The one God proclaimed by the four Gospels was, of course, the same God who was worshipped by the Jews. It was their 'Jewishness' which also set the four (along with the Jewish *Gospel of the Hebrews* and the *Gospel of the Ebionites*) apart from the rest. Jesus and all the first Christians were Jews. The narratives of the four Gospels are embedded in the first-century Palestinian situation, which was not the case with the later gnostic productions. Each of the four presented Jesus in continuity with the hopes of the people of Israel and their Scriptures, as the one sent by the God of Israel to fulfil the words of the prophets. 'Think not', says Jesus in Matthew, 'that I have come to abolish the law and the prophets; I have come not to abolish them but to fulfil them' (5.17). Philip announces in John: 'We have found him about whom Moses in the law and also the prophets wrote, Jesus son of Joseph from Nazareth' (1.45). As summed up by Irenaeus, the handed-down Gospels 'have all declared to us that there is one God, Creator of heaven and earth, announced by the law and the prophets; and one Christ, the Son of God' (*AH* 3.1.2). In fact, Marcion's stated reason for rejecting three of these Gospels and for 'correcting' the one he saved was his charge that they had all been corrupted under Jewish influence. The gnostic Gospels could be even more hostile to the idea that the religion of Jesus could have any real and substantive connection with Judaism, and its God.

Another major area in which the four Gospels were united against the many others had to do with the person of Jesus. For Marcion and his adapted version of Luke, Jesus was neither human nor divine, but inhabited a body composed of a unique spiritual substance. For most of the gnostics and the Valentinians there was indeed a real man named Jesus, but he was only temporarily possessed by a heavenly Christ who used Jesus' humanity as a disposable container (disposable but not 'recyclable'; bodily resurrection was a thing most undesirable). All four of the handed-down Gospels, on the other hand, imply or explicitly teach a real incarnation of a divine Lord, born a real man, Jesus of Nazareth. This meant to early Christians that Jesus Christ's real, human suffering could redeem the entire human person, body and soul.

The gnostic Gospels see the ultimate human predicament as the need for enlightenment. The handed-down Gospels see it as the need for forgiveness, a new orientation, and a place in the people of God. In Matthew, Jesus speaks of his blood as the blood 'of the covenant, which is poured out for many for the forgiveness of sins' (26.28). In Mark, Jesus announces that he came 'not to be served but to serve, and to give his life a ransom for many' (10.45). The Jesus of the handed-down Gospels died and rose again to save the entire person from oblivion. The heavenly Christ of the gnostic Gospels promised salvation to only the non-material human aspect, the contents of the disposable container.

Meeting Jesus and his Self-Attesting Words of Power

The church's embrace of the individuality of the four Evangelists, and its apparent confidence that even the differences among them were a blessing rather than a problem to be overcome, rested on something else as well. Sympathetic readers and hearers of the handed-down Gospels felt that through these books they encountered the real Jesus and divine power.

In his recommendation to Hadrian, Aristides anticipates that the emperor might be able to 'judge the glory of his [Christ's]

presence from the holy gospel writing' (Greek of *Barlaam* 15.1).[6]
Justin, who had heard many a sophist declaim, stresses that Christ
'was not a sophist', but instead 'His word was the power of God'
(*1 Apol.* 14). He believed it was manifest that 'no word or act of
His [Christ's] can be found fault with' (*Dial.* 35). Here is how he
describes to Trypho his own experience of 'the words of Christ'
mediated through the memoirs of the apostles:

Moreover, I would wish that all, making a resolution similar to my own,
do not keep themselves away from the words of the Saviour. For they
possess a terrible power in themselves, and are sufficient to inspire those
who turn aside from the path of rectitude with awe; while the sweetest
rest is afforded those who make a diligent practice of them. If, then, you
have any concern for yourself, and if you are eagerly looking for
salvation, and if you believe in God, you may—since you are not
indifferent to the matter—become acquainted with the Christ of God,
and, after being initiated, live a happy life. (*Dial.* 8.2 ANF)

Again he speaks of the testimony about Christ in the Gospels:
'I shall prove to you as you stand here that we have not believed
empty fables, or words without any foundation, but words filled
with the Spirit of God, and big with power, and flourishing with
grace' (*Dial.* 9). He has Trypho confess that Jesus' words in the
Gospel 'are so wonderful and so great, that I suspect no one can
keep them' (*Dial.* 10). Crescens, he charges, has probably not read
the teachings of Christ in the apostolic memoirs, but if he has, he
'does not understand the majesty that is in them' (*2 Apol.* 3.3). To
Justin, such majesty was self-evident.

Theophilus' reading of the church's inspired Gospels con-
vinced him that they were authored by the same Holy Spirit
who stood behind the prophetical writings of the Old Testament.
His successor Serapion testified that he received the apostles'

writings as if they were Christ's. For him, as for Irenaeus, Jesus' words to his disciples, 'he who hears you hears me', rang true.

Demonstrations of the Indemonstrable

We noted in Chapter 6 that early Christian apologists often used considerable restraint in calling explicitly upon their Christian written sources with which their opponents were not familiar or would not have accepted. But this does not mean that these Christians did not believe their Gospels and other apostolic writings spoke with divine power. As we have noted, they often exhorted opponents to read their Gospels so that they could know that power.

Many have surely had the experience of mounting irritation when Christians try to prove things from the Bible, especially when the thing being proved is not specifically religious! How can they expect others to accept what the Bible says when they have not first demonstrated that everything in the Bible is true, free of mistakes, and worthy of belief? This too is a very old problem, one which annoyed the famous second-century physician Galen. While he admired Christians for their ethics and self-control, he opined in the 160s and 170s that both Jews and Christians were deficient in their use of 'demonstration'.[7] It is not that there were no educated Jews and Christians who were skilled in the use of syllogism and the drawing of proofs.[8] But even educated Jews and Christians in some sense fell under Galen's criticism, for they considered their Scriptures themselves to be the ground of 'demonstration'. The old man who introduced Justin to Christianity told him that the Hebrew prophets 'did not use demonstration in their treatises, seeing that they were witnesses to the truth above all demonstration, and worthy of belief' (*Dial.* 7). For Christians, this 'witness to the truth above all demonstration' was found not only in the writings of the prophets, but in their Gospels as well.

Clement of Alexandria describes this self-attesting quality of Scripture, including the four Gospels, using the philosophical concept of a 'primary premise' or 'first principle'. In Aristotelian philosophy a first principle is what one accepts as the ground of investigation but which by definition is not subject to demonstration.[9] If one has to prove a first principle, it is no longer a first principle. For instance, in order to argue for any point by the use of logic, one must first accept that the use of logic is valid. The validity of logic is conceded as a first principle. For the Christian, God, and God's own voice, constitute the ultimate 'first principle'; how could it be otherwise? Thus, to many a Christian, citing Scripture as the ultimate proof seems self-evident, even though this may leave non-Christians like Galen scratching their heads.

For in the Lord we have the first principle of instruction, guiding us to knowledge from first to last 'in divers ways and divers portions' (Hebrews 1.1) through the prophets and the gospel and the blessed apostles. And, if any one were to suppose that the first principle stood in need of something else, it could no longer be really maintained as a first principle. He then who of himself believes the Lord's Scripture and his actual voice is worthy of belief... Certainly we use it [Scripture] as a criterion for the discovery of the real facts. But whatever comes into judgment is not to be believed before it is judged, so that what is in need of judgment cannot be a first principle. With good reason therefore having apprehended our first principle by faith without proof, we get our proofs about the first principle *ex abundanti* from the principle itself, and are thus trained by the voice of the Lord for the knowledge of the truth. For we pay no attention to the mere assertions of men, which may be met by equally valid assertions on the other side. If, however, it is not enough just simply to state one's opinion, but we are bound to prove what is said, then we do not wait for the witness of men, but we prove the point in question by the voice of the Lord, which is more to be relied on than any demonstration, or rather which is the only real demonstration. (*Stromateis* 7.16.95)[10]

Clement tells why Christians often feel so sure of their knowledge derived from Scripture: 'So too we, obtaining from the Scriptures themselves a perfect demonstration concerning the Scriptures, derive from faith a conviction which has the force of demonstration' (*Stromateis* 7.16.96).

The anonymous, second-century author of a treatise on resurrection[11] reasoned in the same way and began his discourse thus:

The word of truth is free, and carries its own authority, disdaining to fall under any skilful argument, or to endure the logical scrutiny of its hearers. But it would be believed for its own nobility, and for the confidence due to him who sends it. Now the word of truth is sent from God; wherefore the freedom claimed by the truth is not arrogant. For being sent with authority, it were not fit that it should be required to produce proof of what is said; since neither is there any proof beyond itself, which is God. For every proof is more powerful and trustworthy than that which it proves...But nothing is either more powerful or more trustworthy than the truth.

The same conviction permeates the writings of Irenaeus, who says, speaking specifically of the New Testament writings, 'proofs [of the things which are] contained in the Scriptures cannot be shown except from the Scriptures themselves' (*AH* 3.12.9).

The point is that, for Justin, Irenaeus, Clement, and many others, the Gospels of Matthew, Mark, Luke, and John bore the marks of such self-attesting authority. And, holding such an attitude as this towards Scripture, including 'the prophets and the gospel and the blessed apostles', it is only natural that apostolic Christians of the mainstream church should not regard themselves as authorized to choose which books they *wanted* to be Scripture. With Scripture as a self-attesting first principle, the only response for the church is to recognize what God has revealed.

We are bound to say, of course, that questions did arise which prevented these Christians from reaching consensus recognition on the 'self-attesting' marks of a few of the books now in the New Testament until the late fourth century. But the four Gospels seem to have attained general recognition impressively swiftly. Still, even with those books in mind which did not so quickly find consensus (or which moved in and out), the importance of the principle we have just observed should be evident. For it shows just how differently the early Christians thought about such things from the way people typically do today. Christian scholars such as Justin, Irenaeus, Clement, or Origen poured immense critical effort into the application of all manner of literary tools to the study of Scripture. But what they did not seek to do was to sit in judgement over it. For Scripture, including the four handed-down Gospels, spoke with the voice of God.

These Gospels impressed people in the second century, as they still do today, as being truth from God, 'filled with the Spirit of God, and big with power, and flourishing with grace', carrying 'the glory of his power', as being 'the only real demonstration', 'carrying their own authority'. In John's Gospel, Simon Peter confesses that Jesus had the words of eternal life (John 6.69), and Christians of the second century agreed. Jesus said that the world would pass away but that his words would not (Mark 13.31). So far, his prediction is on track! What gave these books containing Jesus' words their self-attesting quality? Such a question, if it can be answered, clearly cannot be answered in the abstract but, I am sure second-century Christians would say, has to be answered from an encounter with that truth itself.

The Conspiracy Exposed

For audiences used to a diet of *The Da Vinci Code*, public unveilings of recovered gnostic Gospels, or dubious docu-dramas about the discovery of the supposed Jesus family tomb, it may be a bit disappointing to learn that the four-Gospel canon did not rise to prominence through a conspiracy of fourth-century bishops determined to squelch threats to their authority. The four well-known Gospels were not even foisted on the church by a second-century, heresy-hunting, book-burning bishop named Irenaeus. This need not, of course, deter any talented journalist, novelist, or Hollywood screenwriter from producing a hypnotic conspiracy (or two, or three) featuring nefarious forces that 'hacked down' a forest of suppressed Gospels in favour of a politically motivated canon of four. But any awards the story might garner would be in the fantasy category. Those who prefer the grittier realism of the documentary might enjoy a script about a modern 'conspiracy' to make the four Gospels look like the product of an ancient one!

Matthew, Mark, Luke, and John emerged from the early Christian mission through the Mediterranean world, a mission spearheaded by Jesus' eyewitness apostles and their associates who were involved in the preservation and dissemination of the tradition about him.[12] Our earliest evidence about these four Gospels associates them with the names of one of these apostles or apostolic associates in the original mission. This is how they were passed down in the churches. But these handed-down books were not set aside as encased relics in those churches. In the growing absence of the preaching of Jesus' earliest representatives, and as reliable oral traditions of his words began to fade into uncertainty and a want of authentication, the written depictions of Jesus' life, words, death, and resurrection contained in these Gospels increasingly formed the life, preaching, and mission of a church which recognized their power and majesty. 'My sheep hear my voice', said Jesus in one of these Gospels, and from their own testimony, readers and hearers of these Gospels experienced in them a divine voice that needed no external demonstration.

In one sense, of course, the answer to the question: 'Who chose the Gospels?' is, everybody who has known something of that indemonstrable power and majesty and, like Aristides, Justin, Irenaeus, Clement, and countless others, has chosen to live by their telling of the story of Jesus. But second-century Christian leaders would have said that neither individuals nor churches had the authority to 'choose' which of the many Gospels they liked, but to receive the ones given by God and handed down by Christ through his apostles.

Christianity, of course, is not the only religion to claim Scriptures which its practitioners receive as revelation from God. But when encountering claims to divine revelation, such as Christians once made and even continue to make concerning their Gospels, one faces the paradoxical necessity of choosing books which one has no authority to choose. And I think I hazard no risk in suggesting this can only be done by heeding the call once heeded by St Augustine: *tolle lege*, take up and read.

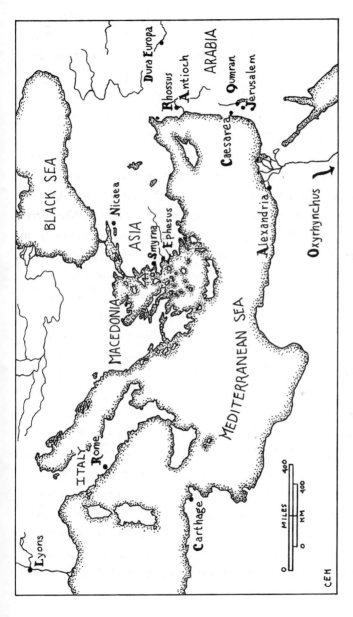

Illustration II.I Map. Significant places and people for the rise of a four-Gospel canon.

APPENDIX: DATES OF THE EARLIEST MANUSCRIPTS OF THE CANONICAL GOSPELS

The Table opposite shows the published judgements of several sources on the dates of the earliest New Testament manuscripts. One might observe that Comfort and Barrett and Jaroš tend to be on the early side and *NTG* and the *Kurzgefasste Liste* tend towards the later side of the estimates. The eccentric late dating by the original editor of P^4 is mostly due to its early discovery at a time when it was thought that the codex form could not have dated from before the fourth century.

Papyrus	First Editor	NTG, Kurz. Liste[a]	Elliott[b]	Lührmann and Schlarb[c]	Hurtado[d]	Roberts and Skeat[e]	Comfort and Barrett[f]	Jaroš[g]
P4 [h] (Luke)	6th cent.	3rd cent.	before 200	c.200	2–3rd cent.	late 2nd cent.	second half of 2nd cent.	c.150
P5 (John)	200–300	3rd cent.		3rd cent.	2–3rd cent.		early 3rd cent.	second half of 2nd cent.
P52 (John)	c.125	2nd cent.	before 200	2nd cent.	2nd cent.	2nd cent.	early 2nd cent.	80–125
P64 + 67 (Matt.)	3rd cent. (P67) late 2nd (P64)	c.200	before 200	c.200	2–3rd cent.	late 2nd cent.	second half of 2nd cent.	c.150
P66 (John)	c.200	c.200	before 200	c.200	2–3rd cent.		c.150	c.100
P75 (Luke; John)	175–225	3rd cent.		3rd cent.	2–3rd cent.		late 2nd or early 3rd cent.	second half of 2nd cent.
P77[i] (Matt.)	late 2nd cent.	2–3rd cent.		2–3rd cent.	2–3rd cent.	late 2nd cent.	first half of 2nd cent.	first half of 2nd cent.
P90 (John)	second half of 2nd cent.	2nd cent.	before 200	2nd cent.	2nd cent.	2nd cent.	middle to late 2nd cent.	near begin. of 2nd cent.
P103 (Matt.)	late 2nd or early 3rd	2–3rd cent.	poss. before 200	2–3rd cent.	2–3rd cent.		middle to late 2nd cent.	first half of 2nd cent.
P104 (Matt.)	second half of 2nd cent.	2nd cent.	poss. before 200	2nd cent.	late 2nd cent.		beginning of 2nd cent.	c. turn of 1st to 2nd cent.

(continued)

Papyrus	First Editor	NTG, Kurz. Liste[a]	Elliott[b]	Lührmann and Schlarb[c]	Hurtado[d]	Roberts and Skeat[e]	Comfort and Barrett[f]	Jaros[g]
P108 (John)	3rd cent.	3rd cent.	3rd cent.	3rd cent.	3rd cent.		late 2nd or early 3rd cent.	c.200
P109 (John)	3rd cent.	3rd cent.	poss. before 200	3rd cent.	3rd cent.		middle to late 2nd cent.	c.150

Notes

[a] Barbara and Kurt Aland, et al., *Novum Testamentum Graece*, 27th edn. (Münster: Deutsche Bibelgesellschaft, 2001), 684–9. These are virtually the same dates given in Kurt Aland, *Kurzgefasste Liste der griechischen Handschriften des neuen Testaments*. Zweite, neubearbeitete und ergänzte Auflage (Berlin and New York, 1994). This list is continually updated on the web at http://www.uni-muenster.de/INTF/continuation_manuscripts. html

[b] J. K. Elliott, 'The Nature of the Evidence Available for Reconstructing the Text of the New Testament in the Second Century', in C.-B. Amphoux and J. K. Elliott (eds.), *The New Testament Text in Early Christianity: Proceedings of the Lille Colloquium, July 2000* (Lausanne: Éditions du Zèbre, 2003), 9–18.

[c] Dieter Lührmann and Egbert Schlarb, *Fragmente apokryph gewordener Evangelien in griechischer und lateinischer Sprache*, Marburger Theologische Studien 59 (Marburg, 2000), 22.

[d] Larry Hurtado, *The Earliest Christian Artifacts: Manuscripts and Christian Origins* (Grand Rapids and Cambridge: Eerdmans, 2006).

[e] C. H. Roberts and T. C. Skeat, *The Birth of the Codex* (London: Oxford University Press, 1983), 40–1, cf. C. H. Roberts, *Manuscript, Society and Belief* (London: Oxford University Press, 1979).

[f] P. W. Comfort and D. P. Barrett, *The Text of the Earliest New Testament Greek Manuscripts: A Corrected, Enlarged Edition of The Complete Text of the Earliest New Testament Manuscripts* (Wheaton: Tyndale House Publishers, Inc., 2001).

[g] Karl Jaroš et al. (eds.), *Das Neue Testament nach den ältesten griechischen Handschriften: Die handschriftliche griechische Überlieferung des Neuen Testaments vor Codex Sinaiticus und Codex Vaticanus* (Vienna and Würburg, 2006).

[h] Many papyrologists now identify P4, P64, and P67 as parts of the same multiple-Gospel codex.

[i] Some papyrologists believe that P77 and P103 are portions of the same codex.

GLOSSARY

Basilideans: followers of Basilides, an early teacher of a gnostic brand of Christianity in Egypt. Unrelated to Basilides the church leader, to whom Dionysius of Alexandria addressed a letter, quoted in Chapter 2.

Cerinthians: followers of Cerinthus, a docetic (see *Docetism*) teacher who Irenaeus says was contemporary with the aged apostle John.

Codex: a new book form taken over by the early Christians for the production of their sacred books in particular. It eventually replaced the scroll in western culture.

Docetism: belief that Jesus Christ was not fully human and there was no real incarnation. Docetism generally took one of two forms: (1) that a man named Jesus was temporarily possessed by a heavenly being (Christ or Spirit), who left him at the cross; or (2) that Jesus was not human at all but his body was some kind of quasi-spiritual substance.

Gnosticism: as used by scholars today, a broad term describing a variety of ancient religious forms. Growing out of Greek theosophical speculation, the best-known forms are the Christian or semi-Christian ones of the second and third centuries CE. They emphasized redemption through spiritual knowledge (gnosis) and displayed a general disdain for the body and things earthly. Hence the tendency for gnostics to be docetists (see *Docetism*).

Gospel Harmony: a book which attempts to combine into a single, unified narrative the words of all four Gospels. Justin Martyr may have used a Harmony of the three Synoptic Gospels, but all other known attempts included the four. The most successful Gospel Harmony was that of Tatian, called the *Diatessaron*, from the second half of the second century.

Gospel of the Ebionites: this gospel is only known to us through quotations by Epiphanius of Salamis writing in the late fourth century. He believed it was the Gospel used by the Ebionites, a Jewish Christian group mentioned by Irenaeus. Epiphanius identifies it in some way with a corrupted version of a presumed Hebrew original of the Gospel according to Matthew. He also calls it the Gospel according to the Hebrews. In fact, it shows signs of being a sort of Gospel Harmony, combining at least Matthew and Luke. Earliest probable date: *c*.125.

Egerton Gospel: the two published scraps of this Gospel are the earliest fragments of a non-canonical Gospel known, dating to the late second century. Though some scholars have proposed that it incorporates material which is independent of and earlier than the canonical Gospels, this is highly unlikely, as it uses both Synoptic and Johannine elements. Probable date: mid-second century.

Gospel of the Egyptians: there are two unrelated works which bear this title, one known only from Nag Hammadi and an earlier one quoted by Clement of Alexandria. Probable date: early to middle second century.

Gospel according to the Hebrews: the most widely known of the so-called Jewish Gospels. One of the sayings it attributed to Jesus is cited twice by Clement of Alexandria, in longer and shorter forms, and was incorporated into the *Gospel of Thomas*. This Gospel was also cited by Origen and Jerome and was known to Eusebius. It was apparently used by Jewish Christians in Egypt. Some of its appeal derived from its presumed relationship to a supposed Hebrew original of Matthew's Gospel. An excerpt used by Jerome seems to show familiarity with 1 Corinthians. Probable date: early second century.

Gospel of Judas: Irenaeus knew of a *Gospel of Judas* by the 180s. A fourth-century Coptic version was unveiled to the world in 2006. Regarded today as a Sethian gnostic production, it mounts a bitter attack on the 'apostolic' church. Probable date: 150–80.

Gospel of Mary: not a Gospel but a discussion between the risen Jesus and some of his disciples about the world and the soul. A Coptic version exists among the Nag Hammadi writings, supported by two third-century Greek fragments. Probable date: second half of the second century.

Gospel of the Nazoraeans: some identify this either with the *Gospel of the Hebrews* or with Jewish Christian tradition from a non-Gospel source. Its separate existence is postulated from some materials used by Jerome in his commentary on Matthew. Some think it originated as an Aramaic translation of the Gospel according to Matthew. Probable date: first half of second century.

Gospel of Peter: a Gospel under the name of Peter was presented to Serapion of Antioch on a visit to nearby Rhossus in the early 190s. He found it to be tinged with docetism (see *Docetism*) but otherwise doctrinally unobjectionable. Besides two or three possible fragmentary Greek representations, we have a manuscript discovered at Akhmim in Egypt containing what is probably the last part of this Gospel. It appears to have combined and rewritten earlier canonical Gospel accounts for its narrative. Probable date: mid-second century.

Gospel of Thomas: not a Gospel, in genre, but a collection of 114 sayings attributed to Jesus. The most celebrated and hotly debated of the non-canonical 'Gospels' (at least until the *Gospel of Judas* reappeared). In its present form it is dependent upon the canonical Gospels. Many, however, believe or allow for the possibility that a portion of its sayings may come from an earlier time. Others think the entire collection is late and even dependent upon Tatian's *Diatessaron*. Probable date: 140–90.

Great Church: a term used by Celsus, the second-century critic of Christianity, for what he considered the standard or majority form of Christianity. It corresponds essentially to the church represented by people like Justin, Irenaeus, and Clement of Alexandria. It is used in this book interchangeably with the terms 'orthodox', 'catholic', and 'mainstream'.

Infancy Gospel of Thomas: not a Gospel but a series of rather bizarre stories about Jesus from age 5 to 12. Existing in multiple forms, most of this work is unrelated to anything in the canonical Gospels, though it shows familiarity with Luke and Acts. Probable date: second half of second century.

Marcionism: named for Marcion, an influential second-century teacher who migrated from Pontus to Rome. Marcion taught an antithesis between what he considered the law-obsessed, wrathful God of the Jewish Scriptures and the gracious God of the Christians. He restricted his 'canon' of Scripture to a modified version of Luke and an abbreviated corpus of Paul's letters.

Opisthograph: writing on the back of a roll (scroll). Customarily rolls were written only on the inside, for the outside was exposed to wear and tear. Occasionally writing was done on the outside as well, usually in order to reuse available writing material for a new text.

Orthodox (see *Great Church* and *Proto-orthodox; Proto-heretical*)

'P': abbreviation for 'papyrus', as in P.Oxy. 4009 or P^{75}. Papyrologists and other scholars use it to refer to ancient manuscripts of all kinds written on papyrus, a writing-material made from the papyrus plant that grew on the banks of the Nile.

Pagan: a term of convenience for a person, group, or religious system that was neither Jewish nor Christian. Paganism in this sense would encompass various types of Greek or Roman religions as well as philosophies.

Pericope: a 'section' or passage of a text.

Proto-orthodox; Proto-heretical: terms used by some contemporary scholars to describe early forms of Christianity. Use of the terms (without inverted commas) usually reflects the belief that in the first, second, and third centuries there was not yet any such thing as 'orthodoxy' (a standard, mainstream, or majority form of Christianity) or 'heresy' (by comparison, deviating forms of Christianity), only forms of Christianity whose later representatives would 'win out' or 'lose out'.

Pseudepigraphy: the practice of writing a book under a false name, usually, in the literature treated in this book, the name of an apostle or disciple of Jesus, or an Old Testament character. A book written under a false name is sometimes called a pseudepigraphon.

'Q': from the German word *Quelle*, meaning 'source'. This is usually taken to be a *written* source which many believe was used by Matthew and Luke when they share common material which has no parallel in Mark. Some scholars believe it was a set of unwritten, memorized, oral tradition; others believe such a source never existed.

Sethian: a particular type of gnostic outlook. It takes its name from the Old Testament figure of Seth, son of Adam and Eve, who played a special role in gnostic speculation. The *Gospel of Judas* is often regarded as a Sethian gnostic document.

Synopsis: a writing which lays out the accounts of the various Gospel writers side by side in parallel columns for comparison. The first one on record was produced by Ammonius in the early or middle third century.

Synoptic: a word meaning 'viewed together', applied to the Gospels of Matthew, Mark, and Luke, which often tell the same or very similar stories of Jesus. The word is only applied to these three Gospels.

Valentinianism: named for Valentinus, a Christian teacher probably from Alexandria who moved to Rome in the mid-second century. According to Irenaeus, he adapted pre-existing gnostic ideas in a more outwardly Christian direction. Valentinians tended to receive all sacred books of the larger church (plus some new ones of their own) and were widely known for supporting their doctrines with creative allegorical interpretations of Scripture.

ENDNOTES

Introduction

1. William L. Petersen, 'The Diatessaron and the Fourfold Gospel', in Charles Horton (ed.), *The Earliest Gospels: The Origins and Transmission of the Earliest Christian Gospels—The Contribution of the Chester Beatty Gospel Codex P⁴⁵* (London and New York: T. & T. Clark International, 2004), 50–68, at 51.
2. Ibid. 52.
3. Elaine Pagels, *Beyond Belief: The Secret Gospel of Thomas* (New York: Random House, 2003), 32. Pagels is talking about the so-called Nag Hammadi texts, discovered near the Egyptian village of Nag Hammadi in 1945. In fact, the entire 'Nag Hammadi library', as it is sometimes called, totalling somewhat more than 1,000 papyrus pages, tumbled out of a single broken urn about two feet high at the time of its discovery, and the standard, modern English translation occupies a single paperback volume that sits comfortably in the palm of one hand. That English edition is: James M. Robinson (general editor), *The Nag Hammadi Library in English* (San Francisco: HarperSanFrancisco, 1990). For the story of the discovery, including the height of the urn, see Bart D. Ehrman, *Lost Christianities* (Oxford: Oxford University Press, 2003), 52; also W. C. van Unnik, *Newly Discovered Gnostic Writings: A Preliminary Survey of the Nag Hammadi Find* (London: SCM Press, 1960), 10. For the number of pages, see Christoph Markschies, *Gnosis: An Introduction*, tr. J. Bowden (Edinburgh: T. & T. Clark, 2003), 49.
4. Stephen Prothero, *American Jesus: How the Son of God Became a National Icon* (New York: Farrar, Straus & Giroux, 2003), 7–8.
5. For an account of the Council and the question of the authenticity of the list, see the still authoritative B. F. Westcott, *A General Survey of the History of the Canon of the New Testament*, 6th edn. (Grand Rapids, Mich.: Baker Book House, 1980; repr. of 1889 original), 431–9. The list of New Testament books is identical to the contents of the traditional New Testament except that it omits the book of Revelation.

6. Bart Ehrman, 'Christianity Turned on Its Head: The Alternative Vision of the Gospel of Judas', in R. Kasser, M. Meyer, and G. Wurst (eds.), *The Gospel of Judas from Codex Tchacos* (Washington, DC: National Geographic, 2006), 77–120, at 118. See also Ehrman, *Lost Christianities*, whose chapters include titles such as 'The Arsenal of the Conflicts: Polemical Treatises and Personal Slurs' and 'Additional Weapons in the Polemical Arsenal: Forgeries and Falsifications'.

7. For an accessible account of the debate and its consequences, see John Barton, *Holy Writings, Sacred Text: The Canon in Early Christianity* (Louisville, Ky.: Westminster/John Knox, 1997), 2–14.

8. The term itself in Greek (κανών) does not appear to have been used for the contents of Scripture until the middle of the fourth century. But long before the words 'canon' and 'canonical' were employed for the writings now in the New Testament, Christian preachers and theologians were referring to most if not all of them (as well as occasionally some other books) as 'Scripture,' and with the use of adjectives such as divine, holy, and as covenantal or 'testamental'.

9. Barton, *Holy Writings, Sacred Text*, 12–14.

Chapter I

1. J. K. Elliott, *The Apocryphal New Testament. A Collection of Apocryphal Christian Literature in an English Translation* (Oxford: Clarendon Press, 1993).

2. William L. Petersen, 'The Diatessaron and the Fourfold Gospel', in Charles Horton (ed.), *The Earliest Gospels: The Origins and Transmission of the Earliest Christian Gospels—The Contribution of the Chester Beatty Gospel Codex P⁴⁵* (London and New York: T. & T. Clark International, 2004), 50–68, at 51. In another publication Petersen even constructs an argument that two of these (*Gospel of the Nazoraeans, Gospel of the Ebionites*) and possibly a third (*Gospel according to the Hebrews*) are actually different names for the same Gospel (William L. Petersen, *Tatian's Diatessaron: Its Creation, Dissemination, Significance, and History in Scholarship* (Leiden, New York, and Cologne: E. J. Brill, 1994), 40–1). This would bring the number of rival Gospels down to eight or possibly seven. It must be said, however, that few if any

scholars have been persuaded by these arguments, and most continue to identify three separate 'Jewish' Gospels. For a recent, balanced assessment of the data on the number of Jewish Christian Gospels, see Andrew Gregory, 'Jewish Christian Gospels', in Paul Foster (ed.), *The Non-canonical Gospels* (London: T. & T. Clark, 2008), 54–67.

3. Andrew Cockburn, 'The Judas Gospel', *National Geographic* (May 2006), 78–95, at 88.

4. Ibid.

5. James M. Robinson, 'The Nag Hammadi Gospels and the Fourfold Gospel', in Charles Horton (ed.), *The Earliest Gospels: The Origins and Transmission of the Earliest Christian Gospels—The Contribution of the Chester Beatty Gospel Codex P⁴⁵* (London/New York; T. & T. Clark International, 2004), 69–87, at 86.

6. Cyril of Jerusalem says the Manichees wrote a Gospel according to Thomas (*Catechetical Lectures* 4.36), but this is probably not our GT.

7. For a very readable review of Oxyrhynchus and its treasures see Peter Parsons, *City of the Sharp-nosed Fish: Greek Lives in Roman Egypt* (London: Weidenfeld & Nicolson, 2007).

8. Robinson, 'The Nag Hammadi Gospels', 86.

9. Ibid. 87. Actually, while the word 'canonical' was not yet used to describe Scriptural documents, Irenaeus of Lyons (*AH* 1.20.1) speaks of 'apocryphal and spurious writings' in around 180 CE.

10. See, for instance, J. W. Pryor, 'Fragment from the Unknown Gospel', in S. R. Llewelyn (ed.), *New Documents Illustrating Early Christianity*, Vol. 9, *A Review of the Greek Inscriptions and Papyri Published in 1986–87* (Grand Rapids and Cambridge: Eerdmans, 2002), 99–101.

11. See E. J. Epp, 'The Codex and Literacy in Early Christianity and at Oxyrhynchus: Issues Raised by Harry Y. Gamble's *Books and Readers in the Early Church*', Critical Review of Books in Religion 10 (1997), 15–37, at 22.

12. For example, by C. H. Roberts and T. C. Skeat, *The Birth of the Codex* (London: Oxford University Press, 1983), 40–1; T. C. Skeat, 'The Oldest Manuscript of the Four Gospels?' *New Testament Studies*, 43 (1997), 1–34. The date is also accepted in B. M. Metzger and B. D. Ehrman, *The Text of the New Testament: Its Transmission, Corruption, and Restoration*, 4th edn. (New York and Oxford: Oxford University Press, 2005), 53.

13. J. K. Elliott, 'The Nature of the Evidence Available for Reconstructing the Text of the New Testament in the Second Century', in C.-B. Amphoux and J. K. Elliott (eds.), *The New Testament Text in Early Christianity: Proceedings of the Lille Colloquium, July 2000* (Lausanne: Éditions du Zèbre, 2003), 9–18, at 10. Elliott actually gives a list of the fragments of all the New Testament books which he says experts date from 'before 200 AD', a list which includes both Gospels and other NT literature. The total number is either ten or eleven, as he includes 'two or three of the recently published Oxyrhynchus manuscripts $P^{103,104,105}$' (in which P^{105} must be a misprint for P^{109}). The Gospels are represented in two and possibly three texts of Matthew ($P^{64/67}$, and one or both of P^{103} and P^{104}); one text of Luke (P^4); and three or possibly four texts of John (P^{52}, P^{66}, P^{90}, and possibly P^{109}).

14. M. Hengel, 'The Four Gospels and the One Gospel of Jesus Christ', in Charles Horton (ed.), *The Earliest Gospels: The Origins and Transmission of the Earliest Christian Gospels—The Contribution of the Chester Beatty Gospel Codex P^{45}* (London and New York: T. & T. Clark International, 2004), 13–26 at 15.

15. P. W. Comfort and D. P. Barrett, *The Text of the Earliest New Testament Greek Manuscripts: A Corrected, Enlarged Edition of* The Complete Text of the Earliest New Testament Manuscripts (Wheaton: Tyndale House Publishers, Inc., 2001), 651.

16. Epp, 'The Codex and Literacy', 26.

17. To see the evaluations of several scholars and how I have determined a 'consensus', see the Appendix.

18. See Paul Foster, 'Are there any Early Fragments of the So-Called *Gospel of Peter*?', *New Testament Studies*, 52 (2006), 1–28.

19. Robinson, 'The Nag Hammadi Gospels and the Fourfold Gospel', 86.

20. Bart D. Ehrman, *Lost Christianities* (Oxford: Oxford University Press, 2003), 22–3.

21. Hengel, 'The Four Gospels', 18, citing the work of D. Lührmann and E. Schlarb, *Fragmente apokryph gewordener Evangelien in griechischer und lateinischer Sprache* (Marburg, 2000), 23. Lührmann and Schlarb count sixteen manuscripts of John, twelve of Matthew, seven of Luke, and one of Mark.

22. Larry Hurtado, *The Earliest Christian Artifacts: Manuscripts and Christian Origins* (Grand Rapids and Cambridge: Eerdmans, 2006), 20–3, who

lists the same numbers of manuscripts of canonical Gospels as Lührmann, Schlarb, and Hengel. His list of non-canonical Gospels: three of *Gospel of Thomas*; one of *Protevangelium of James*; two of *Gospel of Mary*; two of *Gospel of Peter*; one of Egerton; one unidentified (Fayum) Gospel (228).

23. They are P.Oxy. 4803 (P^{119}) and P.Oxy. 4806 (P^{122}). See Nick Gonis (ed.), *The Oxyrhynchus Papyri LXXI* (London: Egypt Exploration Society, 2008).

24. Robinson, 'The Nag Hammadi Gospels and the Fourfold Gospel', 87.

25. Bart Ehrman, *The Orthodox Corruption of Scripture* (New York, 1993), 7, a judgement he has repeated in several publications. Bauer's book was published in 1935, republished in 1964, and was only translated into English in 1971.

26. Bart Ehrman, 'Christianity Turned on Its Head: The Alternative Vision of the Gospel of Judas', in R. Kasser, M. Meyer, and G. Wurst (eds.), *The Gospel of Judas from Codex Tchacos* (Washington, DC: National Geographic, 2006), 77–120, at 118.

27. Ehrman, *Lost Christianities*, 174.

28. Kurt and Barbara Aland, *The Text of the New Testament: An Introduction to the Critical Editions and to the Theory and Practice of Modern Textual Criticism*, tr. Erroll Rhodes, 2nd edn. (Grand Rapids, Mich.: Eerdmans, 1995, from the 1981 German edition), 59.

29. Eldon J. Epp, 'The Significance of the Papyri for Determining the Nature of the New Testament Text in the Second Century: A Dynamic View of Textual Transmission', in W. L. Petersen (ed.), *Gospel Traditions in the Second Century: Origins, Recensions, Text, and Transmission*, Christianity and Judaism in Antiquity 3 (Notre Dame and London: University of Notre Dame Press, 1989), 71–103, at 73.

30. Though many scholars doubt the tradition, Eusebius, the early fourth-century church historian, relates that Mark, the disciple of Peter and Paul and putative author of the Gospel of Mark, came very early to Alexandria and founded churches there. See Eusebius, *Ecclesiastical History* (henceforth *EH*) 2.16.1–2.

31. The influence of Christianity on the wider adoption of the codex form has been often recognized, though the recent book by Roger S. Bagnall, *Early Christian Books in Egypt* (Princeton and Oxford: Princeton University Press, 2009), calls for a nuanced reassessment. While

denying that Christianity played the critical role, Bagnall concedes, 'there is no doubt at all that the church routinely and uniformly used the codex for scripture in the period from the end of the second to the beginning of the third century ... a century before society at large seems to have reached even the point of moderately widespread use of the codex, and it highlights the distinctiveness and specificity of Christian practice. It is in this sense that we may still consider that the codex has an association with Christianity' (pp. 88–9).

32. Hurtado, *Earliest Christian Artifacts*, 58.

33. Ibid. 81.

34. *Gospel of Thomas*: codex (P.Oxy. 1); unused roll (P.Oxy. 655); opisthograph (P.Oxy. 654). *Gospel of Mary*: codex (P.Ryl. 463); roll (P. Oxy. 3525). *Gospel of Peter*: codex (P.Oxy. 4009); roll (P.Oxy 2949).

35. Chiefly Eric Turner, *The Typology of the Early Codex* (Philadelphia: University of Pennsylvania Press, 1977). Turner's data has been analysed insightfully by Hurtado, *Earliest Christian Artifacts*.

36. Hurtado, *Earliest Christian Artifacts*, 155.

37. C. H. Roberts, *Manuscript, Society and Belief* (London: Oxford University Press, 1979), 10–11; Gamble, *Books and Readers*, 235–6.

38. D. Lührmann and P. J. Parsons, in R. A. Coles *et al.* (eds.), *Oxyrhynchus Papyri LX* (London: Egypt Exploration Society, 1994), 1.

39. The dimensions of the existing fragment are 8.9 by 9.9 cm, but using C. H. Roberts's calculations about the original length of the column, one may say that the original dimensions of the codex were about 8.9 by 13.4 cm. Hurtado, *Earliest Christian Artifacts*, 163, considers 'compact' codices, the next step up from 'miniatures', to be between about 10–15 cm wide and 15–20 cm high.

40. Harry Y. Gamble, *Books and Readers in the Early Church: A History of Early Christian Texts* (New Haven: Yale University Press, 1995), 231–7, argues that most of the Christian texts which exist in the miniature format are apocryphal works. This, however, was denied by Thomas J. Kraus, at the meeting of the Society of Biblical Literature, November 2007. There are more miniature codices of biblical than of non-biblical texts, just as there are more 'regular'-sized codices of biblical than of non-biblical texts.

41. Even Ehrman has acknowledged that 'most of the early Christian texts do appear to have been produced for public reading, as suggested, for

instance, by their frequent employment of lectional aides: accents, breathing marks, and occasional separation of words': 'The Text as Window: New Testament Manuscripts and the Social History of Early Christianity', in Bart D. Ehrman and Michael W. Holmes (eds.), *The Text of the New Testament in Contemporary Research: Essays on the* Status Quaestionis. *A Volume in Honor of Bruce M. Metzger* (Grand Rapids, Mich.: Eerdmans, 1995), 361–79, at 373. Study of the size of the manuscripts only seems to confirm this observation with regard to the Gospels.

42. This was recently the conclusion of Christoph Markschies in a paper read at the Fifteenth International Conference on Patristic Studies, held in Oxford in August 2007. He refers, for instance, to the *Gospel of Peter* (Akhmim Codex) as expressing 'popular or folksy piety'. Markschies observes that various versions of this view have been held by Franz Lietzmann and Wilhelm Schneemelcher. See Schneemelcher's essay in the General Introduction to Wilhelm Schneemelcher (ed.), *New Testament Apocrypha*, rev. edn., translation ed. R. McL. Wilson, 2 vols. (James Clarke & Co.: Cambridge and Louisville: Westminster/John Knox Press, 1991), i. 50–69.

43. Bauer, *Das Leben Jesu im Zeitalter der neutestamentlichen Apokryphen* (Tübingen, 1909, repr. Darmstadt, 1967), 521; the English translation is cited from Hans-Joseph Klauk, *Apocryphal Gospels: An Introduction*, tr. Brian McNeil (London and New York: T. & T. Clark International, 2003), 232.

Chapter 2

1. G. N. Stanton, 'The Fourfold Gospel', *New Testament Studies*, 43 (1997), 317–46, at 322.

2. e.g. Lee Martin McDonald, *The Biblical Canon: Its Origin, Transmission, and Authority* (Peabody, Mass.: Hendrickson Publishers, 2007), 294.

3. R. W. Funk, 'The Once and Future New Testament,' in Lee Martin McDonald and James A. Sanders (eds.), *The Canon Debate* (Peabody, Mass.: Hendrickson Publishers, 2002), 541–57, at 543.

4. McDonald, *The Biblical Canon*, 291.

5. 'Fanciful' is the word of Lee Martin McDonald and Stanley E. Porter, *Early Christianity and its Sacred Literature* (Peabody, Mass.: Hendrickson Publishers, 2000), 615; 'tortured' is the word of G. M. Hahneman, *The Muratorian Fragment and the Development of the Canon*, Oxford Theological Monographs (Oxford: Oxford University Press, 1992), 101.

6. Eric Osborne, *Irenaeus of Lyons* (Cambridge: Cambridge University Press, 2001), 175.

7. Translation of R. M. Grant, *Irenaeus of Lyons* (London: Routledge, 1997).

8. Osborn, *Irenaeus*, 18–20.

9. Ibid. 177.

10. *AH* 3.1.1, ANF translation, modified.

11. Lee Martin McDonald, 'The Gospels in Early Christianity: Their Origin, Use, and Authority', in Stanley E. Porter (ed.), *Reading the Gospels Today* (Grand Rapids and Cambridge: Eerdmans, 2004), 150–78, at 170.

12. Elaine Pagels, *Beyond Belief: The Secret Gospel of Thomas* (New York: Random House, 2003), 111. Irenaeus 'welded the Gospel of John to the far more widely quoted gospels of Matthew and Luke' (112).

13. Arthur Bellinzoni, 'Luke in the Apostolic Fathers', in A. Gregory and C. Tuckett (eds.), *Trajectories through the New Testament and the Apostolic Fathers* (Oxford: Oxford University Press, 2005), 45–68, at 49, n. 17.

14. Grant, *Irenaeus*, 1, 34, does not think it included Hebrews, but according to Eusebius, Irenaeus cited Hebrews in a lost work. It is likely that Irenaeus did not attribute Hebrews to the apostle Paul, as some others did. We cannot tell if Irenaeus' collection included James or Jude, because he does not quote them. Grant sees an allusion to 2 Peter 3.8 in 5.28.3, but this is doubtful. In addition, some believe that Irenaeus held *The Shepherd* of Hermas to be Scriptural (see 4.20.2), but Grant, *Irenaeus*, 38, probably correctly, thinks this is not the case.

15. Harry Gamble, 'The New Testament Canon: Recent Research and the Status Quaestionis', in *Canon Debate*, 268–94 at 281.

16. McDonald, 'The Gospels in Early Christianity', 172.

17. Pagels, *Beyond Belief*, 112.

18. Ibid. 172.

19. Ibid. 97.

20. Pagels (ibid.) curiously says that Athanasius lists 'virtually all of our present "New Testament"'. Athanasius lists exactly our present New Testament. On the same page Pagels says that in his letter Athanasius

'demanded that Egyptian monks destroy all such writings, except for those he specifically listed as "acceptable," even "canonical"'. In fact, Athanasius recommended a number of books not in the New Testament canon as worthy of reading by Christians.

21. Ibid. 176.

22. The text is preserved in Slavonic. The English translation is that of Reidar Hvalvik, 'Christ Proclaiming his Law to the Apostles: The *Traditio Legis*-Motif in Early Christian Art and Literature', in John Fotopoulos (ed.), *The New Testament and Early Christian Literature in Greco-Roman Context: Studies in Honor of David E. Aune*, NovTSupp 122 (Leiden: Brill, 2006), 430.

23. The editor points out that Origen's phrase is 'Gospels to be received'.

24. Preface, recorded in Eusebius, *EH* 6.25.4.

25. See Charles Lett Feltoe, *St Dionysius of Alexandria, Letters and Treatises* (London and New York: SPCK/Macmillan, 1918), 76–81.

26. G. W. Clarke (translator and annotator), *The Letters of St. Cyprian of Carthage*, 4 vols., Vol. IV, *Letters 67–82*, Ancient Christian Writers 47 (New York and Mahwah: Newman Press, 1989), 59.

27. M. Dulaey, *Victorin de Poetovio. Sur l'apocalypse, suivi du* Fragment chronologique *et de* La construction du monde. *Introduction, Texte critique, traduction, commentaire et index*, Sources Chrétiennes 423 (Paris: Les Éditions du Cerf, 1997), 16.

28. Harry Y. Gamble, *Books and Readers in the Early Church: A History of Early Christian Texts* (New Haven: Yale University Press, 1995), 147, 149, 298, n. 8.

29. See also W. H. C. Frend, *Martyrdom and Persecution in the Early Church: A Study of a Conflict from the Maccabees to Donatus* (Grand Rapids, Mich.: Baker, 1981 repr. of 1965 original), 442.

30. For Greek and Latin texts, and translations, see Herbert Musurillo, *The Acts of the Christian Martyrs*, Oxford Early Christian Texts (Oxford: Oxford University Press, 1972), 310–19.

Chapter 3

1. The name goes back to Adam and Eve's third son, Seth, perceived as a revealer of gnostic truth.

2. April DeConick, *The Thirteenth Apostle: What the Gospel of Judas Really Says* (London and New York: Continuum, 2007), 20.

3. Frank Williams, 'The Gospel of Judas: Its Polemic, its Exegesis, and its Place in Church History', *Vigiliae Christianae*, 62 (2008), 371–403 at 395.

4. Ibid. 398.

5. The charges surface again later in the document, where the sobering reality of the prejudice they created is evident. Under torture and just before she was killed, a Christian woman named Biblis spoke out in defence of her community: 'How would such men eat children, when they are not allowed to eat the blood even of irrational animals' (*EH* 5.1.26). Blandina similarly cried out, 'I am a Christian woman and nothing wicked happens among us' (5.1.19). As he was being burned alive, Attalus addressed the crowd of onlookers: 'Lo, this which you are doing is to eat men, but we neither eat men nor do anything else wicked' (1.5.52).

6. Elaine Pagels, *Beyond Belief: The Secret Gospel of Thomas* (New York: Random House, 2003), 142.

7. Clement of Alexandria actually wanted to retrieve the name from such people, as he thought that 'gnostic' or 'one who knows' rightly belonged to those of the apostolic church who really knew the truth.

8. As Bart D. Ehrman, *Lost Christianities: The Battles for Scripture and the Faiths We Never Knew* (Oxford: Oxford University Press, 2003), 247, puts it: 'If the Marcionite Christians had gained ascendancy, would people still ask, "Do you believe in God?" Or would they ask, "Do you believe in the two Gods?" '

9. Irenaeus, *AH* 1.5.4. See also the use of Isaiah 45.5 in the gnostic *Trimorphic Protennoia*, the *Apocryphon of John*, and *Second Apocalypse of James*.

10. Denis Minns, 'Irenaeus', in Margaret M. Mitchell and Frances M. Young (eds.), *The Cambridge History of Christianity*, Vol. 1, *Origins to Constantine* (Cambridge: Cambridge University Press, 2006), 261–73 at 266.

11. Pagels, *Beyond Belief*, 147–8.

12. Ibid. 142.

13. Peter Lampe, *From Paul to Valentinus: Christians at Rome in the First Two Centuries*, tr. Michael Steinhauser, ed. Marshall D. Johnson (Minneapolis: Fortress Press, 2003), 389, thinks that at this time

Florinus was still in communion with Victor, playing the part of an orthodox Christian but circulating his Valentinian opinions in his writings. Irenaeus' letter to Victor, however, says nothing about expelling Florinus, only his writings, and it is possible that Florinus had already been 'turned out of the presbytery', as Eusebius says (*EH* 5.15).

14. For more on this incident see Lampe, *From Paul to Valentinus*, 389–90; C. E. Hill, *From the Lost Teaching of Polycarp* (Tübingen: Mohr Siebeck, 2006), 12–13.

15. Raymond J. Starr, 'The Circulation of Literary Texts in the Roman World', *Classical Quarterly*, 37 (1987), 213–23, at 219.

16. After reviewing modern analysis of Irenaeus' reliability in describing Valentinianism, Mary Ann Donovan, *One Right Reading? A Guide to Irenaeus* (Collegeville, Minn.: Liturgical Press, 1997), writes: 'If read with attention to his goal and methodology the work of Irenaeus can yield a fair appreciation of the Valentinians. Study of the Nag Hammadi material has not thus far raised substantial challenges to this opinion.'

17. Denis Minns, *Irenaeus* (Washington, DC: Georgetown University Press, 1994 [2007 reprint]), 26–7, says: 'It should not be too readily supposed that he resorts to cheap misrepresentations of his opponents' views in order to score rhetorical victories. When he does present a distorted picture of his opponents' positions this owes much to his own inability or refusal to achieve any kind of sympathetic insight into their religious outlook'.

18. Ehrman, *Lost Christianities*, 198.

19. Ismo Dunderberg, 'The School of Valentinus', in Antti Marjanen and Petri Luomanen (eds.), *A Companion to Second-Century Christian 'Heretics'*, Supplements to *Vigiliae Christianae* 76 (Leiden and Boston: Brill, 2005), 64–99, at 83. See also as representing this view Minns, *Irenaeus*, 12, and in particular Niclas Förster, *Marcus Magus. Kult, Lehre und Gemeindeleben einer valentinianischen Gnostikergruppe* (Tübingen: Mohr Siebeck, 1999), 123–6, 135–7. Two scholars who accept Irenaeus' report are Giovanni Filoramo, *A History of Gnosticism*, tr. Anthony Alcock (Oxford: Basil Blackwell, 1990), 168, 175–6, 181, and Eric Osborne, *Irenaeus of Lyons* (Cambridge: Cambridge University Press, 2001), 240, n. 13, who judges, 'Irenaeus

would not raise harmful rumour for the sake of scoring a point against his opponents'.

20. *The Works of Lucian*, tr. H. W. Fowler and F. G. Fowler, 4 vols. (Oxford: Oxford University Press, 1905).

21. Earlier, in *AH* 1.6.3, Irenaeus had made these charges of immorality when describing the practices of Valentinians without mentioning Marcus or his followers by name. Yet even here he is careful enough to say that these charges only pertain to 'some' of them, likely pointing ahead to his treatment of Marcus. In 1.6.4 he claims to reproduce the very words by which they defend their actions. Two groups Irenaeus does blanket with the accusation of licentious living are the Carpocratians (*AH* 1.25.3–4) and the Nicolaitans (1.26.3). Other groups, Irenaeus says, practiced asceticism.

22. The text seems to signify that the incident took place in Asia. Marcus may or may not have emigrated to Gaul along with some of his followers.

23. I will refrain from naming names at this point, but the scholars know who they are!

24. e.g. Pamela Cooper-White, *The Cry of Tamar: Violence Against Women and the Church's Response* (Minneapolis: Fortress Press, 1995).

Chapter 4

1. Lee Martin McDonald, *The Biblical Canon: Its Origin, Transmission, and Authority* (Peabody, Mass.: Hendrickson Publishers, 2007), 294. See also Lee Martin McDonald, 'The Gospels in Early Christianity: Their Origin, Use, and Authority', in Stanley E. Porter (ed.), *Reading the Gospels Today* (Grand Rapids and Cambridge: Eerdmans, 2004), 150–78.

2. In the preface to *Against Heresies* Irenaeus mentions his residence among the Celts, who used a barbarous dialect; his position as a Christian leader would also have made associations with society's elite in and near Lyons, where there had recently been open persecution of Christians, difficult at best. On Clement's being at home in 'the educated, civilized strata of society which he seeks to win for the gospel', see Henry Chadwick, *Early Christian Thought and the Classical Tradition* (Oxford: Oxford University Press, 1966), 36.

3. 'Liberal use', G. M. Hahneman, *The Muratorian Fragment and the Development of the Canon*, Oxford Theological Monographs (Oxford, 1992), 105, 109; 'frequent reference', Robert M. Price, *The Pre-Nicene New Testament: Fifty-four Formative Texts* (Salt Lake City, Utah: Signature Books, 2006), p. xv.

4. Van den Hoek says six times: Annewies van den Hoek, 'How Alexandrian was Clement of Alexandria? Reflections on Clement and His Alexandrian Background', in *Heythrop Journal*, 31 (1990), 179–94 at 186.

5. McDonald, 'The Gospels in Early Christianity', 172.

6. While it may possibly be different for Clement's use of the *Epistle of Barnabas*, it surely cannot be said that his citations of *1 Clement*, the *Shepherd* of Hermas, Sirach, Tatian's *Against the Greeks*, the *Preaching of Peter*, the *Apocalypse of Peter*, and the *Sibylline Oracles* mean that he placed them on the same level with the four Gospels, as McDonald, 'The Gospels in Early Christianity', 172, infers.

7. Bernard Mutschler, *Irenäus als johanneischer Theologe*, Studien und Texte zu Antike und Christentum 21 (Tübingen: Mohr Siebeck, 2004), 101.

8. Clement cites what he calls the *Gospel of the Hebrews* twice (*Strom.* 2.9.45.5; 5.14. 96.3, naming it so only in the first instance), but what he cites corresponds closely to saying 2 of the *Gospel of Thomas*. The saying may have been contained in both Gospels (so Hans-Josef Klauck, *Apocryphal Gospels: An Introduction*, tr. Brian McNeil (London and New York: T. & T. Clark, 2003), 38). Although we cannot be sure that he had never seen *Thomas*, because Clement cites this saying as from *Gospel of the Hebrews* and never mentions a *Gospel of Thomas*, and because Origen later cites other material from the *Gospel of the Hebrews* which is *not* contained in the *Gospel of Thomas*, we cannot say there is any good evidence that Clement knew the latter.

9. Annewies van den Hoek, 'Clement and Origen as Sources on "Non-canonical" Scriptural Traditions during the Late Second and Earlier Third Centuries', in Gilles Dorival and Alain le Boulluec (eds.), *Origeniana Sexta. Origène et la Bible/Origen and the Bible. Actes du Colloquium Origenianum Sextum Chantilly, 30 aut–3 septembre 1993*, BETL 118 (Leuven: Leuven University Press, 1995), 93–113 at 104.

10. Annewies van den Hoek, 'How Alexandrian was Clement?', 187–8.

11. The word is ἀνωμολογημένοις. The perfect tense implies a settled opinion.

12. The translation of Henry Chadwick in Henry Chadwick and J. E. L. Oulton (eds.), *Alexandrian Christianity: Selected Translations of Clement and Origen* (Lousville and London: Westminster John Knox Press, 1954).

13. If Stephen C. Carlson, 'Clement of Alexandria on the "Order" of the Gospels', *New Testament Studies*, 47 (2001), 118–25, is correct, προγεγράφθαι here means not 'written before' but 'published openly'. This would mean that Matthew and Luke were written for wide public dissemination while Mark was written originally for a private audience in Rome. Carlson is correct, I believe, in surmising that Clement is quoting what an elder of a previous generation, most likely Pantaenus, used to teach.

14. Ronald E. Heine, *Origen: Commentary on the Gospel according to John Books 13–32* (Washington, DC: Catholic University of America Press, 1993), 89. The words are γνήσοιόν, νόθον, and μικτόν.

15. Origen puts such discriminating principles to use when he speaks of the apocryphal work *The Prayer of Joseph* which he says Jews of his day were using. Origen calls it 'apocryphal', but nonetheless finds it to be 'a writing that is worthy of consideration' (*Comm. John* 2.188).

16. Origen, *Commentary on the Song of Songs*, Prologue (Rufinus' translation), from *Origen: The Song of Songs. Commentary and Homilies*, tr. and annotated R. P. Lawson, Ancient Christian Writers 26 (New York and Ramsey: Newman Press, 1956), 56.

17. McDonald, 'The Gospels in Early Christianity', 173.

18. Much of what follows is reworked from Charles E. Hill, 'Serapion of Antioch, the *Gospel of Peter*, and a Four Gospel Canon', *Studia Patristica*, forthcoming 2010.

19. McDonald, 'The Gospels in Early Christianity', 173.

20. Bart Ehrman, *Lost Christianities: The Battles for Scripture and the Faiths We Never Knew* (Oxford: Oxford University Press, 2003), 15, 261, n. 17.

21. Ibid. 27.

22. Ibid. 15.

23. Harry Y. Gamble, 'The New Testament Canon: Recent Research and the Status Quaestionis', in Lee Martin McDonald and James A. Sanders (eds.), *The Canon Debate* (Peabody, Mass.: Hendrickson, 2002), 267–94,

at 280–1; McDonald, 'The Gospels in Early Christianity', 173; Ehrman, *Lost Christianities*, 16.

24. Harry Y. Gamble, *The New Testament Canon: Its Making and Meaning* (Philadelphia, 1985), 35; McDonald, 'The Gospels in Early Christianity', 173.

25. See Peter van Minnen, 'The Akhmim *Gospel of Peter*', in Thomas J. Kraus and Tobias Nicklas (eds.), *Das Evangelium nach Petrus. Text, Kontexte, Intertexte* (Berlin and New York: Walter de Gruyter, 2007), 53–60.

26. Paul Foster, 'Are there any Early Fragments of the So-Called *Gospel of Peter*?', *New Testament Studies*, 52 (2006), 1–28.

27. J. K. Elliott, *The Apocryphal New Testament* (Oxford: Oxford University Press, 1993), 151. See page 150 for a list of features it borrows from each of the four. Bruce M. Metzger, *The Canon of the New Testament* (Oxford: Oxford University Press, 1987), 172, also says the author 'shows acquaintance with all four canonical Gospels'. One attempt to argue otherwise is that of J. D. Crossan, *Four Other Gospels* (Minneapolis: Winston Press, 1985); id., *The Cross that Spoke* (San Francisco: Harper & Row, 1988).

28. Ehrman, *Lost Christianities*, 18, writes: 'This fragmentary Gospel is far more virulently anti-Jewish than any of those that made it into the New Testament'; see also Elliott, *Apocryphal New Testament*, 151.

29. See Wilhelm Schneemelcher, 'The Gospel of Peter: Introduction', in *New Testament Apocrypha*, rev. edn., 2 vols., tr. Robert McLachlan Wilson (Cambridge: James Clarke & Co., 1991), i. 216–22 at 220.

30. Joseph Verheyden, 'Some Reflections on Determining the Purpose of the "Gospel of Peter"', in *Das Evangelium nach Petrus*, 281–99 at 298–9. He quotes approvingly Kathleen Corley's assessment, 'the Gospel of Peter should be considered a late novelistic account of the crucifixion and the empty tomb' (K. E. Corley, 'Women and the Crucifixion and Burial of Jesus', *Forum*, 1 NS (1998), 181–225 at 211).

31. Elliott, *Apocryphal New Testament*, 150: 'In many ways the Gospel of Peter can be compared with P. Egerton 2 . . . Both betray early knowledge of the canonical Gospels but with differences that may be due to the influence of oral traditions.'

32. Reidar Aasgaard, *The Childhood of Jesus: Decoding the Apocryphal Infancy Gospel of Thomas* (Eugene, Oreg.: Cascade Books, 2009).

33. Ehrman, *Lost Christianities*, 261, n. 17.
34. Translation from R. M. Grant, *Theophilus of Antioch: Ad Autolycum* (Oxford: Oxford University Press, 1970).
35. This is recognized by G. Downey, *A History of Antioch in Syria from Seleucus to the Arab Conquest* (Princeton: Princeton University Press, 1961), 302.
36. Grant concludes, 'Theophilus seems to know Matthew, John, and Luke, though he prefers the apostolic gospels of Matthew and John' (R. M. Grant, 'The Bible of Theophilus of Antioch', *Journal of Biblical Literature*, 66 (1947), 173–96 at 185). After forty more years of scholarship, Grant repeated this same conclusion in *Greek Apologists of the Second Century* (Philadelphia: The Westminster Press, 1988), 163. The proposal that Theophilus, as late as the 170s, might have been using (hypothetical) earlier sources of the Gospels and not the Gospels themselves seems like special pleading.
37. Epistle 121.6.15, *To Algasius*, cited from William L. Petersen, *Tatian's Diatessaron: Its Creation, Dissemination, Significance, and History in Scholarship* (Leiden, New York, and Cologne: Brill, 1994), 32, who also gives the Latin.
38. Grant, *Irenaeus of Lyons*, 34; id., *Greek Apologists*, 164.
39. McDonald, 'The Gospels in Early Christianity', 173.
40. Any who wish to delve deep into the scholarly saga of the ever-changing Alogi, may consult C. E. Hill, *The Johannine Corpus in the Early Church* (Oxford: Oxford University Press, 2004), 172–204.
41. The translation is that of Bruce Metzger, *The Canon of the New Testament* (Oxford: Oxford University Press, 1987), 305–6, who provides clarifying expansions in square brackets. The numbers in parentheses are the line numbers of the manuscript.
42. The word can also mean 'recognize', as in: recognize its authority.
43. Ehrman, *Lost Christianities*, 241: 'It is fairly clear that it began by mentioning Matthew and Mark.'
44. A. C. Sundberg, 'Towards a Revised History of the New Testament Canon', *Studia Evangelica*, 4/1 (1968), 452–61; id., 'Canon Muratori: A Fourth-Century List', *Harvard Theological Review*, 66 (1973), 1–41; Hahneman, *Muratorian Fragment*; most recently in 'The Muratorian Fragment and the Origins of the New Testament Canon', *Canon Debate*, 405–15.

45. See the reviews of E. Ferguson, 'Canon Muratori: Date and Provenance', *Studia Patristica*, 17. 2 (Oxford, 1982), 677–83; idem, 'Review of Geoffrey Mark Hahneman, *The Muratorian Fragment and the Development of the Canon*', *Journal of Theological Studies*, NS 44 (1993), 696; and in particular, Joseph Verheyden, 'The Canon Muratori: A Matter of Dispute', in J.-M. Auwers and H. J. de Jonge (eds.), *The Biblical Canons* (Leuven: Leuven University Press, 2003), 488–556.

46. Visible in the *Apology* of Quadratus (Eusebius, *EH* 4.3.2); Hegesippus (*EH* 4.22.9); Irenaeus (*AH* 5.30.3), all from the second century; and in the work of an anonymous writer from the early third century (*EH* 5.28.8). For more on these arguments see Hill, *JCEC* 129–34.

47. Verheyden, 'The Canon Muratori', 504.

48. Ibid. 556.

Chapter 5

1. I have chosen to relegate to a long endnote the controversy surrounding a report by Victor of Capua, who discovered in the sixth century a Latin translation of Tatian's work and had a beautiful and expensive copy of it made. Writing in a preface to this copy, now called the Codex Fuldensis, Victor reports that Tatian gave his composition the name *Diapente* '(one) through five'. This has sent scholars on a heroic search to find what Tatian's mysterious 'fifth source' might have been. But no other Gospel has ever been discovered which can supply a consistent source for any of the peculiarities of the *Diatessaron*. The search appears to be a wild-goose chase. 'Diapente' probably represents either an innocent mental slip—both Diapente and Diatessaron were common terms for the musical intervals we today call 'a fifth' and 'a fourth'—or simply a mistake in copying by Victor or his scribe. I say this for three reasons. First, other early sources, like Theodoret, writing seventy or more years earlier, call Tatian's work *Diatessaron*, while *no one else* calls it *Diapente*. Second, Victor is not making an independent claim about what Tatian called his work but rather reporting that Eusebius in his *Ecclesiastical History* said that Tatian called his work *Diapente*. But every existing manuscript of Eusebius' *History*, even the Syriac and Latin translations, says *Diatessaron* not *Diapente*! If, perchance, Victor thought he was correcting Eusebius,

he must have understood the word *Diapente* as meaning something like, 'one new Gospel out of four, that is, a fifth'. For, third, and most conclusively, it is clear that Victor himself, who had the manuscript before him and had studied it very carefully, believed it was composed from four Gospels, not five. Ignored by most critics is the fact that in the very place where Victor uses the word *Diapente*, he himself describes the work as 'one composite gospel out of the four', and repeats this description three more times. Even when reporting what Eusebius wrote in his *History*, he says: 'It became clear to me also from his [Eusebius'] *History* that Tatian . . . combined one gospel out of the four, for which he composed the title "Diapente".' After a close examination of the manuscript, Victor speaks of the way Tatian arranged the Gospel materials, saying that, 'for the most part he joined the words of the remaining three to the gospel of Saint Matthew'. Again, it is the 'remaining three' which are joined to Matthew, not the remaining four. All the relevant data (but not this explanation) can be found in William L. Petersen, *Tatian's Diatessaron: Its Creation, Dissemination, Significance, and History in Scholarship* (Leiden, New York, and Cologne: Brill, 1994).

2. Bruce M. Metzger, *The Canon of the New Testament: Its Origin, Development, and Significance* (Oxford: Oxford University Press, 1987), 115.

3. Lee Martin McDonald, 'The Gospels in Early Christianity: Their Origin, Use, and Authority', in Stanley E. Porter (ed.), *Reading the Gospels Today* (Grand Rapids and Cambridge: Eerdmans, 2004), 150–78 at 175.

4. Namely, Helmut Koester, *Ancient Christian Gospels: Their History and Development* (Philadelphia and London: Trinity Press International/SCM Press, 1990), 365–402.

5. McDonald, 'The Gospels in Early Christianity', 174, n. 57.

6. The 'foreign' elements are so minor that H. J. W. Drijvers thinks it 'extremely unlikely that Tatian made use of extracanonical material or even of an apocryphal gospel in composing his Diatessaron' (H. J. W. Drijvers, 'Facts and Problems in Early Syriac-Speaking Christianity', *The Second Century*, 2 (1982), 173, n. 64). See also Metzger, *Canon*, 115–16.

7. Harry Y. Gamble, 'The New Testament Canon: Recent Research and the Status Quaestionis', in Lee Martin McDonald and James A. Sander (eds.), *The Canon Debate* (Peabody, Mass.: Hendrickson, 2002), 267–94, at 280.

8. Petersen, 'Fourfold Gospel,' 67.

9. Ibid.

10. Ibid. 68.

11. An example is the document known as 4Q175 (the notation '4Q' means the work was discovered in cave number four at Qumran).

12. Petersen, 'Fourfold Gospel', 54.

13. See C. E. Hill, *The Johannine Corpus in the Early Church* (Oxford: Oxford University Press, 2004), 79.

14. Loraine Boettner, *A Harmony of the Gospels* (Phillipsburg, NJ: Presbyterian and Reformed Publishing Co., 1979).

15. That this is a fragment from Tatian's *Diatessaron* has been challenged, but recently reaffirmed by Jan Joosten, 'The Dura Parchment and the Diatessaron', *Vigiliae Christianae*, 57 (2003), 159–75. It is not, however, impossible that this Greek fragment represents the Harmony of Theophilus instead.

16. The translation is taken from Bruce Metzger, *The Early Versions of the New Testament: Their Origin, Transmission, and Limitations* (Oxford: Oxford University Press, 1977), 11. I have eliminated the bracketed parts of Metzger's translation, which indicated elements reconstructed from the damaged manuscript, and have changed the Roman numerals to Arabic.

17. C. H. Roberts, 'Books in the Graeco-Roman World and in the New Testament', in P. R. Ackroyd and C. F. Evans (eds.), *The Cambridge History of the Bible*, Vol. 1, *From the Beginnings to Jerome* (Cambridge: Cambridge University Press, 1970), 48–66, at 56.

18. Ibid. 57.

19. Translation of Harold H. Oliver, 'The Epistle of Eusebius to Carpianus: Textual Tradition and Translation', *Novum Testamentum*, 3 (1959), 138–45 at 144. See also Petersen, *Tatian's Diatessaron*, 33.

20. J. K. Elliott, 'Manuscripts, the Codex and the Canon', *Journal for the Study of the New Testament*, 63 (1996), 105–23, at 107.

21. D. C. Parker, *An Introduction to the New Testament Manuscripts and their Texts* (Cambridge: Cambridge University Press, 2008), 316–17.

22. Elliott, 'Manuscripts, the Codex and the Canon', 107.

23. Frederick G. Kenyon, *The Chester Beatty Biblical Papyri: Descriptions and Texts of Twelve Manuscripts on Papyrus of the Greek Bible*, 3 fascicles, fascicle I, *General Introduction* (London: Oxford University Press, 1933), 13.

24. P. W. Comfort and D. P. Barrett, *The Text of the Earliest New Testament Greek Manuscripts: A Corrected, Enlarged Edition of* The Complete Text of the Earliest New Testament Manuscripts (Wheaton: Tyndale House Publishers, Inc., 2001), 504.

25. T. C. Skeat, 'The Origin of the Christian Codex', *Zeitschrift für Papyrologie und Epigraphik*, 102 (1994), 263–8.

26. C. H. Roberts, *Manuscript, Society and Belief* (London: Oxford University Press, 1979), 12–13.

27. T. C. Skeat, 'The Oldest Manuscript of the Four Gospels?', *New Testament Studies*, 43 (1997), 1–34 at 31–2.

28. Notably Joseph van Haelst, *Catalogue des papyrus littéraires juifs et chrétiens*, Série papyrologie 1 (Paris: Sorbonne, 1976), no. 403.

29. P. M. Head, 'Is P4, P64 and P67 the Oldest Manuscript of the Four Gospels? A Response to T. C. Skeat', *New Testament Studies*, 51 (2005), 450–7; S. D. Charlesworth, 'T. C. Skeat, P64 + 67 and P4, and the Problem of Fibre Orientation in Codicological Reconstruction', *New Testament Studies*, 53 (2007), 582–604.

30. C. H. Roberts, *Manuscript, Society and Belief*, 13, said it is 'a thorough-going literary production'; Skeat, 'The Oldest Manuscript', 26, called it an '*édition de luxe*'; G. N. Stanton, 'The Fourfold Gospel', *New Testament Studies*, 43 (1997), 317–46 at 328, says it was a 'high-class codex, a splendid "pulpit edition" intended for liturgical use'; cf. G. N. Stanton, 'The Early Reception of Matthew's Gospel', in David E. Aune (ed.), *The Gospel of Matthew in Current Study: Studies in Memory of William G. Thompson, S.J.* (Grand Rapids and Cambridge: Eerdmans, 2001), 42–61 at 49.

31. Stanton, 'Fourfold Gospel', 328.

32. Victor Martin and Rodolphe Kasser, *Papyrus Bodmer XIV–XV: Evangiles de Luc et Jean*, Vol. 1, *Papyrus Bodmer XIV: Evangile de Luc chap. 3–24* (Cologny-Geneva: Bibliotheca Bodmeriana, 1961), 13.

Chapter 6

1. Helmut Koester, *Ancient Christian Gospels: Their History and Development* (Philadelphia and London: Trinity Press International/SCM Press, 1990), 377, 402.

2. C. H. Cosgrove, 'Justin Martyr and the Emerging Christian Canon: Observations on the Purpose and Destination of the Dialogue with Trypho', *Vigiliae Christianae*, 36 (1982), 209–32, at 226.

3. Oskar Skarsaune, 'Justin and His Bible', in Sara Parvis and Paul Foster (eds.), *Justin Martyr and His Worlds* (Minneapolis: Fortress Press, 2007), 53–76.

4. M. Hengel, 'Four Gospels and the One Gospel of Jesus Christ', in Charles Horton (ed.), *The Earliest Gospels: The Origins and Transmission of the Earliest Christian Gospels—The Contribution of the Chester Beatty Gospel Codex P[45]* (London and New York: T. & T. Clark International, 2004), 13–26, at 14. For others, see C. E. Hill, *The Johannine Corpus in the Early Church* (Oxford: Oxford University Press, 2004), 338.

5. G. N. Stanton, 'The Fourfold Gospel', *New Testament Studies*, 43 (1997), 317–46, at 330–1. Another who thinks that a fourfold Gospel was established in Rome by mid-century is Francis Watson, 'The Fourfold Gospel', in Stephen Barton (ed.), *The Cambridge Companion to the Gospels* (Cambridge: Cambridge University Press, 2006), 34–52, at 40.

6. Some scholars seem to prefer the theory that what Justin was citing here was not Mark but a (hypothetical) earlier source which Mark used in writing his Gospel. While we may not ignore the possibility that Mark used one or more written sources, this theory looks desperately implausible. Whatever 'Memoir' Justin was using was, like Mark, known as a Gospel (for Justin indicates that the Memoirs were known as Gospels); like Mark, it was a Gospel which had a special connection to Peter; like Mark, it mentioned Jesus' renaming of Peter; like Mark, it told of Jesus' renaming the sons of Zebedee as 'sons of thunder' and even used the transliterated Aramaic term 'Boanerges' in doing so. The theory would require not only that such a Gospel-of-Mark lookalike once existed but that it survived as an independently known Gospel until at least the mid-second century and was at that time closely identified in Rome with the Gospels of Matthew and Luke (also John, as we'll see). It seems that the only reason for advancing such a theory would be to avoid the conclusion that Justin was using Mark's Gospel.

7. For example, Arthur J. Bellinzoni, *The Sayings of Jesus in the Writings of Justin Martyr* (Leiden: E. J. Brill, 1967), 136–7; Koester, *Ancient Christian Gospels*, 361.

8. For more on this, see Hill, 'Was John's Gospel among Justin's *Apostolic Memoirs?*', in Sara Parvis and Paul Foster (eds.), *Justin Martyr and His Worlds* (Minneapolis: Fortress Press, 2007), 88–9; id. *JCEC* 320–5.

9. C. T. Lewis and C. Short, *A Latin Dictionary* (Oxford: Oxford University Press, 2002 (1879 original), '*ago*' II.C.12.c.II.2.B.

10. See Hill, 'Was John's Gospel among Justin's *Apostolic Memoirs?*', 90–1.

11. This is perhaps why Everett Ferguson speaks of a 'curious scholarly blindness' which professes 'to find no evidence that Justin knew the Fourth Gospel' (Everett Ferguson, 'Factors Leading to the Selection and Closure of the New Testament Canon: A Survey of Some Recent Studies', in Lee Martin McDonald and James A. Sanders (eds.), *The Canon Debate* (Peabody, Mass.: Hendrickson Publishers, 2002), 295–320 at 302).

12. Hengel states that the use of any apocryphal Gospel in Justin's works 'cannot be demonstrated convincingly' (Martin Hengel, *The Four Gospels and the One Gospel of Jesus Christ: An Investigation of the Collection and Origin of the Canonical Gospels* (Harrisburg, Pa.: Trinity Press International, 2000), 20); Stanton likewise thinks, 'there is no clear evidence for Justin's knowledge of any gospels other than the canonical four' (Stanton, 'Fourfold Gospel', 330–1).

13. Koester, *Ancient Christian Gospels*, 386.

14. Skarsaune, 'Justin and his Bible', 184, n. 63. Skarsaune cites for this view also P. Henne and D. Vigne.

15. Paul Foster, 'The Relationship between the Writings of Justin Martyr and the So-called *Gospel of Peter*', *Justin Martyr and His Worlds*, 104–12 at 112.

16. Tjitze Baarda, 'Διαφωνία—Συμφωνία, Factors in the Harmonization of the Gospels Especially in the Diatessaron of Tatian', *Essays on the Diatessaron* (Kampen: Kok Pharos, 1994), 29–47, at 35. Andrew Gregory, 'Jewish Christian Gospels', in Paul Foster (ed.), *The Non-canonical Gospels* (London: T. & T. Clark, 2008), 54–67, at 61, says Epiphanius' excerpts of the *Gospel of the Ebionites* 'appear to contain material that depends on at least Matthew and Luke' and 'the presence of material that comes from Luke strongly suggests that this gospel may be better thought of as a gospel harmony rather than as a version of Matthew' (p. 62).

17. For example, Bart Ehrman, *Lost Christianities: The Battles for Scripture and the Faiths We Never Knew* (Oxford: Oxford University Press, 2003), 141–2; 175, 238.

18. It is probably to this very notice that Eusebius had reference when he said elsewhere that he knew that Clement's letter had been read publicly in churches. The fact that *1 Clement* and *2 Clement* are appended to the great fifth-century codex Alexandrinus is often cited as proof of their Scriptural status in some churches. Sinaiticus, a great fourth-century Biblical codex, contains *Barnabas* and *The Shepherd* at the end of the New Testament instead of *1* and *2 Clement*. All four books belong to a loose category which Eusebius, Athanasius, and others considered 'catechetical' or 'recommended' and not 'canonical'. They are probably best considered as appendices to the New Testament.

19. Mary Ann Donovan, *One Right Reading? A Guide to Irenaeus* (Collegeville, Minn.: Liturgical Press, 1997), 14.

20. Skarsaune, 'Justin and His Bible', 54.

Chapter 7

1. Justin was no doubt aware of the martyrdom of Polycarp which had recently taken place in Smyrna. The ancient account of Justin's trial before the prefect Q. Junius Rusticus may be read in Herbert Musurillo, *The Acts of the Christian Martyrs*, Oxford Early Christian Texts (Oxford: Oxford University Press, 1972), 43–7 (Recension A).

2. Robert Grant, *Greek Apologists of the Second Century* (Philadelphia: Westminster Press, 1988), 138.

3. Including Martin Hengel, *Die johanneische Frage. Ein Lösungsversuch*, with a contribution on the Apocalypse by Jörg Frey, WUNT 67 (Tübingen: Mohr Siebeck, 1993), 28, n. 48.

4. See the translation of H. Chadwick, *Origen: Contra Celsum* (Cambridge: Cambridge University Press, 1965), 'some believers . . . alter the original text of the gospel three or four or several times over, and they change its character to enable them to deny difficulties in face of criticism'.

5. Bentley Layton, *The Gnostic Scriptures: A New Translation with Annotations and Introductions* (New York: Doubleday, 1987), 250.

6. Harold W. Attridge, 'The Gospel of Truth as an Exoteric Text', in C. W. Hedrick and R. Hodgson, jun. (eds.), *Nag Hammadi, Gnosticism, and Early Christianity* (Peabody, Mass.: Hendrickson, 1986), 229–55, at 239–40.

7. The seminal study is W. C. van Unnik, 'The "Gospel of Truth" and the New Testament', in F. L. Cross (ed.), *The Jung Codex* (London: A. R. Mowbray, 1955), 79–129. Writing thirty years later, Attridge, 'Exoteric', 242, agrees. He finds evidence of the author's knowledge of Matt. 5.48 at *Gospel of Truth* 1.3.27, 24–5; Matt. 11.25 at 19.25; Mark 14.24 at 20.15–16; Luke 2.46–9 at 19.19–20; John 3.19 at 3.24–5; John 10.3–4 at 21.33–4, 22.21–2; John 11.37 at 30.15–16. It also seems to know some letters of Paul, Hebrews, 1 John, and Revelation.

8. See Jacquelin A. Williams, *Biblical Interpretation in the Gnostic Gospel of Truth from Nag Hammadi*, SBL Dissertation Series 79 (Atlanta, Ga.: Scholars Press, 1988), 177–8.

9. Frank Williams, 'The Gospel of Judas: Its Polemic, its Exegesis, and its Place in Church History', *Vigiliae Christianae*, 62 (2008), 371–403 at 373–4.

10. Ibid. 375.

11. Williams (ibid. 387–8) shows that while the author accepted some things in the Gospels as true, he or she implies 'that the violent events in Gethsemane and Judas' embarrassing kiss of Jesus, never took place' because the disciples 'hid themselves' and 'are disqualified as witnesses for any events that may have followed the supper'.

12. Pheme Perkins, *Gnosticism and the New Testament* (Minneapolis: Fortress Press, 1993), 183.

13. Ibid. 185.

Chapter 8

1. Four of these are fragments of John: P^{119} (P.Oxy. 4803, 3rd cent.), P^{120} (P.Oxy. 4804, 4th cent.), P^{121} (P.Oxy. 4805, 3rd cent.), P^{122} (P.Oxy. 4806, 4th/5th cent.), published in R. Hatzilambrou, P. J. Parsons, and J. Chapa, *The Oxyrhynchus Papyri LXXI* (London: Egypt Exploration Society, 2007). One fragment each from 1 Corinthians (P^{123} (P.Oxy. 4844, 4th cent.)) and 2 Corinthians (P^{124} (P.Oxy. 4845, 6th cent.)) have

also been published in *The Oxyrhynchus Papyri LXXII* (London: Egypt Exploration Society, 2008).

2. e.g. Martin Hengel, *The Johannine Question* (London and Philadelphia: SCM Press, 1989); id., *Die johanneische Frage. Ein Lösungsversuch*, with a contribution on the Apocalypse by Jörg Frey, WUNT 67 (Tübingen: Mohr Siebeck, 1993); Titus Nagel, *Die Rezeption des Johannesevangeliums im 2. Jahrhundert. Studien zur vorirenäischen Auslegung des vierten Evangeliums in christlicher und christlich-gnostischer Literatur*, Arbeiten zur Bibel und ihrer Geschichte 2 (Leipzig: Evangelische Verlagsanstalt, 2000); C. E. Hill, *The Johannine Corpus in the Early Church* (Oxford: Oxford University Press, 2004).

3. Wolfgang G. Röhl, *Die Rezeption des Johannesevangeliums in christlich-gnostischen Schriften aus Nag Hammadi*, Europäische Hochschulschriften. Publications Universitaires Européennes, Series XXIII. Theologie, 428 (Frankfurt am Main, Bern, New York, and Paris: Peter Lang, 1991), and in particular, Hill, *JCEC*.

4. For its use of John, see Hill, *JCEC*, 250–8.

5. The translation of F. E. Williams, 'The Apocryphon of James: I, 2:1.1–16.30' in H. W. Attridge (ed.), *Nag Hammadi Codex I (The Jung Codex): Introductions, Texts, Translations, Indices*, Nag Hammadi Studies 22 (Leiden: Brill, 1985), 13–53.

6. *Commentary on John*, 10 (301–302). Translation from Ronald E. Heine (tr.), *Origen: Commentary on the Gospel according to John Books 1–10*, The Fathers of the Church 80 (Washington, DC: Catholic University of America Press, 1989).

7. Except possibly in the one it mentions as written previously by James. Most scholars regard this too as fictitious.

8. Helmut Koester, *Ancient Christian Gospels: Their History and Development* (Philadelphia and London: Trinity Press International/SCM Press, 1990), 196–7. While he indicates some doubt about some of these identifications, he says, 'In any case, reference seems to be made to parables of all three Synoptic Gospels' (p. 197). Christopher Tuckett, *Nag Hammadi and the Gospel Tradition: Synoptic Tradition in the Nag Hammadi Library* (Edinburgh: T. & T. Clark, 1986), 97, believes the *ApocJas* presupposes Matthew's and Luke's finished Gospels and possibly Mark's.

9. Pheme Perkins, *Gnosticism and the New Testament* (Minneapolis: Fortress Press, 1993), 72, '*Apocryphon of James* intends to invoke the authority of

the canonical Gospels to bolster the esoteric, gnostic teaching presented in the treatise'.

10. Paraphrased from Hill, *JCEC* 258.

11. Perkins, *Gnosticism and the New Testament*, 191.

12. Philip Vielhauer, *Geschichte der urchristlichen Literatur* (Berlin: Walter De Gruyter, 1975), 687, says the *EpApost* is 'an attempt to combat the gnostic opponents with their own weapons'.

13. On this last point see now Darrell D. Hannah, 'The Four-Gospel "Canon" in the *Epistula Apostolorum*', *Journal of Theological Studies*, NS 59 (2008), 598–632.

14. In Irenaeus the Old Testament passages Isaiah 11.2 f. and Psalm 24.7 are used, and perhaps 1 Cor. 2.8 standing behind it all.

15. Ronald F. Hock, *The Infancy Gospels of James and Thomas* (Santa Rosa, Calif.: Polebridge Press, 1995), 90, 92; Hans-Josef Klauck, *Apocryphal Gospels: An Introduction* (London and New York: T. & T. Clark, 2003), 73. For a recent, short treatment see Tony Chartrand-Burke, 'The *Infancy Gospel of Thomas*', in Paul Foster (ed.), *The Non-Canonical Gospels* (London: T. & T. Clark, 2008), 126–38, who decides on the originality of one of the shorter recensions of the book. This original was clearly dependent upon the canonical Gospel of Luke and Acts.

16. Reidar Aasgaard, *The Childhood of Jesus: Decoding the Apocryphal Infancy Gospel of Thomas* (Eugene, Oreg.: Cascade Books, 2009), 168.

17. Ibid. 203.

18. Ibid. 176, who also cites Chartrand-Burke's 2001 University of Toronto Ph.D dissertation for this view. Hannah, 'The Four-Gospel "Canon"', 627, supposes that the author has domesticated a gnostic legend, but is not confident that it came from a written source.

19. See C. E. Hill, 'The *Epistula Apostolorum*: An Asian Tract from the Time of Polycarp', *Journal of Early Christian Studies*, 7 (1999), 1–53.

20. Hannah, 'The Four-Gospel "Canon"', also decides for a time prior to 150.

21. John Barton, 'Marcion Revisited', in Lee Martin McDonald and James A. Sanders (eds.), *The Canon Debate* (Peabody, Mass: Hendrickson Publishers, 2002), 341–54, at 342–3.

22. See Hill, *JCEC* 396–402.

23. The Syriac translation, made in the fourth or fifth century, has it addressed to Hadrian's successor Antoninus Pius (138–61). But

fragments of a fifth-century Armenian translation of the work have been discovered and they agree with Eusebius.

24. The author who incorporated Aristides' apology into *Barlaam* transferred this section to a later part of his dialogue (ch. 15). The Syriac and Armenian have the original placement. The translation is that of D. M. Kay in ANF 10.

25. See Justin, *Dial.* 10.2; 100.1; *2 Clement* 8.5; Theophilus, *To Autolycus* 3.12; Irenaeus, *AH* 1.7.4; 3.5.1; 3.11.7; 4.34.1.

Chapter 9

1. Bart D. Ehrman (ed. and tr.), *The Apostolic Fathers: I Clement, II Clement, Ignatius, Polycarp, Didache* (Cambridge, Mass. and London: Harvard University Press, 2003); Michael W. Holmes (ed. and tr.), *The Apostolic Fathers: Greek Texts and English Translations*, 3rd edn. (Grand Rapids, Mich.: Baker Academic, 2007). Both collections include *The Martyrdom of Polycarp* even though, while Polycarp is a rightful Apostolic Father, strictly speaking, the author of the *Martyrdom* is not. A recent and readable introduction to these writers is Paul Foster (ed.), *The Writings of the Apostolic Fathers* (London: T. & T. Clark, 2007).

2. A Committee of the Oxford Society of Historical Theology, *The New Testament in the Apostolic Fathers* (Oxford: Oxford University Press, 1905).

3. Andrew Gregory and Christopher Tuckett (eds.), *The New Testament and the Apostolic Fathers*, 2 vols.: Vol. 1, *The Reception of the New Testament in the Apostolic Fathers* (Oxford: Oxford University Press, 2005); Vol. 2, *Trajectories Through the New Testament and the Apostolic Fathers* (Oxford: Oxford University Press, 2005) [henceforth *RNTAF* and *TNTAF*].

4. Andrew F. Gregory, '*1 Clement* and the Writings that Later Formed the New Testament', *RNTAF* 129–57, at 157.

5. Helmut, Köster, *Synoptische Überlieferung bei den Apostolischen Vätern*, Texte und Untersuchungen 65 (Berlin: Akademie Verlag, 1957).

6. Like the hypothetical source nicknamed 'Q' from the German word *Quelle*, meaning simply 'source', which many believe was used by Matthew and Luke.

7. John Barton, *Holy Writings, Sacred Text: The Canon in Early Christianity* (Louisville, Ky.: Westminster John Knox Press, 1997), 92.

8. e.g., John Whittaker, 'The Value of Indirect Tradition in the Establishment of Greek Philosophical Texts, or the Art of Misquotation', in John N. Grant (ed.), *Editing Greek and Latin Texts: Papers Given at the Twenty-Third Annual Conference on Editorial Problems, University of Toronto 6–7 November 1987* (New York: AMS Press, 1989), 63–95; Sabrina Inowlocki, *Eusebius and the Jewish Authors: His Citation Technique in an Apologetic Context* (Leiden and Boston: Brill, 2006).

9. For what follows see Charles E. Hill, *From the Lost Teaching of Polycarp*, WUNT 186 (Tübingen: Mohr Siebeck, 2006). For some reason, *Diognetus* was not included in *RNTAF*.

10. See Per Franco Beatrice, 'Der Presbyter des Irenäus, Polykarp von Smyrna und der Brief an Diognet', in Eugenio Romero-Pose (ed.), *Pléroma Salus Carnis. Homenaje a Antonio Orbe, S. J.* (Santiago de Compostella, 1990), 179–202; Hill, *Lost Teaching*, 128–65.

11. See Hill, *Lost Teaching*, 106–27.

12. e.g. compare 7.5 and 10.2 to John 3.16–17. See C. E. Hill, *The Johannine Corpus in the Early Church* (Oxford: Oxford University Press, 2004), 361–6.

13. Cf. Matt. 5.44 in 6.6; Matt. 6.25–31 in 9.6; Matt. 3.17 in 11.5.

14. James Carleton-Paget, 'The *Epistle of Barnabas* and the Writings that Later Formed the New Testament', *RNTAF* 229–49, at 229.

15. Ibid. 249. He also notes: 'As Köhler implies . . . it is very difficult to demonstrate that *Barnabas* did not know the gospels. After all, if we admit that the author aims to make his subject Old Testament promise and Christian fulfillment, then the need to cite from NT texts is, as noted, diminished' (p. 239).

16. Ibid. 233.

17. See Chapter 10.

18. See *AH* 3.3.4 and his letters to Florinus and to Victor (excerpted in Eusebius, *EH* 5.20.6; 5.24.16). See also *AH* 4.27.1 and Hill, *Lost Teaching*, 37–40; 80–1; 171–7.

19. Helmut Koester, *Introduction to the New Testament*, Vol. 2, *History and Literature of Early Christianity* (Berlin and New York: Walter de Gruyter, 1982), 306.

20. Michael W. Holmes, 'Polycarp's *Letter to the Philippians* and the Writings that Later Formed the New Testament', *RNTAF* 187–227, at 197; cf. 194.

21. Ibid. 188, 194, 196.

22. J. N. Sanders, *A Commentary on the Gospel According to St. John*, ed. and completed by B. A. Mastin (New York, 1968), 35; Robert M. Grant, *Irenaeus of Lyons* (London and New York: Routledge, 1997), 37; Hill, *JCEC* 416–20.

23. Some of the Greek manuscripts of the letter say 'you' instead of 'us', but both Ehrman and Holmes decide for the originality of 'us'.

24. There is a long history of debate about both the genuineness of his letters and their date. Most scholars accept the so-called 'middle recension' of his letters (as I do, with Holmes and Ehrman) as genuine. I accept Eusebius' date of 107–8. Others argue for a somewhat later date.

25. R. M. Grant, 'Scripture and Tradition in St. Ignatius of Antioch', *Catholic Biblical Quarterly*, 25 (1963), 322–35, at 327.

26. Paul Foster, 'The Epistles of Ignatius of Antioch and the Writings That Later Formed the New Testament' *RNTAF* 159–86. In response to Foster's scepticism about John's Gospel, see Charles E. Hill, ' "The Orthodox Gospel". The Reception of John in the Great Church Prior to Irenaeus', in Tuomas Rasimus, *The Legacy of John* (Leiden: Brill, 2009).

27. C. E. Hill, 'Ignatius and the Apostolate: The Witness of Ignatius to the Emergence of Christian Scripture', in M. F. Wiles and E. J. Yarnold (eds.), *Studia Patristica* 36 (Leuven: Peeters, 2001), 226–48, at 234.

28. See C. E. Hill, 'Ignatius, "the Gospels" and the Gospel', *TNTAF* 267–85.

29. In *Magnesians* 13.1 he also tells his readers to 'be confirmed in the decrees of the Lord and of the apostles', where 'decrees of the Lord' seem to stand in the place of 'the gospel'. *Didache* 11.3–4 apparently refers to Jesus' instructions in Matt. 10.40–1 as 'decrees of the gospel'. See J. A. Kelhoffer, ' "How Soon a Book" Revisited: $EYAΓΓEΛION$ as a Reference to "Gospel" Materials in the First Half of the Second Century', *ZNW* 95 (2004), 1–34.

30. Graham N. Stanton, 'Matthew: $BIBΛOΣ$, $EYAΓΓEΛION$, or $BIOΣ$?' in *The Four Gospels 1992: Festschrift Frans Neirynck*, BETL 2 (Leuven: Peeters, 1992), 1187–1201, at 1192.

31. See in particular, H. van de Sandt (ed.), *Matthew and the Didache: Two Documents from the Same Jewish-Christian Milieu?* (Assen: Royal Van Gorcum; Minneapolis: Fortress Press, 2005). The relevant bibliography can be found in Holmes, *Apostolic Fathers*, or Christopher M. Tuckett, 'The *Didache* and the Writings that Later Formed the New Testament', *RNTAF* 83–127.

32. Tuckett, '*Didache*', 127.

33. Ehrman, *Apostolic Fathers*, i. 25.

34. Gregory, '*1 Clement*', 131. Speaking of the string of teachings attributed to Jesus in 1 *Clem.* 13, Gregory says, 'the material may depend on Matthew and Luke (and perhaps also on Mark), either directly or indirectly, or on some of the sources and/or traditions on which the evangelists drew'.

35. Ibid. 133–4.

36. Ibid. 139.

Chapter 10

1. See the brief discussion in Michael W. Holmes, *The Apostolic Fathers: Greek Texts and English Translations*, 3rd edn. (Grand Rapids, Mich.: Baker Academic, 2007), 724–7.

2. Scholars debate whether Papias' words mean that Matthew's Gospel was composed in Hebrew (Aramaic) and later translated into its present Greek form, or simply that he wrote in Greek but in a Hebrew style. Most seem to favour the former, though the latter would seem to fit better the Gospel of Matthew as we know it.

3. The translation is that of Holmes, *The Apostolic Fathers*.

4. See C. E. Hill, *The Johannine Corpus in the Early Church* (Oxford: Oxford University Press, 2004), 385–6.

5. On this see ibid. 407–8.

6. F. Siegert, 'Unbeachtete Papiaszitate bei armenischen Schriftstellern', *New Testament Studies*, 27 (1981), 605–14.

7. This is fragment 24 in Holmes's edition of *The Apostolic Fathers*, fragment 23 in J. Kürzinger, *Papias von Hierapolis und die Evangelien des Neuen Testaments* (Regensburg: Pustet, 1983).

8. Walter Bauer, *Rechtgläubigkeit und Ketzerei im ältesten Christentum* (Tübingen: Mohr/Siebeck, 1934), translated as *Orthodoxy and Heresy in Earliest Christianity* (Philadelphia: Fortress Press, 1971), 186–7.

9. C. E. Hill, 'What Papias Said About John (and Luke): A "New" Papian Fragment', *Journal of Theological Studies*, NS 49 (1998); id., *JCEC* 385–94; 409–16.

10. Eusebius often (though not always) uses the Greek word for 'they say' to refer to a written source (e.g. *EH* 1.12.1, 3; 2.2.2; 2.15.1, used of Clement and Papias).

11. 'If the author of the source in 3.24.6–8, 11, is Papias, then Papias could be citing what he had heard that the elders had said or what he had heard that John the Elder had said', Richard Bauckham, *Jesus and the Eyewitnesses: The Gospels as Eyewitness Testimony* (Grand Rapids and Cambridge: Eerdmans, 2006), 435.

12. Note how this parallels John 21.24, 'This is the disciple who is testifying to these things and has written them, and we know that his testimony is true'.

13. My translation.

14. See Hill, 'What Papias Said'; id., *JCEC* 383–96, 407–16. One may now read a sympathetic but critical response to this argument in Bauckham, *Jesus and the Eyewitnesses*, 433–7, and my rejoinder to Bauckham in Hill, ' "The Orthodox Gospel": The Reception of John in the Great Church prior to Irenaeus', in Tuomas Rasimus (ed.), *The Legacy of John* (Leiden: Brill, 2009).

15. For (a), compare *EH* 2.15.1; 3.24.6, 7, 15; 3.39.15; for (b) compare *EH* 2.15.1; 3.24.5, 6, 11, 15; 3.39.15; for (c) compare *EH* 2.15.1; 3.24.5; 3.39.15; for (d) compare *EH* 3.24.7–13; 3.39.15, 16; for (e) compare *EH* 2.15.2; 3.24.7–11; 3.39.17.

16. The first two of these in fact were anticipated by Richard J. Bauckham, 'Papias and Polycrates on the Origin of the Fourth Gospel', *Journal of Theological Studies*, NS 44 (1993), 24–69, who speculated on what Papias must have said about John, based on the reports of those who had read his comments on Mark and Matthew. We can now confirm these two points, and others, if *EH* 3.24.5–13 is dependent upon Papias.

17. See Bauckham, *Jesus and the Eyewitnesses*, 427–8, for more arguments that this section of the *Muratorian Fragment* reveals its knowledge of Papias.

18. Some have argued that 'John the Elder', a historical disciple of Jesus, was in fact the real author of books commonly but erroneously assigned to John the apostle, including the Gospel according to

John. But if the identification of Eusebius' source in *EH* 3.24 as John the Elder is correct, this argument fails. For it is John the Elder who is delivering to Papias the circumstances that led 'John', obviously a person different from himself, to write his Gospel.

19. The *Muratorian Fragment* even allows Andrew and some others a role in 'recognizing' John's Gospel.

Chapter 11

1. Bruce Metzger, *The New Testament, Its Background, Growth and Content*, 3rd revised and enlarged edn. (Nashville, Tenn.: Abingdon Press, 2003), 318.

2. See the long note 1 in Chapter 5.

3. April DeConick, *The Thirteenth Apostle: What the Gospel of Judas Really Says* (London and New York: Continuum, 2007), 5.

4. Pheme Perkins, *Gnosticism and the New Testament* (Minneapolis: Fortress Press, 1993), 194.

5. The followers of both Basilides and Valentinus each claimed a 'succession' from otherwise unknown disciples of apostles (in Basilides' case, one Glaucias, said to be a follower of Peter; in Valentinus', a man named Theudas, said to be a student of Paul).

6. This is the reading of the Greek of *Barlaam*. It is possible that the Syriac preserves the original more closely: 'This is taught in the gospel . . . and you also if you will read therein, may perceive the power which belongs to it' (2.4).

7. R. Walzer, *Galen on Jews and Christians* (London: Oxford University Press, 1949), 11–15.

8. See, for example, on Clement, Silke-Petra Bergjan, 'Logic and Theology in Clement of Alexandria: The Purpose of the 8th Book of the *Stromata*', *Zeitschrift für antikes Christentum*, 12 (2008), 396–413.

9. 'Things are true and primary that are convincing on the strength not of anything else but of themselves', Aristotle, *Topics* 100b19, cited from Bergjan, 'Logic and Theology', 405.

10. Translation from Henry Chadwick and J. E. L. Oulton (eds.), *Alexandrian Christianity: Selected Translations of Clement and Origen* (Louisville and London: Westminster John Knox Press, 1954), 155.

11. Attributed by a medieval source (John of Damascus) to Justin, this treatise, Moreschini and Norelli say, 'fits perfectly into the debates at the end of the second century': Claudio Moreschin and Enrico Norelli, *Early Christian Greek and Latin Literature: A Literary History*, 2 vols.: Vol. I, *From Paul to the Age of Constantine*, tr. Matthew J. O'Connell (Peabody, Mass.: Hendrickson, 2005; Italian original 1995), 202.

12. On this see in particular Richard Bauckham, *Jesus and the Eyewitnesses: The Gospels as Eyewitness Testimony* (Grand Rapids and Cambridge: Eerdmans, 2006).

INDEX

289